CHICCA ALBERTINI

THE
Great
Book
OF
Family
Games

STERLING PUBLISHING CO., INC.
New York

Translated by the Translation Team at Binghamton University's Center for Research in
Translation/Translation Research and Instruction Program (CRIT/TRIP)

Library of Congress Cataloging-in-Publication Data Available
Albertini, Chicca.
[Grande libro dei giochi in famiglia, English]
The great book of family games / Chicca Albertini
p. cm.
Translation of: Il grande libro dei giochi in famiglia.
Includes index.
ISBN 1-4027-0123-3
1. Games. 2. Family recreation. I. Title

GV1201 .A522 2001
790.1'91—dc21

2001049188

10 9 8 7 6 5 4 3 2

First paperback edition published in 2002 by
Sterling Publishing Company, Inc.
387 Park Avenue South, New York, N.Y. 10016
Originally published and © 1998 by
Edizioni Piemme S.p.A., Italy
Under the title *Il grande libro dei Giochi in Famiglia*.
English Translation © 2001 by Sterling Publishing Company, Inc.
Distributed in Canada by Sterling Publishing
c/o Canadian Manda Group, One Atlantic Avenue, Suite 105
Toronto, Ontario, Canada M6K 3E7
Distributed in Great Britain and Europe by Chris Lloyd at
Orca Book Services, Stanley House, Fleets Lane, Poole, BH15 3AJ England
Distributed in Australia by Capricorn Link (Australia) Pty. Ltd.
P.O. Box 704, Windsor, NSW 2756 Australia

Sterling ISBN 0-8069-2845-X Hardcover
ISBN 1-4027-0123-3 Paperback

THE
Great
Book
OF
Family
Games

CONTENTS

THE GREAT CLASSICS

CARD GAMES

GAMES OF CHANCE

SOLITAIRE GAMES

CHILDREN'S CARD GAMES

DICE GAMES

PEN & PAPER GAMES

OLD FAVORITES

PUZZLES

Introduction

Games are a fundamental component of our existence, serving as a means of recreation and diversion, which together allow us to both challenge ourselves and relate to others. It is all this and much more. It is enough just to observe a child when he is a toddler and holding onto any little plaything, to perceive the intimate complexity of an activity that is apparently so simple as a game.

During their early years of life young children learn most of the things they know through games: "educational methodology" for children (specifically that which is applied by educators in pre-school, kindergarten, and elementary school) is based exclusively on games that educate children gradually about shapes, colors, and relationships with other children.

Then, for whatever reason, there comes an age when many of us cease to play. This is due to a number of reasons: lack of time; the company with whom we share our leisure for an hour or two; and the less "trying" alternatives such as the loved-hated television, all decrease the time we dedicate to play in our daily lives.

Nonetheless, human beings have always played, from time immemorial. Some pastimes, like the Royal Game of Ur, have precise testimonies that go back to far earlier civilizations (in this case, to the Sumerians). On the contrary, others have ever uncertain origins. The latter are games with traditions that are often millenary, transmitted orally throughout the centuries and played with only a few elements, most often improvised. For example, a chessboard traced on the ground and a few pebbles were enough for the ancestors of our ancestors, for challenges that were memorable and engaging.

In the nine chapters of this volume we have gathered together many of these pastimes, the ancient origins of which render them even more fascinating. Alongside these we have also gathered other recent and contemporary ones, some of which are barely known and others which are more widespread.

In conclusion, we have sought to create a panorama that is wide enough to furnish the reader with ample documentation while at the same time offering a range of games that is rich in possibilities.

By excluding games such as bridge or chess, whose entries would have required additional monographs of their own, we have privileged those we would characterize as "familiar," and have therefore included games for children, outdoor games, and parlor games.

Of course we have not forgotten those "little" games of chance (that is, those not played exclusively in the casino), the most important of which is poker. These games are adapted for meetings among friends who wish to add a bit of thrill, which never hurts, to pure and simple game-playing.

Therefore, for every game presented here there are brief introductory and/or historical notes, appropriate descriptions of the game equipment (which, alongside the illustrations, will stimulate the most creative among us to construct homemade playing boards, panels, and chessboards), basic rules, little hints and basic strategies.

We do have one recommendation that borders on specification: once the game rules are established, playing is another thing altogether. Indeed, only practice will lead one to truly master the many shrewd strategies required for each game, which furthermore are not really an integral part of the game. These include the number of pieces and scoring.

Well then, on to the fun!

SYMBOLS

One player

Two players

Three players

Four players

Four players in pairs

Five players

Family

Group of players

Easy game

Moderately difficult game

Difficult game

THE GREAT CLASSICS

TOURNAMENT

*Tournament is a genuinely strategic game, a truly astute competition
between two Queens and their respective armies in conquest of a throne.
It enjoyed moderate popularity in England during the 1800s. It still has numerous
admirers, due of course to the many possibilities of carrying out a match.*

Players
Two

Game Equipment
- Hexagonal board, with 91 spaces
laid out in concentric bands *(Fig. 1)*
- The central space, different from the
others, is the throne
- 2 sets of 6 playing pieces of two different colors, which represent the soldiers
- 2 queens, of two different colors

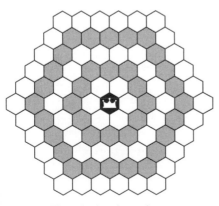

Fig. 1 - The playing board.

▦ Start & Object of the Game

Players decide by luck of the draw who
goes first. Each player takes turns moving his own pieces (soldiers and Queen)
freely along the perimeter of the hexagonal board *(Fig. 2)*.

The object of the game is to place
one's own Queen on the throne (i.e., the
central space), surrounded by her soldiers in the six adjacent spaces.

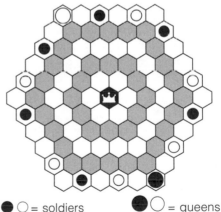

● ○ = soldiers   ●○ = queens
*Fig. 2 - Diagram of one possible way to
start the match.*

▦ The Play

The pieces, including the Queen, can be
moved toward the center into a free
adjacent space, diagonally or laterally,

but not backward *(Fig. 3),* except in the case of imprisonment (see IMPRISON-MENT below). Players cannot jump over their own nor their opponent's pieces, therefore no pieces can be taken.

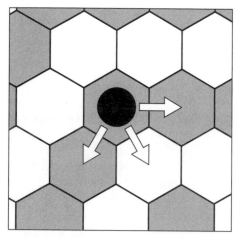

Fig. 3 - Possible movements for soldiers and Queen.

IMPRISONMENT

When two pieces surround and enclose an opponent piece in the middle, thereby imprisoning it *(Fig. 4),* that piece must, at its turn in the game, retreat into a free space on the outermost band.

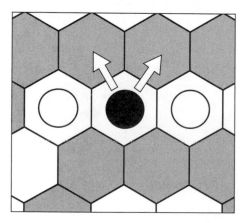

Fig. 4-Imprisonment: the prisoner piece must retreat.

This is the only occasion on which a piece must move backward. If there are more than one imprisoned piece, a player can decide on the order in which they will be freed. On the other hand, if the Queen is one of those pieces, she must be moved first. When carrying out a move, a player should never put himself in a position of imprisonment.

FINAL PHASE

The throne can be occupied only by the Queen. A player loses the match if he finds that his own pieces surround the throne, without having placed the Queen there first.

■ Strategy

Players can choose a typical line-up at the start, with the two Queens placed on opposite corners of each other and the soldiers alternating at the sides, in such a way that the spaces are alternately filled and vacant.

The simplicity of the moves and the impossibility of eliminating opponent pieces from the game make Tournament a refined game of pure strategy.

In order to slow down the advance of the opponent it is always good to take advantage—as soon as the opportunity arises—of the option to imprison one or more of the opponent's pieces, especially if the Queen is among them.

If you want to make the game more complex, you can introduce the following rule: when a player imprisons the opponent Queen, he can order her to a specific space wherefrom she will be freed.

Finally, if through practice you are able to master the game well, it will not be difficult to oblige the opponent to surround the throne before he conquers it with his own Queen.

BACKGAMMON

A very ancient game which, according to legend, was probably invented in India and which reproduced on a board the hours of a day (24, like the total of the narrowed triangles), the months of the year and signs of the zodiac (12, like the triangular points projecting from opposite sides toward the center), the days of the month (30, like the total of pieces present on the board at the beginning of the game).

Players
Two

Game Equipment
- Rectangular board, on which there are 24 narrowed triangles drawn of alternating colors. One half is called the Home Board, and the other half is called the Outer Board *(Fig. 1)*
- 2 sets of 15 pieces each, in white and red
- 2 dice, numbered from 1 to 6
- The "doubling cube" with the numbers 2, 4, 8, 16, 32, and 64 imprinted on the six sides

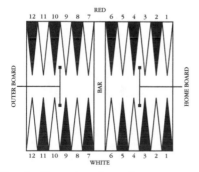

Fig. 1 - The game-board.

Start & Object of the Game

The players set up their pieces on the board as shown in Figure 2.

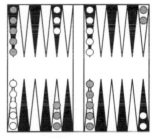

Fig. 2 - Setup of the start of the game.

White plays with the Home Board at her right and will move clockwise. Red plays with the Home Board at her left and will move counterclockwise *(Fig. 3)*.

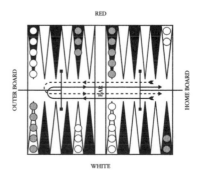

Fig. 3 - Movements of white and black.

The object of the game is to move all of one's own pieces through the entire board until reaching the Home Board from which one's opponent initially left and to remove all the pieces from the board. The winner is the player who is able to first remove all her own pieces.

■ The Play

The triangular points are not numbered on the Backgammon board. We have only done it here in order to facilitate the explanations of the game.

Each player throws a die onto the table in turn. Whoever has the highest number begins play. Each player, on her turn, throws the dice on her own half of the board, and only after the opponent has concluded her move. If these conditions are not respected, then the throw is void and must be executed again.

Based on the numbers rolled, one or two pieces are advanced on the board, following precise rules. The two counts of the dice can allow players to singly advance one piece each or both advance the same piece. In other words *(Fig. 4)*: if White throws the dice and obtains a 4 and a 3, she can move one piece 4 positions and another piece 3 positions from the 1-point; or, she can move one piece first 3 positions and then 4 positions, for a total of 7 positions, from the 12-point to the 6-point. White cannot move a piece 4 + 3 positions from the 1-point, because she would end up on the 8-point, occupied by more than one opponent piece, a move that is not allowed.

Be careful! It is true that with a 4 + 3 one can move a piece 7 positions, but only if the intermediate spots are not occupied by more than one opponent piece, in which case the situation already described above will occur.

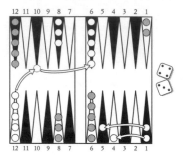

Fig. 4 - Examples of possible moves.

On the contrary, the player who finishes on a point occupied by only a single opponent piece in one move, takes that opponent's place (hits the blot), thus making the opponent leave the game. The eliminated pieces get placed on the Bar.

The player who ends up with one or more pieces on the Bar cannot continue the game until they have been made to reenter.

To this aim, she throws the dice when it is her turn: the player's piece on the Bar can reenter the game only if the count on one of the two dice lets her reach a point that is vacant or occupied by one of her own pieces *(Fig. 5)*.

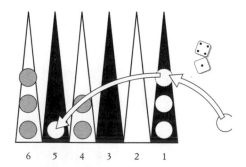

Fig. 5 - The player's piece on the Bar reenters the game only if the count on one of the two dice lets her reach a point that is vacant or occupied by one of her own pieces.

In this case, the count on the second die can be used for the piece that reenters or for another option, but only after the piece on the Bar reenters. Otherwise the player must wait until her next turn, without moving this time, waiting until she obtains the ideal count with the dice.

DOUBLE COUNT

If in the throw of the dice, the same number is obtained on both, the count doubles, as does the possibility of moving. In other words: if a double 4 is obtained, it is possible to advance four pieces 4 positions, or one piece 4 positions and another one 12, or even 2 pieces 8 positions each or, finally, a single piece 16 positions. Even in this case, be careful at the intermediate spots, which need to be free of opponent pieces or occupied only by one opponent piece that would end up on the Bar

"MAKING THE POINT"

When a player positions at least two pieces on the same point, she has made the point: in other words she is in a safe position, without risk of having her piece hit, in addition to blocking the opponent who cannot stop on that point. On the contrary, when a single piece occupies a point, it is called a "blot," because it is vulnerable to attacks by the opponent.

END GAME

Once all of a player's own pieces are gathered in her own Home Board, she begins to bear them off according to precise rules.

A piece is moved out according to the count of the dice *(Fig. 6)*, for instance, if she obtains a 3 and a 2, one piece would be moved out onto a 3-point and one piece onto a 2-point.

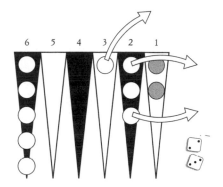

Fig. 6 - A piece is borne off according to the count of the dice, for instance: with a 3 and 2, one piece goes out from the 3-point and one from the 2-point.

If on the count of the dice one obtains numbers corresponding to points that are unoccupied, then the pieces can be advanced from the points with higher numbers *(Fig. 7)*.

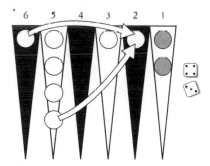

Fig. 7 - If on the count of the dice one obtains numbers corresponding to points that are unoccupied, then the pieces can be advanced to the point with the number that is highest.

If, as illustrated in Figure 7, one obtains a 4 and a 3 and the points corresponding to those numbers are vacant, then two pieces can still be advanced, choosing those pieces located on the 5-point and 6-point, and which can be moved 3 and 4 positions.

One can choose either to remove the pieces corresponding to the numbers obtained on the dice or advance pieces.

If the numbers obtained with the dice are higher than the highest numbered occupied point, then two pieces can be removed from that point. For example, let's suppose we throw a 4 and a 5 *(Fig. 8)* and we only have pieces on the 3-, 2-, and 1-points, then we can remove from the board two of the pieces on the 3-point.

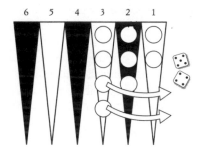

Fig. 8 - If the numbers that are obtained with the dice are higher than the highest occupied point, as indicatd by the numbers on the diagram above, then two pieces can be made to leave from that point.

If during this phase of the game, a piece is eliminated by an opponent (either remaining in the Home Board or in phase of reentry) then it must reenter and begin its trajectory from scratch until it reaches the Home Board. Only at this point can the player begin removing her pieces again. Finally, it must absolutely be kept in mind that if a player obtains a dice count that corresponds to a move which is not possible, then she must skip her turn.

SCORING & DOUBLING

The winner is the player who first manages to remove (bear off) all of her own pieces. If the opponent removes at least one piece on a turn, then the winner is allocated one point. If the loser still hasn't removed any of her own pieces, then the winner has won a "gammon" and is allocated 2 points.

If in addition to not having removed any of her own pieces, the loser still has some in the opponent's Home Board or on the Bar, then the winner has won a "backgammon" and is allocated 3 points.

The doubling cube serves to indicate the doublings of the stake that are agreed on from time to time as the match progresses. That is, if a stake is established at the beginning of the game. Doubling can be proposed by one player to another at any time during the match, but before throwing the dice. If the player who is challenged accepts, the die will be turned over in a way that the face with the number 2 imprinted on it is showing (successively for the numbers 4, 8, etc.). Otherwise, she concedes victory to the challenger.

Every successive doubling can only be requested by the player who is challenged, that is, by the one to whom it was previously proposed. From doubling to doubling, the final score can be multiplied (1, 2 in the case of "gammon" or 3 in the case of "backgammon") 64 times!

Traditionally, if the dice on the first throw of the match are two equal numbers, then the players automatically proceed to the first doubling.

■ Strategy

Backgammon is a game that is actually easy and fun to learn despite the seeming complexity of the explanations. However, it is not so easy to play Backgammon well. In short, as often happens in board games, only practice and experience will make the player a skillful one, even if it is possible to point out strategies to keep in mind during the match.

Above all, avoid leaving any pieces vulnerable to being hit, and make the point as soon as possible. This way, in addition to having to defend her own pieces, the opponent is efficiently blocked, since by finding the points occupied she will have to play according to the count of the dice.

Try not to leave too many pieces behind, and instead advance them in a compact way. When you near the final phase of the game, carefully evaluate if it is worth eliminating an opponent piece: having an opponent piece able to reenter

could mean that one of yours will be eliminated in turn, perhaps when you are already in the bearing-off phase. This means you would have to start from scratch (which is the English meaning of the term Backgammon, from back = to go back and gammon = game).

When all of your pieces are gathered together in your Home Board, try to move them ahead, and to occupy the points with the lowest numbers.

Indeed, the pieces on a 6-point can only leave on this count, perhaps obtained using both dice, while those on a 3-point (if 4, 5, and 6 are already free) will be able to take advantage of more options.

Be careful to understand the stake and future doublings or you might have some unpleasant surprises: for instance, 3 times 64 is 192 . . .

CLOSE THE BOX

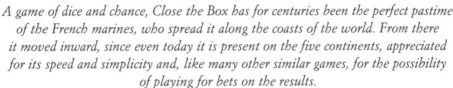

A game of dice and chance, Close the Box has for centuries been the perfect pastime of the French marines, who spread it along the coasts of the world. From there it moved inward, since even today it is present on the five continents, appreciated for its speed and simplicity and, like many other similar games, for the possibility of playing for bets on the results.

Players
One, two or more

Game Equipment
- Board that has a series of "boxes," closed with little doors, numbered from 1 to 9, and a mat on which to throw the dice (Fig. 1)
- 2 dice, numbered from 1 to 6

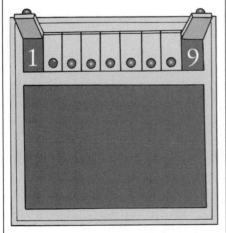

Fig. 1 - Game equipment

■ Start & Object of the Game

The game is played in turns, one player at a time playing a complete hand. Each player must conclude with his hand before passing the dice to the next player.

The game begins with all nine of the little doors open for the boxes along the top of the board.

The object of the game is to close all the little doors to the boxes, according to the count each player obtains by the thrown dice.

■ The Play

The player throws the dice and can choose between two possibilities: either—depending on one's own strategy—to close the box that corresponds to the sum obtained, or to close the two boxes corresponding to the points obtained on each one of the two dice.

For example: if a player throws the dice to obtain a 1 and a 4, he can close box 1 and box 4, or close only box 5 (*Figs. 2 and 3*).

When the sum of all numbers on the boxes that have remained open is equal to or less than 6, then the game shifts from using thw two dice to the throwing of only a single die.

Fig. 2

Fig. 3

CLOSING THE HAND & SCORING

The player's hand concludes when a throw of the die doesn't give the player the option of closing any box. Thus when no door can be closed, the player's hand is over and play moves to the next player. The player whose hand has ended adds up the score of the boxes that have remained open, keeping in mind that a low score is desirable.

Naturally, if you manage to close all the boxes, then the score is 0.

The scores of the hands are added up: whoever goes over 45 points goes out of the game. The last remaining player is declared the winner.

■ Strategy

While this is a game of chance that depends on the fate cast by every throw of the dice, it is a good strategy to first close the boxes with the highest numbers. The reasoning is that if the boxes remain open, the higher the corresponding points the more likely the player is to reach 45 and be removed from the game.

Before starting the game, the players can agree to establish a "bonus" to be given to the player who manages to close all the boxes during his hand, and such a bonus could be, for example, subtracting 5 points from the player's score.

CONQUEST

*Among the many variants of the traditional game of checkers,
Conquest deserves to be recognized for its particularly strategic characteristic
(indeed, one needs to conquer a hypothetical fortress) which surely renders it
an exciting and engaging game.*

Players
Two

Game Equipment
- Checkerboard divided into 9 squares on each side, for a total of 81 squares, and with a central section of 9 squares, marked off with a bolder line which represents the fortress *(Fig. 1)*
- 2 sets of 8 pieces of two different colors
- 2 Kings, of two different colors

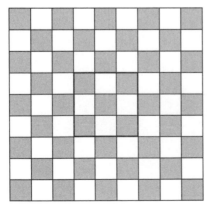

Fig. 1-Diagram of the game board.

◼ Start & Object of the Game

The player who goes first is decided by luck of the draw. The players set up their own pieces as shown in *Fig. 2,* around their own King.

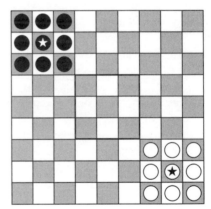

Fig.2-Initial layout of the pieces. The pieces marked with an asterisk are the Kings.

The object of the game is to take over the fortress with the King and some of his pieces, forming, as shown in Figures 3, 4, 5, and 6, the so-called lines of attack.

◼ The Play

As in the game of checkers, the pieces can move only one square at a time and only diagonally, such that each one

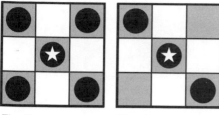

Fig. 3.   Fig. 4.

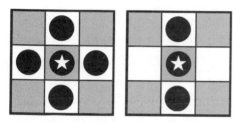

Fig. 5.   Fig. 6.

always ends up in squares that are of the same color as the one of departure. However, unlike what happens in the game of checkers, all pieces can move backward too (*Fig. 7*).

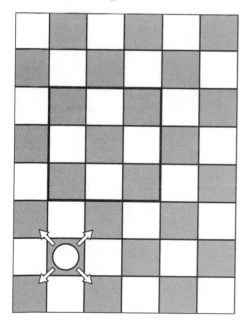

Fig. 7-Example of possible moves for a piece.

The opponent's pieces are neither jumped over nor taken.

If a player closes off an opponent piece between two pieces, in a diagonal line (*Fig. 8*), he can put the surrounded piece into exile, by banishing it to a square of his choice that is vacant and of the same color as the square of departure.

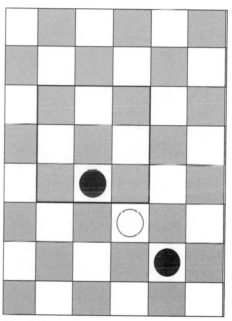

Fig. 8-Example of a surrounded white piece.

■ Strategy

It is good strategy to play offensively and to not close oneself up in defense, taking well into account the fortress but, at the same time, attempting to banish the opponent pieces which, once they are put far from the position they had conquered, must obligatorily begin from scratch, often obliging the player to rethink his strategy.

Whoever carries out the first move is not really at an advantage. Nonetheless, it is good to alternate from match to match.

CHECKERS

A board game that is greatly diffused throughout the world, with a few variants, Checkers is famous like chess and is only simpler in appearance. Among the many hypotheses as to its origins, one sees Checkers as a "softer" version of chess. The most well known version, played in international tournaments, is the one devised by a French officer in 1723. There are numerous national variations: Spanish, German, Russian, Canadian, Turkish, Polish, and Italian.

Players
Two

Game Equipment
- Checkerboard with 8 squares on each side, a total of 64 squares, in colors alternating between black and white (Fig. 1)
- Two sets, one white and one black, of 12 pieces

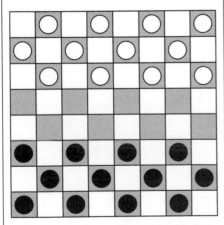

Fig. 1 - Game setup and initial layout of pieces.

■ Start & Object of the Game

The checkerboard is placed so that each player has a black square at the lower left corner. Both players lay out their pieces in three rows of 4 pieces each, only on the black squares *(Fig. 1)*.

The object of the game is to eliminate all the opponent's pieces or, alternatively, to immobilize them.

■ The Play

Whoever gets the Black by the luck of the draw will initiate the game. In later matches, the colors of the players' pieces will be switched, and so, likewise, will the player initiating the first move.

The pieces can move diagonally forward, only on the black squares *(Fig. 2)* and only one square at a time.

KING
When a piece reaches the farthest limit of the opponent's field, it becomes "King" and, in order to distinguish it from the others, another piece of the same color is placed on top of it as a crown. Unlike the simple pieces, the King can also move backward *(Fig. 2)*.

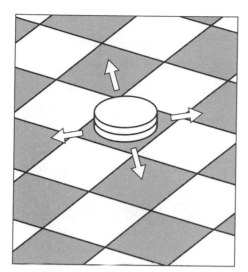

Fig. 2 - Unlike the simple pieces, the King can also move backward.

ELIMINATING THE OPPONENT'S PIECES

When a piece (or a King) ends up next to an opponent, and the next square in a straight line is vacant, it jumps over that piece and eliminates it from the game *(Fig. 3)*.

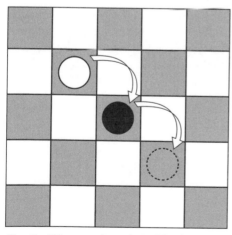

Fig. 3 - When a piece (or a King) ends up next to an opponent, and the next square in a straight line is vacant, it jumps over that piece and eliminates it from the game.

Multiple jumps are allowed whenever they are possible. If after having made a jump, the piece ends up next to another opponent piece that has, in turn, an adjacent vacant square, then this other piece can also be taken *(Fig. 4)*.

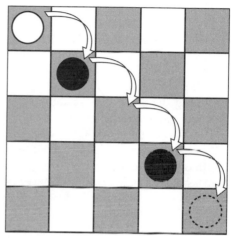

Fig. 4 - Example of a multiple jump.

Every jump must necessarily be done in a straight line even if, at the end of the move, the line of multiple jumps might result in a broken one.

Jumps are mandatory: whenever a piece has the possibility of jumping. In the standard game of Checkers played today, the pieces must jump; there are no exceptions.

■ Strategy

As has been noticed with regard to Alquerque (from which it is said Checkers might have its origins), two players of equal ability might easily find themselves in a stalemate situation, where each player's own pieces are immobilized by those of the opponent and vice versa. In this case, the match is a draw.

■ Italian Checkers

The Italian version of the game is comprised of a few, but significant, differences:

The checkerboard is set up so that the square at the left of each player is white (even while the game is still played on the black squares), as shown in Figure 5.

The simple pieces cannot capture a King.

When a player has multiple options of capturing, he must choose the option that will eliminate the greatest number of his opponent's pieces. Otherwise, the piece that has disregarded this move gets "huffed" and eliminated from the game. The same thing happens whenever a multiple jump is interrupted or he has possible jump but fails to make the manditory jump.

Careful: It is up to the opponent to "huff" the pieces of an unwary player who doesn't realize that there is a capture to be carried out.

However, the players can agree before starting play on rules to allow certain possibilities regarding "huffing": 1) a player can correct the error of another, forcing it to capture (perhaps when this would put the piece in a posi-

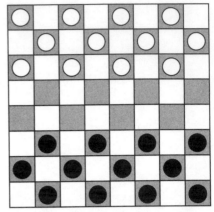

Fig. 5 - The initial layout of pieces on the checkerboard in the Italian version of Checkers has a white square at the lower end to the players' left, but play is still only on the black squares.

tion favorable to the player correcting it); (2) he can "ignore" the opponent's error, if this puts him at an advantage; (3) or finally, he can "huff" the piece that should have carried out the capture.

When a player has multiple possibilities of moving and capturing the same number of pieces with a King, he must choose the move that will allow him to eliminate the most important pieces (the opponent Kings, if there are any).

CHINESE CHECKERS (or STAR HALMA)

Similar, in rules, to the game of Halma, Chinese Checkers supposedly (for once!) reached the East from Europe, via Japan, rather than the other way around. Certainly today it is widespread in all of China, but likewise is it so in the West.

Players
From one to six

Game Equipment
- Board in the form of a star, crossed with lines that form intersecting points (usually holes) in which the pieces are put in *(Fig. 1)*
- Six sets of 15 pieces (usually pegs), of 6 different colors

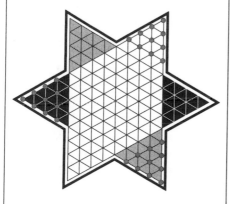

Fig. 1 - Game board and layout of pieces for 3 players.

■ Start & Object of the Game

For a single player, 15 pieces are placed on a selected point on the star *(Fig. 2)*.

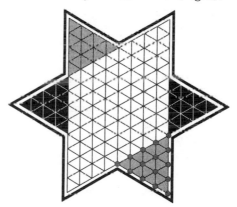

Fig. 2 - Layout of the 15 pieces for a game played by a single player.

For a match between two players, 15 pieces each are placed at any two points that are opposite each other. If the match is among three players, one point is filled and the next point is left vacant. For a match among four or five, the points can be filled as wished. For a game among six, all the star's points are filled by the pieces.

It is possible to play in pairs if the number of players is 4 or 6. In this case, the members of a pair depart from opposite points.

If three or more players are playing, only 10 pieces are used.

The object of the game is to get all of one's own pieces to a point that is diametrically opposite.

■ The Play

The pass move consists in moving a piece to a vacant adjacent intersecting point of one's choice (*Fig. 3*).

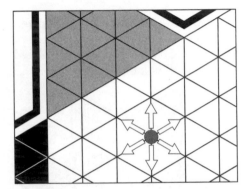

Fig. 3 - The pass move consists in moving a piece to a vacant adjacent intersecting point of one's choice.

The jump move consists in jumping a piece (it doesn't matter if it is one's own or the opponent's), which, nonetheless, will not be eliminated from the game, provided it lands on an intersecting point that is vacant (*Fig. 4*).

Multiple leaps are allowed, even in diverse directions, but always and only if, between the piece that is jumped and another, it can land on a vacant spot.

Jumps are not mandatory. Multiple leaps can be interrupted whenever the player wishes.

Combining a pass and a jump is not allowed in single moves. When playing in three or more, moves are by turns and done in a clockwise direction.

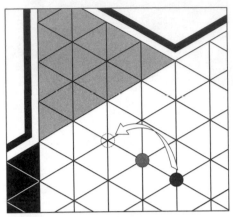

Fig. 4 - Jump move.

When playing in pairs, and in the event that one of the players in the pair has completed the moves of his own pieces, he can move the pieces of his companion on his next turn.

SINGLE PLAY

In single play, the player must get his 15 pieces into the opposite corner with the least possible number of moves.

■ Strategy

One widespread strategy is to advance one's own pieces by ladders, in order to favor the line-up at the point of arrival (from one to four or five pieces in a row).

Keep in mind, however, that in doing so, you will favor the opponent who will also find that the spaces he needs are left open and free . . .

One variant consists in making the jump mandatory, or alternatively, making it mandatory to proceed with multiple leaps. If this rule is established, the player having to carry out an alternative move would have to cancel it and proceed with a jump. Provided that the companion, or companions, realize it.

DOMINOES & VARIANTS

A game of unmistakable pieces, derived from dice, and no doubt one of the most appreciated games in the world among the great and small alike. Like many others, Dominoes also has its origins in ancient China, where it was born not as a game but as a divinatory method, that is, depending on how the tiles were combined, the future was foretold. Today children play with dominoes made of wood and decorated with animals, Eskimos carve them out of splinters of walrus ivory, and in every corner of the world they are made with the most diverse materials, from bone to stone, with wood that was considered more or less valuable, and even made of plastic, which are the most common and widespread.

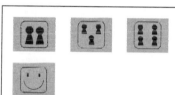

Players
Two, three or four

Game Equipment
- 28 tiles (bones) divided in half with each half (end) having points marked on it, from zero to six, like on the common dice *(Fig. 1)*

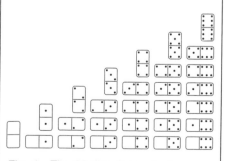

Fig. 1 - The 28 tiles (bones) of dominoes.

▇ Start & Object of the Game

The domino tiles (bones) are set out facedown on the playing area. Each player chooses 7 tiles randomly and keeps them hidden, laying them out standing on the long edge *(Fig. 2)*.

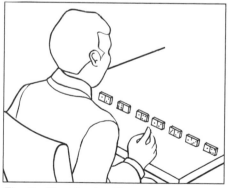

Fig. 2 - The domino tiles are set out facedown. Each player chooses 7 tiles randomly and keeps them hidden from the other players, laying them out standing on the long edge.

If there are two or three players in the game, the first player to move is decided by the luck of the draw.

In a game between two or three players, the surplus tiles (bones) will be left, facedown, in the center of the table: they will constitute the so-called boneyard from which all the players can "dig" (or fish).

When playing among four players, the player who has the double-6 tile will initiate the game by putting it faceup on the playing are of the table.

The object of the game is to lay down all of one's own tiles (bones) according to the rules described below.

■ The Play

The game is played in a counterclockwise direction from player to player.

We will begin by looking at the rules of Dominoes for four players.

The player next to the one who has laid down a double-6 tile, gives the go-ahead to set up the line by putting down one of his own tiles that has a 6 end, for example, a 6:1 (*Fig. 3*).

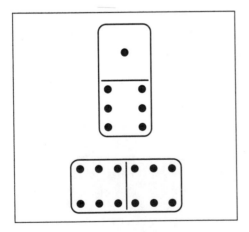

Fig. 3 - Example of a game start: the player next to the one who has laid down a double 6 gives the go-ahead to set up the line by putting down one of his own tiles of 6, for example, a 6:1.

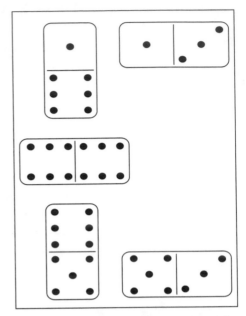

Fig. 4 - A tile with a 1 end (above right) or a tile with a 5 end (below right) can be coupled to the matching tiles laid down against the double 6 (left side).

The next player will now have the option to continue on from either the 1 end or the 6 end, and could lay down, for example, a 1:3, or a 6:5 (*Fig. 4*).

And so on and so forth, the game continues in this manner. Doubles get placed sideways to the line (*Fig. 4*).

When the line gets very long, it can change directions, creating a right angle.

Any player who cannot attach any of his tiles to the line must pass on his turn.

If any player who can attach a tile chooses not to do so (and the opponents realize it), he automatically loses his hand.

The same happens if a player attaches a wrong tile to the line. However, if his opponents do not realize the error right away, and proceed to attach, then the tile in question will be accepted as "good" and retain its place in the line.

CLOSING THE HAND & SCORING

When a player has finished placing down all of his own tiles, then the total sum of values of the remaining tiles of the opponents is calculated: this number is marked to the advantage of the player who has closed his hand. If a stalemate situation is reached, in which none of the players can attach any of his tiles to the line, the winner of the hand is the player who has the least number of points.

In such a case, the winner of the hand is allocated a score that corresponds to the sum of the remaining tiles of his opponents minus the number of his tiles.

Whoever reaches 200 points first is the winner of the game.

"OPEN" DOMINOES

We will now see the rules of play for two or three players, the so-called Open Dominoes, where the surplus tiles (14 if there are two players, 7 if there are three) remain facedown (in the boneyard) and at the disposal of each of the players (*Fig. 5*).

Fig. 5 - In open dominoes, the surplus tiles remain facedown—in the so-called boneyard—at the disposal of each of the players.

The player who—decided on the luck of the draw—starts first, puts down one tile of his choice.

By turns, the tiles are attached following the rules of the game for four.

When a player does not have, among his tiles, a tile to attach to the line, he digs one out of the boneyard. If the tile dug out of the boneyard can be played, it is attached to the line. Otherwise he keeps it among his own tiles and digs again, until he finds the one to play or until two tiles remain facedown on the table, in which case he can no longer take them and is obliged to pass.

When only two tiles remain in the boneyard and no one can attach one of his own, the hand is closed. If, at this point, the players are left with the same number of unplayable tiles, the hand will be canceled. Scores are calculated according to rules for a game among four.

■ Strategy

The success of a match largely depends on the pieces one has. Nevertheless, it is also true that good pieces can be played poorly and vice versa.

As a general rule, it is a good idea to keep the opponent's moves in mind, trying to guess his weaknesses (that is, the numbers he lacks), in order to then "attack" with the right piece, forcing him to pass on a turn.

A favorable situation to take advantage of is when, after randomly choosing tiles, a player discovers that he has many pieces with one end the same. If, for example, one finds he has 5:5, 5:3, 5:1, 5:0, it means that there are another three pieces with a 5 end in circulation, and by playing one's own 5 ends in a strategic way, one can force an opponent to miss a have to pass on a turn.

▣ Variants

The rules explained up to this point deal with traditional Dominoes, also called "Block Dominoes," for which infinite variants exist.

A warning: they are so numerous (and can coexist very well together) that it is a good idea to clarify with game companions what rules are to be adopted before the beginning of the match, so as not to break up the game each time with a discussion as to whether or not a move is valid . . .

"OPEN" DOMINOES AMONG THREE OR FOUR PLAYERS

Playing among three or four game companions, 5 tiles apiece are taken, instead of 7, leaving the surplus ones facedown and at the disposal of everyone.

The difference, obviously, is that playing in three, each player will have more tiles among which to dig and choose, and playing in four, there will be an "open-face" match instead of a "closed-face" one.

In both cases, the rule that is almost always valid is that when only two tiles are remaining in the boneyard, no player will be allowed to dig, and if none of the players has any more valid tiles, the hand will be considered finished.

OPENING

It can be decided, even in a domino game among four, to have a player to open the first hand who has been chosen by the draw, instead of the one who has drawn a double 6. The player initiating the game can lay down any one of his own tiles, as he wishes.

Whoever wins the first hand opens the following one.

This latter rule (whoever wins a hand opens the next one) can be applied to any kind of Dominoes variant.

DOUBLE DOMINOES

It can be established that whoever has a double will have the right to attach another tile (only if he can) immediately: in this way, a player can lay down two tiles in one single turn.

In regards to this, it can be established that the double tiles will give the player laying them down as many points as are on the faces of the tiles (of course, a double zero gives zero!).

DOMINOES IN PAIRS

A game of Dominoes among four players can be played in pairs, with 7 or 5 tiles chosen (in which case four would remain to be dug out of the boneyard).

Pairs are formed by the two players facing each other and, when one of the two finishes up his own tiles, the hand is won by the pair, who are allocated the points corresponding to the sum total of the tiles still in hand of the opponents.

In a stalemate situation, when no one can attach a tile to the line, the pair who wins is the one which, adding up the values of the tiles that remain in their possession, ends up with the lowest total.

The winning pair is awarded as points the difference between their own tiles and those of their opponents.

Finally, in the event that the sum total of remaining tiles between the two pairs is the same, the hand is considered null and void.

BERGEN DOMINOES

This is a domino game "of draws" in which a certain number
of tiles are available for all the players. Furthermore,
there are points that are "gathered" during the hand
and others are allocated to whoever wins.

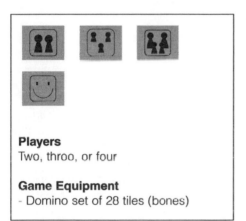

Players
Two, throo, or four

Game Equipment
- Domino set of 28 tiles (bones)

■ Start & Object of the Game

The tiles are laid out facedown. If the game is played between two or three players, 6 tiles apiece are randomly chosen; for four players, only 5.

Surplus tiles are left facedown, at the disposal of everyone, in the so-called boneyard.

The player who starts is the one who has the highest double.

The object of the game is to lay out all of one's own tiles.

■ The Play

A player who cannot or does not want to attach one of his own tiles can dig one out of the boneyard.

A player is awarded 2 points when he attaches to the extreme end of the line a tile that depicts the same value as the one on the opposite end. For example, a player who, in Figure 1, has laid down a 3:2, matches with a 6:2 on the extreme opposite end.

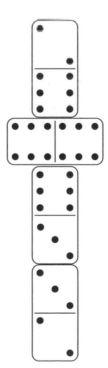

Fig. 1 - Example of a play (extreme ends having the same value) that earns 2 points.

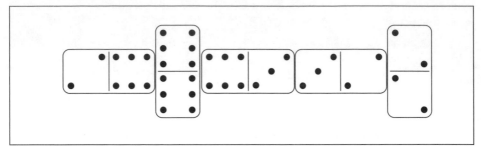

Fig. 2 - Example of a play (a double equal to the number of points on the opposite extreme end) that earns 3 points.

A player is awarded 3 points when he attaches to the extreme end a double that is equal to the opposite extreme end. This is shown in Figure 2, where the player who laid down a double 2 matvhing the 2 at the extreme opposite end is awarded 3 points. Whoever wins the hand, laying down all of his tiles, is allocated 2 points.

When no one can lay down all of his tiles, being unable to attach a tile to the line, whoever has the least number of doubles left in his hand wins; if the number of doubles is the same, it is whoever has tiles of a least overall value; finally, if no one has a double in hand then the winner is the one who has tiles with an overall score that is lower than that of his opponents. The winner of the match is the one who first reaches a total of 10 or 15 points, as agreed by the players before they start a match.

BINGO DOMINOES

In this game the traditional tiles of dominoes are used in the manner of cards.
It is an adaptation of dominoes that is quite widespread, and which
testifies to the versatility of the game Dominoes.

Players
Two

Game Equipment
- Dominoes of 28 tiles

■ Start & Object of the Game

Tiles are laid out, facedown, in the center of the game table.

Each player turns over one tile to decide who will open the hand. The one whose tile has the highest total opens.

The luck-of-the-draw tiles are returned to the boneyard, and both players then choose 7 tiles apiece, keeping them hidden from the opponent's view.

The player who opens, turns over a tile picked out of the boneyard: the highest of his numbers becomes the trump suit of that hand. For example, in Figure 1, for the turned-over tile 2:1, the 2 becomes the trump.

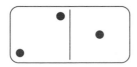

Fig. 1 - In the example here, the
2 becomes the trump of the hand.

The object of the game is to accumulate points, through captures, as in a typical game of cards.

■ The Play

The player who opens the game plays one of his tiles, and the opponent responds. Of course, every play must be carried out with the object of executing a capture, according to the rules that are explained below.

The captured tiles are put aside.

After every capture, the two players each dig out a tile from the boneyard. Whoever has executed the capture digs first and leads the hand. When only two tiles, the trump and the one that is facedown, are left in the boneyard, whoever has won the preceding capture can choose which one of the two to dig.

WIN THE CAPTURES
The neutral tile (double zero) is the "bingo" and wins over all of the captures.

If there are no trumps played, the winning tile is the one that is largest, i.e., which depicts the highest total of points. For example, the 4:5 (a total of 9) wins over the 6:1 (total of 7).

The trump wins over a non-trump tile. For example, if the 2 is a trump, the 2:0 wins over the 5:6.

If two trumps are played, the winner is the one that is largest, i.e., one that, besides the trump, has the highest number of points. Continuing with our hypothetical 2 trump, the 2:5 would win over the 2:4 (Fig. 2).

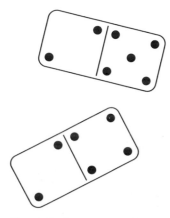

Fig. 2 - The 2:5 wins over the 2:4.

If no trumps are played and the total of points is the same, the winner is the player leading the hand.

SCORES

Points are recorded as the captures are carried out.

Keeping in mind the trump (as in our example, the 2, in Figure 3), the following values are recorded:

- Double trump is worth 28 points;
- Bingo has a value of 14 points, except when zero is the trump (a double zero would bring 28 points);
- The non-trump doubles have a value of the total of their points;
- Non-double trumps have a value of the total of their points;
- The tile 6:4 has a value of 10 points, even if neither the 6 nor 4 are trumps;
- The tile 3:0 has a value of 10 points, even if the 3 or 0 were to be trumps.

"HONOR" POINTS

The doubles, also called "honors," can help the player win extra points throughout the course of the match, if this player has in hand more than one.

This occurs when a player, playing a double tile, declares to the opponent that he has others in hand and shows him:

- If he has 2, he declares "double" (=20 points);
- If he has 3, he declares "triple" (=40 points);
- If he has 4, he declares "double double" (=50 points);
- If he has 5, he declares "king" (=60 points);
- If he has 6, he declares "emperor" (=70 points);

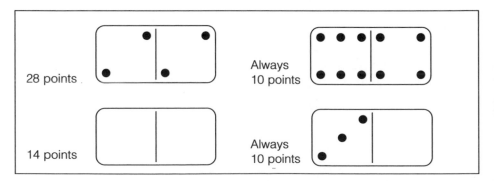

28 points

Always 10 points

14 points

Always 10 points

Fig. 3 - Combination values with the 2 as trump.

- If he is fortunate enough to have 7, he can declare "unbeatable" (=210 points) which is the maximum score;
- If among the doubles there is a bingo, then he is awarded 10 supplementary points.

In order to have a right to record honor points, a player must declare the double at the moment of playing, and in any event, win the hand.

CLOSE THE MATCH

At any moment, a player can "close the match" by declaring that he has obtained 70 points, including captures and/or doubles.

Naturally, in order to close he must have in hand the amount that he has declared.

In this case, the trump in the bone yard is turned over and neither one of the two can dig up any more tiles.

When the match is closed, whoever plays second must respond "in kind" to the opponent, within the limits possible:
- If one plays a trump, the opponent must also play a trump;
- If one plays a tile that isn't a trump, the opponent must respond with a tile that depicts a number that is higher than the tile played by the opponent or, if not

able to do so, with the lowest number possible. For example, a player plays a 6:5, and the other responds with a tile that has a 6, and only if he doesn't have a tile with 6 can he answer with a tile having 5;
- If one doesn't have a tile with either 6 or 5, a trump can be played (and the capture is won);
- Only if a player can no longer respond to the opponent in any of the ways listed above can he play with any kind of tile, the so-called dud; naturally, he loses the capture.

WINNING THE MATCH

A match is won by a player when he is allocated 7 of the so-called sets. Sets are allocated when:
- 70 points are had during a single hand (with captures and/or doubles);
- 70 points are reached and the opponent has at least 30;
- A double trump is taken with bingo.

Two sets are awarded when a player reaches 70 points after the opponent has carried out at least one capture but still hasn't reached a total of 30 points.

Three sets are awarded when a player reaches 70 points before the opponent has carried out at least one capture.

MEDIEVAL MILL GAME (or MILL BOARD)

Universally known and played everywhere, the Mill game has origins rooted in antiquity. It was invented by the Phoenicians or the Trojans, appreciated in ancient Rome and widespread during Medieval times, as its name indicates.

Players
Two

Game Equipment
- Square board with horizontal and vertical lines forming 24 intersection points *(Fig. 1)*
- Two different-colored sets of 9 pieces (also known as "merels")

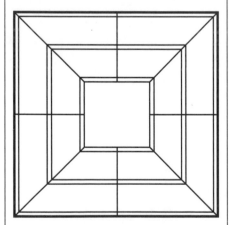

Fig. 1 - The playing board.

■ Start & Object of Game

Players decide by luck of the draw who goes first.

Each player takes turns moving his own pieces, one at a time, onto the vacant intersection points as he wishes, seeking to create a mill, or in other words, to place three pieces in a straight row on three adjacent intersection points. They can be horizontal or vertical, but not diagonal (Fig. 2).

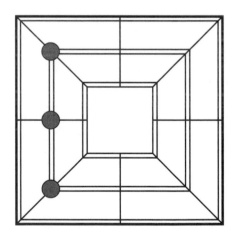

Fig. 2 - Example of a mill: three pieces in a straight row on three adjacent intersection points.

The object of the game is to succeed in eliminating at least seven of the opponent's pieces (the two remaining ones, therefore, cannot create a mill) or to make it impossible for the player to make a move.

■ The Play

In the initial phase of setting up the pieces, every closed mill gives the player the option to take any one of the opponent's pieces. The piece that is taken is eliminated from the game.

MOVING THE PIECES

Once the pieces are set up, the players begin to move.

Every piece can be moved from one intersection point to an adjacent one that is free, in a straight horizontal or vertical line (Fig. 3). Even in this phase, it is necessary to try to close the mills in order to take the opponent's pieces.

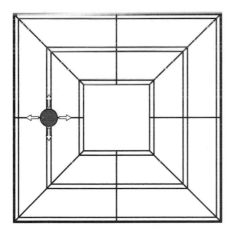

Fig. 3 - Every piece can be moved from one intersection point to an adjacent one that is free, in a straight horizontal or vertical line.

Pieces making up part of a mill cannot be taken. Opponent's pieces cannot be taken through jumps.

The only exception to this rule is when a player is left with only three pieces, and then he can jump, moving onto any vacant intersection point of his choice.

■ Strategy

One widespread strategy is to open up a mill, moving one piece to a vacant intersection point adjacent to the threesome, and, on the following move, close it again, thereby eliminating an opponent piece. Careful, however: the three pieces in a row are not able to be attacked, except when the threesome is opened, which then gives the opponent the opportunity to eliminate one of them.

MILL WITH DIAGONALS

One interesting variation is to also use the diagonal lines either for moving or for creating a mill. Whoever is left with the three pieces and begins to jump, can change the outcome of the game, having many more possibilities for moves, and winning a hand that was given up for lost. For this reason, it can be decided to exclude the jumping rule, thereby complicating the final phase of the game.

JUMP OF THE "KING"

It can also be established to introduce the jump of the "king": one piece adjacent to another (one's own or the opponent's) can jump it if the player has the possibility of landing on a vacant intersection point. In this case, however, the pieces that have been jumped are not taken: the only way to eliminate them is still to close the mills.

THE ROYAL GAME OF GOOSE

The extremely popular Royal Game of Goose has its origins in Florence toward the end of the 1500s. Following a gift made by Ferdinand of Medici to Philip II, King of Spain, it began to spread to the courts of Europe, especially in France and England. The sudden changes of fortune throughout the game contributed in no small degree to making it a successful game, as well as an excuse to richly decorate the boards on which one's own true adventures were narrated, famous battles were reproduced, and historical episodes, fables, myths and legends were recounted. This was done with such great abundance that some models of the Royal Game of Goose from past centuries can be considered as true works of art in their own right.

Players
Two or more

Game Equipment
- A large board divided into 63 squares, some of which have symbols corresponding to the rules of the game *(Fig. 1 on the following page)*
- A place card for each player
- Two dice, numbered from 1 to 6

■ Start & Object of Game

Players decide by luck of the draw who goes first.

The game is played in a clockwise direction. The players line up the place cards at the beginning of the game (outside of the first square, the one with the number 1). The object of the game is to make it through the entire board to square 63 before your opponents do.

■ The Play

Each player takes a turn throwing the dice and advances the number of squares corresponding to the total of the dice. It doesn't matter if one player ends up on a square occupied by one or more of the opponents' place cards.

FOLLOWING THE SIGNS
There are signs on some of the squares that are mandatory for the player to follow; common ones are described below.

Throw the dice again and advance according to the number obtained. Sometimes this rule corresponds to the symbol of the goose; other times, the geese designed on some of the squares of the trajectory are purely decorative.

Stop for one, two, or more turns, youare "imprisoned". In some Royal Games of Goose, when one is imprisoned for more than one turn, a player landing on the same square can free you. In turn, this player will be imprisoned for the turns indicated or until another player lands on the same square.

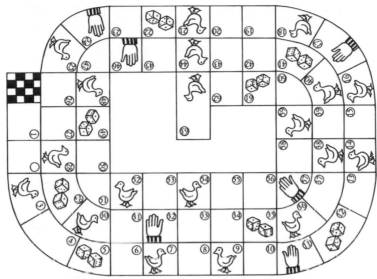

Fig. 1 - A typical panel board for the Royal Game of Goose.

Go back to the square from which you departed after throwing the dice; or, go back a preestablished number of squares, or go back to the starting square at the beginning of the game.

Go forward a preestablished number of squares, or a number equal to those just passed. If in going forward and back you end up on a square with a sign, you must follow it.

Reach a specific square. For example, if a player reaches a square where it is announced that he has won the lottery, then he goes to another square farther ahead in order to claim his prize. Naturally, if the player happens to end up on this "prize" square by chance, nothing happens.

WINNING THE GAME

In order to win, the player must reach square 63 on an exact throw of the dice. Otherwise, he must go back the number of squares that exceed the number he would have needed to land on that square.

If, for example, a player finds himself on square 60 and with a total of 5 points, he would advance to 63 and return to square 61 *(Fig. 2)*.

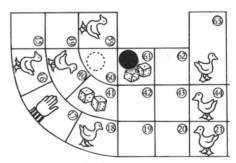

Fig. 2.

■ Strategy

The playing of the Royal Game of Goose absolutely depends on only on chance, since it relies on the numbers on the dice and on the signs on the squares one happens to land on. This is certainly the secret of its success. There is no strategy, only chance, and that is what makes it so much fun to play!

THE ROYAL GAME OF UR

*The Royal Game of Ur was the favorite game of the Sumerian nobility,
who resided more than 4,500 years ago in Mesopotamia, the region
located between the Tigris and Euphrates rivers. Like many other peoples,
the Sumerians had the custom of entombing with the dead
all that was dearest to them in life: different articles, jewels,
pottery, and even their favorite game, so they would have
some distraction in the world beyond. Numerous game boards, in fact,
were recovered in the tombs of the royal family and high priests,
during important archaeological digs in the biblical site of the city of Ur
at the beginning of the 20th century. A beautiful model is still preserved today
at the British Museum in London, a precious piece due to its richly elaborated
inlaid work, and an invaluable testimony to that ancient culture.*

Players
Two

Game Equipment
- A board divided into 20 squares, marked with rosettes *(Fig. 2)*
- 2 sets of 7 different-colored pieces, with front and back
- 6 special pyramid-shaped dice, each one with two marked corners and two unmarked corners *(Fig. 1)*

Fig. 1 - The pyramid-shaped dice (3 per player), each with two marked corners and two unmarked corners.

This is a racing game: the object is to move through the entire board and then remove all of one's own pieces.

SCORE OF THE DICE
Once the special dice are thrown, three corners, marked or unmarked, will be touching the table. According to the game, there are four different scores:
- 3 marked corners: 5 points;
- 3 unmarked corners: 4 points;
- 2 unmarked corners: 0 points;
- 2 marked corners: 1 point.

■ Start & Object of Game

Players decide by luck of the draw who goes first. Each player throws his own three dice and in accordance with the numbers, tries to make his own pieces enter the board.

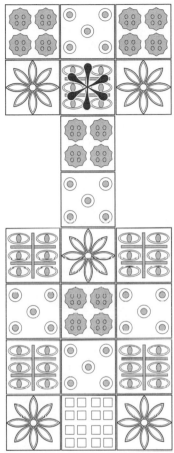

Fig. 2 - An example of a typical game board that is richly decorated. Note the five squares marked with rosettes.

▨ The Play

In accordance with the numbers obtained, one piece at a time will enter and successively advance in the game. Before beginning to advance, the pieces must all have entered onto the game board. The trajectory of the two players, outlined in Figure 3, shows one entering on the right and one on the left, with each one moving along his own lateral track (i.e., the squares on the upper level) and then moving down the central path, until reaching the exit square that is the central one of the first lower line (indicated below with an arrow).

The pieces enter the board showing their front side up. When they reach the central square in the lower part of the upper section (indicated by an asterisk in the diagram) and then begin to descend along the path, the back is turned up, in order to distinguish them from those that are ascending.

Entrances are only onto the rosettes in the lower section of the board, and only with a dice score of 1 or 5.

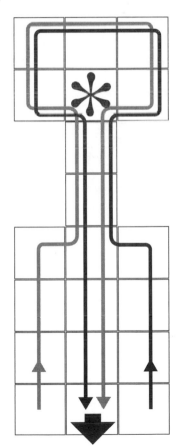

Fig. 3 - Display of the game trajectory of two players.

SAFE SQUARES & ATTACK

The 5 rosettes of the board (3 in the lower section and 2 in the upper section) mark the safe squares: pieces found there cannot be attacked. The same can be said for the exit square.

All the pieces in the upper section or path are open to attack by the opponent. This happens when a piece lands on an unsafe square, occupied by one or more of the opponent's pieces, which must be taken out and start from the beginning (that is, enter from the lower rosettes with 1 or 5 points). The pieces that are face-up can only attack pieces that are face-up while those face-down can attack only those opponents that are also face-down. There is no limit to the number of pieces that can occupy a square.

REENTRY OF THE PIECES

If a player has one or more pieces taken out of the game, they must reenter before the others can be moved again. If a player does not obtain 1 or 5 points on the dice so that a piece taken out can reenter, then he can not play that turn.

EXITING THE BOARD

When a piece that is face-down ends up, with exact numbers, on the exit square, it has the option, on the next throw, of leaving the board completely.

If, in the vicinity of the exit square, there is an excess of total of points, it goes there and then goes back the number of points that exceed the exit square. A piece on the exit square leaves if the points for the dice throw are exactly 4. If there are many pieces together on the exit square, all of them leave at once when the total number of points is 4.

■ Strategy

The Royal Game of Ur is a racing game, similar to the well-known game of Backgammon. While the game does depend to a great extent on the throw of the dice, players can nonetheless develop a clever and efficient strategy.

In contrast what typically happens in Backgammon, it is good not to accumulate too many pieces on the same square (unless it is a safe one) because they could be attacked and made to leave the game all at once.

On the other hand, it is good to accumulate them on the exit square, where they cannot be attacked and from where they can depart all at once when the total points for the throw of the dice is 4.

In the interest of removing the peices from the game, it is important to know that opponents' pieces can share the same safe squares.

GO

*Rightly considered the oldest game in the world, it is known for certain that
Go was already in vogue among the Chinese nobility more than 2,000 years ago,
taught by true and proper masters and wise men considered as holy men.
Toward the eighth century A.D., it was introduced in Japan,
where it was just as popular, so much so that until 1600
it was one of the disciplines taught at military schools. Finally, it arrived
in Europe only at the end of the last century but was immediately appreciated,
especially by the great chess players, for its rigorous logic.*

Players
Two

Game Equipment
A board divided into squares crossed
by 19 horizontal lines and 19 vertical
lines, forming 361 intersection points.
Of these, 9 are marked with a dot and
are called "handicap" points (Fig.1)
- 181 black pieces
- 180 white pieces

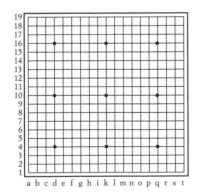

Fig. 1 - Playing board.

▓ Start & Object of Game

Players decide by luck of the draw who
begins to play first with Black, which
opens the game. In the game that follows, the roles will be reversed. Black
moves a piece onto any point of the
board, followed by White who does the
same.

The object of the game is to conquer
and win the greatest number of points,
by surrounding the opponent's pieces
with one's own pieces.

▓ The Play

Once in position, a piece can no longer
be moved. The pieces can be positioned
in any free point on the board, except in
the place called "Ko," as shown below.

Adjacent points are understood to
mean points that are contiguous in a
straight line that can be either horizontal
or vertical.

CAPTURING OPPONENT'S PIECES
In order to capture an opponent's piece
(or group of pieces), the player must surround it with his own, thereby cutting off

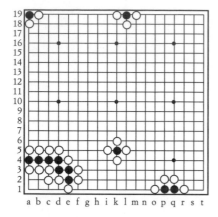

Fig. 2.

all possible means of escape, i.e., the free adjacent points *(Fig. 2)*. The captured pieces are eliminated from the game and put aside for the final score of points. Since the object of the game is not to capture opponent pieces but rather to accumulate as many points as possible, paradoxically a game can be won even without eliminating any opponent pieces.

WAYS TO EXIT & THE "KO" RULE

As is shown in Figure 3, a piece can have a maximum of 4 ways out; if it is positioned along the edge of the board the ways out are reduced to 3; if found in a corner, it has only 2 ways out.

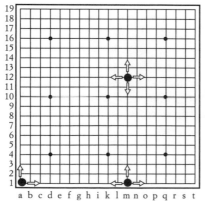

Fig. 3.

Groups or chains of pieces of the same color naturally increase the ways out.

The "Ko" situation is illustrated in Figure 4. In the first layout of the diagram, Black can put a piece on the point labeled with an "X" and in so doing capture the White located below; at this point, however, White can put a piece on the point labeled with an "X" in the second layout of the diagram, thereby returning to the initial situation.

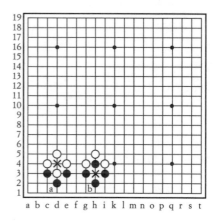

Fig. 4.

It is obvious that these situations could keep going infinitely, and that is why the "Ko" rule establishes that, in this case, White cannot execute the move described above, but must obligatorily choose another.

If on the next turn Black fails to fill in the vacant point (labeled with an "X" in the second layout of the diagram), White, on its turn, will be able to take the opponent's piece.

SUICIDE

Suicide could be said to occur were a player to purposely position his piece within a circle of opponent pieces. In that case, the piece would automatically be eliminated *(Fig. 5).*

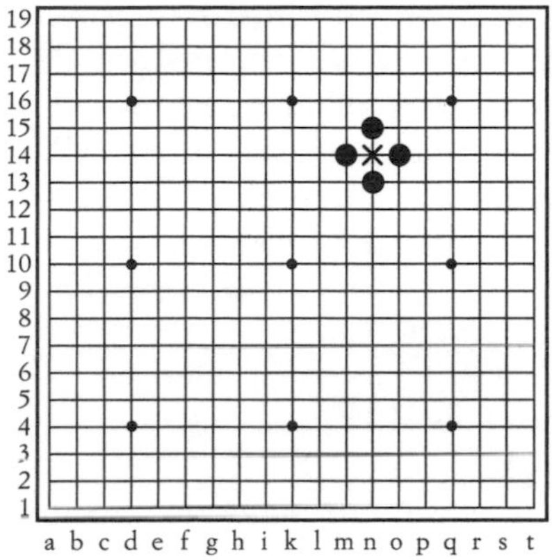

Fig. 5.

For this reason, it is forbidden to put oneself in such a situation. A piece cannot be positioned in territory surrounded by the opponent, unless this move results in the capture of one or more enemy pieces.

In Figure 6 it is shown, in fact, that if White's only way out is the point labeled with an "X" because it is itself surrounded by Black pieces, then it is eliminated by a piece that apparently intended to commit suicide.

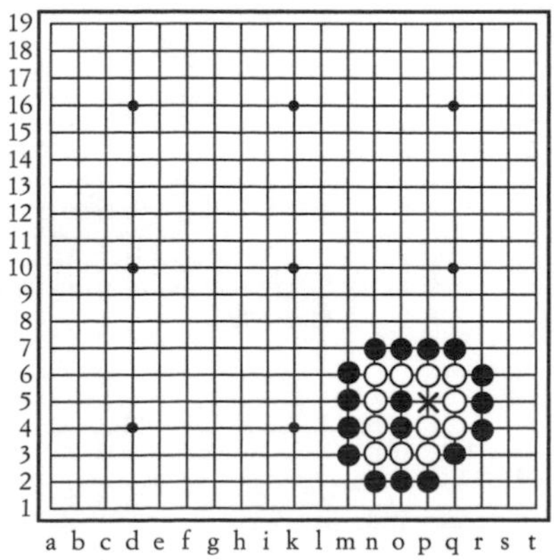

Fig. 6.

Figure 7 has the same layout as Figure 6 but with one fewer Black piece which then gives White the option of capturing three of the opponent's pieces if Black makes a wrong move and ends up occupying the point labeled with an "X."

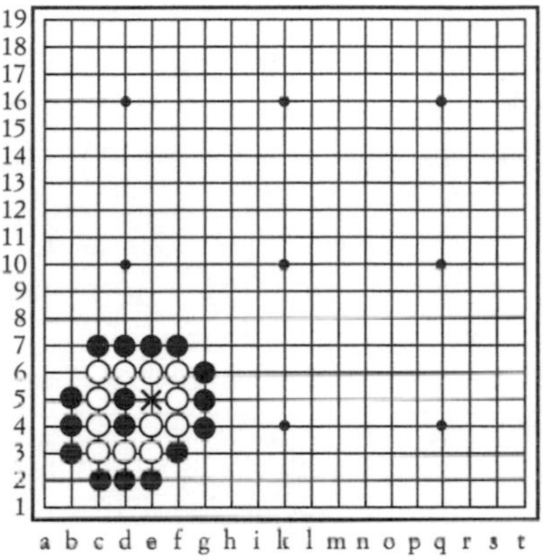

Fig. 7.

Finally, in the illustration of Figure 8 the situation called "Seki" occurs when two groups of opponent pieces are put in a situation such that neither of the players can position any of their own pieces without the risk of compromising his own pieces (or his own game).

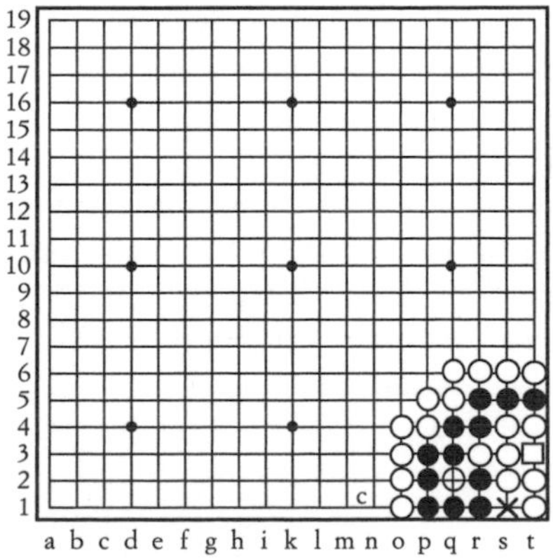

Fig. 8.

If Black puts a piece on the point labeled with an "X," on the next throw White will position itself on the point marked with a circle and capture the opponent's chain. If Black positions itself on the point marked with a "X," it commits suicide, like the White on the point with the circle; but if White positions itself on the point with the "X," Black only has to be put on the point marked with a circle in order to capture the White chain . . .

In short, however you look at it, the Seki situation is impossible to manage. For that reason it is left until the end of the game. In our example, the point marked with a circle will be ascribed to Black, the point with the square to White, and the one labeled with an "X" to neither one of the two.

END OF THE GAME

At a certain point of the game, a situation is reached where it is impossible to attack the opponent, protect oneself—except for suicide—or restrict one's own territory. On the game board, there are always vacant points remaining that will not be able to be claimed or conquered by the two players. These points are called "Queens." When players reach the impossible situation described above and can no longer move, they will occupy the Queen points with their own pieces on their respective turns.

Remember that the pieces can make connections between their respective formations, but will not be able to surround any new territory or capture opponents, and where the Queens are—as in the example—is indicated with the numbers and letters.

When the Queens are also occupied, then the game is truly finished. If there are still pieces enclosed within the oppo-

nent formations, they are eliminated and players proceed to count their points and add them to the opponent's pieces that have been eliminated.

In order to facilitate the task, Black puts together all the White pieces captured in opponent territory, while White does likewise. Then, only the points that have remained free in both territories have to be counted. Whoever has the most wins the game.

ADVANTAGE OF BLACK & THE HANDICAP POINTS

Black, which carries out the first move, has an advantage. If the two players are at the same level, they will alternate in playing with the Black. On the other hand, if one of the two players is less experienced, then it can be established that that player always plays with Black. If that does not balance the game enough, then he can play with a specific number of handicap pieces (from 2 to 9) positioned first at the start of the game on specific points. This is shown in Table 1, which refers to the game board coordinates as in all of the Figures.

In this case, once the handicap pieces are placed, White then moves first.

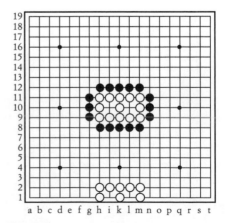

Fig. 9.

■ Table 1

Handicap	Position
2 pieces	D4, Q16
3 pieces	D4, Q4, Q16
4 pieces	D4, D16, Q4, Q16
5 pieces	D4, D16, K10, Q4, Q16
6 pieces	D4, D10, D16, Q4, Q10, Q16
7 pieces	D4, D10, D16, K10, Q4, Q10, Q16
8 pieces	D4, D10, D16, K4, K16, Q4, Q10, Q16
9 pieces	D4, D10, D16, K4, K10, K16, Q4, Q10, Q16

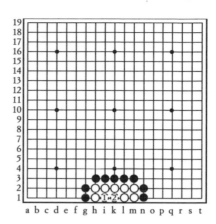

Fig. 10.

■ Strategy

The rules for Go are both easy and complicated at the same time. A game usually lasts one-and-a-half hours, and the more skilled the players are, the longer it can run. There are many strategies and modes of reasoning to consider for each of the moves.

For example, think well ahead before positioning a piece that would lengthen your chain, determining if the move would give you an additional way out, or if it predisposes you to encirclement of territory. As the game proceeds, complex shapes are formed which, at a glance, are not always easy to grasp.

EYES

One unbeatable way out is through the so-called eyes, illustrated in Figure 9. In both cases Black cannot occupy the two free points inside the White formation.

Eyes are efficient if there are two open points, separated by at least one piece, as in Figure 9. An eye of two points, as in Figure 10, is useless because Black attacks (at the spot labeled 1), and White responds (at 2), allowing Black to eliminate all the Whites.

A longer eye (*Fig. 11*) does not need to be divided because it is wide enough to allow White to defend itself from enemy attacks.

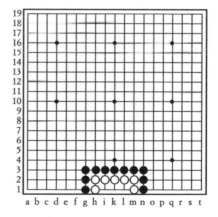

Fig. 11.

GROUPS

The key strategy is to not have a group that is either too dense or too scanty and not to change the structure of the group. Positioning one's own pieces on points adjacent to the group gives one new ways out; however, doing so also presents many options for closing to the opponent.

GO-MOKU

This is a variant of the more noble game Go, simple and quick
like the traditional Mill Game, from which this is perhaps the Eastern variant.
It can be played at the end of a long and contended game of Go,
but also drafted on a piece of blocked notebook paper
on which dots and crosses, like in Tic-Tac-Toe, can be marked.

Players
Two

Game Equipment
- A square board divided into
18 squares on each side *(Fig. 1)*
- 2 sets, one White, the other Black,
of 180 pieces

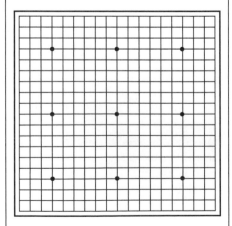

Fig. 1 - Playing board.

▦ Start & Object of Game

Players decide by luck of the draw who will play with Black. Similar to what happens in Go, Black positions a piece on one of the intersection points. The object of the game is to succeed in putting five of one's own pieces in a row called a mill, along a horizontal, vertical or diagonal line *(Fig. 2)*.

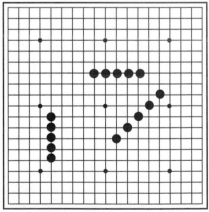

Fig. 2 - The object of the game is to put five of one's own pieces in a row.

▦ The Play

Players proceed in turns, positioning their pieces one at a time on a vacant intersection point.

Once the pieces are positioned they cannot be moved, nor at any moment eliminated by the opponent.

A move can consist in constructing one's own mill or in seeking to stop the opponent's.

The game ends when either of the two players has completed a mill or, alternately, it can continue until there are no pieces left. In the first case, the one who is first to make a mill wins the game. In the second case, once there are no pieces left, the one who has made the most mills wins the game. In both cases, the winner of the game concedes the Black to the loser who then initiates the following game.

▨ Strategy

As mentioned earlier, this is a pastime that is quick and very simple and which, given the vastness of the game board and the number of available pieces, truly allows the two players a free hand in playing. They can continuously initiate new mills, and in the meantime calmly dedicate themselves to stopping the opponent.

It is also true, especially in the case of players playing until there are no pieces left, that when the game board begins to be crowded one needs to have a thousand eyes in order to control all the moves left open to the opponent.

BARRIERS

One interesting variant to be adopted if players wish to complicate things a bit is

to put up "barriers" on the game board, before the start of the game.

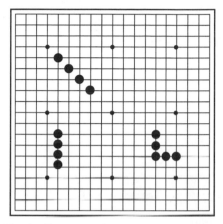

Fig. 3 - Example of "barriers" that can be put in place before the start of the game.

This means to put an indefinite number of pieces, as one wishes, in rows that are horizontal, vertical or diagonal, but which are not necessarily in a straight line, as seen in Figure 3. For example, a player can opt to put two barriers apiece, of a variable number of pieces agreed upon among the players before beginning the hand.

The barriers cannot be jumped over nor can they be used to help create a mill; naturally, the squares occupied by the barrier pieces cannot hold those of other players.

Barriers imply an extra strategic effort; one little strategy that is simple but should be kept in mind is to move from the barrier out and not in the opposite direction.

HALMA

*This game was very popular in England during the last century,
and owes its name to the Greek word meaning "jump,"
which is one of the two moves available to the pieces.
Today it is widespread in Germany and parts of Switzerland.*

Players
One, two, three or four

Game Equipment
- A square board divided into
16 squares on each side *(Fig. 1)*.
In each corner, there are sections of
13 squares marked off, two of which
are opposite each other and have
an ulterior line that widens them
to 19 squares
- Two sets of 19 pieces and two sets
of 13 pieces (of four different colors)

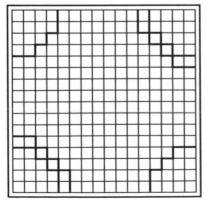

Fig. 1 - Playing board.

■ Start & Object of Game

For a game by a single player, there are
19 pieces in the special section. For a
game between two players, each player
has 19 pieces in their respective sections,
opposite each other *(Fig. 2)*.

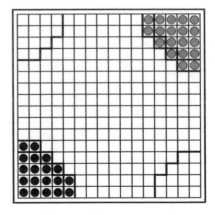

*Fig. 2 - Initial setup of pieces in a game
played by two.*

When playing among three or four,
13 pieces apiece are used *(Fig. 3)*. In a
game among four, it is possible to play in
teams of two against each other. In this
case, the components of a playing pair
play together side by side.

The object of the game is to bring all
one's own pieces into the corner section
that is opposite to the starting corner.

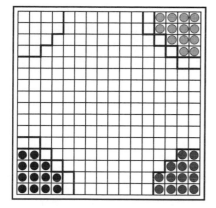

Fig. 3 - Example of initial setup of pieces for a game among three players.

A game played between two or four is won also when one or more of the opponent's pieces are blocked before they have departed from their own section.

▨ The Play

The pass move consists in moving a piece into an adjacent square of one's choice (horizontally, vertically or diagonally), if the square is vacant (Fig. 4).

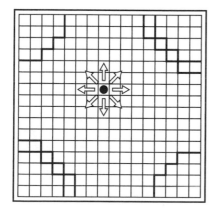

Fig. 4 - A pass move: moving the piece into an adjacent square.

The jump move (from where the game takes its name in Greek) consists in jumping a piece (it does not matter if it is one's own or the opponent's), which, however, doesn't get eliminated from the game, provided that it lands on a vacant square (Fig. 5).

Jumping is not mandatory.

Multiple leaps are allowed, even in different directions (Fig. 5), but only if, between one piece jumped and another, the land is on a vacant square.

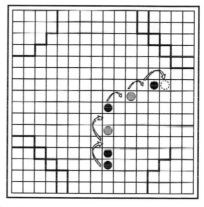

Fig. 5 - A jump move: consists in jumping a piece (one's own or the opponent's)—which doesn't get eliminated—provided that it lands on a vacant square.

During a multiple leap, one can stop wherever one wishes, even if there is a possibility of continuing.

Combining a pass move and jump move in a single turn is not allowed.

PLAYING WITH THREE, FOUR, OR PAIRS
When the game is played with three or four individuals, moves are made in a clockwise direction. When the game is played in pairs, if one of the team players has exhausted possibilities of moving his pieces, he can move his companion's pieces on his turn.

SINGLE PLAY

If a single player is playing, he must move his 19 pieces into the opposite corner in the least possible number of moves.

In another version for a game played by a single player, the player must manage to create the lineup illustrated in Figure 6 in no more than 19 moves.

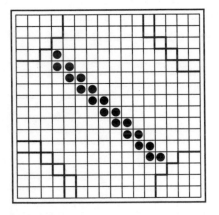

Fig. 6 - Representation of the end lineup in this single-player version.

There are about a hundred possible solutions and any player who is somewhat skillful can manage to find about half of the various methods without too much difficulty.

■ Strategy

Halma is a game with such simple rules that, as often happens, it offers an infinite number of variables, so many that mathematicians have not yet managed to delineate a winning strategy.

Certainly, other than having succeeded at accomplishing the goal (to reach the section opposite to the section of departure), it is also good to try to create as many obstacles as possible for the opponent, forcing him, if possible, to withdraw or prevent him moving one or more pieces. In a game played by a single player, the player should carry out the least number of moves possible. Remember that the more he jumps, especially multiple ones, the fewer moves are needed to reach the end.

ALQUERQUE (or WINDMILL)

An illustration depicting this game, which can be considered as a full precursor to modern Checkers, was recovered in an Egyptian temple going back to 1400 B.C. At the end of A.D. 1200 it was integrated into the "Book of Games" by Alfonso X in Spain, where, most probably it was introduced by the Arabs. From here it spread throughout all of Europe and was appreciated, like Chess, for its noteworthy dose of astuteness, skill, and intelligence needed to conquer the opponent.

Players
Two

Game Equipment
- A square board divided into
4 squares on each side, yielding
a total of 16 squares *(Fig.1)*.
-2 sets of 12 pieces, as in Checkers

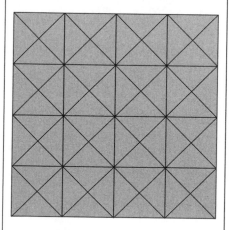

Fig. 1 - Playing board.

Start & Object of Game

Each player puts his own pieces on the intersection points of the squares, as shown in Figure 2.

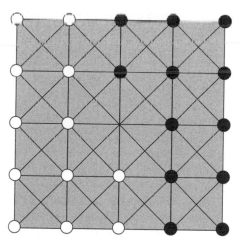

Fig. 2 - Initial set-up of the pieces.

The central point is left vacant in order to allow the first move, which the player with White pieces is entitled to. In successive games, players alternate in making the first move.

The object of the game is, as in Checkers, to succeed in eliminating all of the opponent's pieces or, alternatively, to immobilize them.

The Play

The player can move horizontally, vertically, or diagonally, along the intersection lines, and continue to advance, moving from one intersection point to an adjacent one that is vacant *(Fig. 3)*.

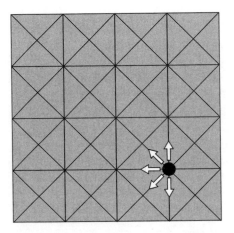

Fig. 3 - Example of possible movements for the pieces.

If the point adjacent to a piece happens to be occupied by an opponent, and the next one in a straight line is vacant, then the player can jump the opponent's piece and eliminate it from the game.

Jumps are mandatory: whenever a piece has the possibility of jumping and does not do it, it is "huffed" and eliminated from the game.

Multiple leaps are allowed. If, for example, after having jumped the piece ends up next to an opponent piece that has, in turn, the space adjacent to it vacant, then even this piece can be taken, and must be.

Every jump should necessarily be done in a straight line even if, at the end of the move, the line of the multiple leap ends up as a broken one.

Strategy

According to what is reported in the previously mentioned "Book of Games" by Alfonso X, the favored player is the one who plays second. For this, at the beginning of the game, the luck of the draw will determine who first plays with the White pieces and, in successive games, the two players alternate in their turns at playing iwht White and making the first move.

Two players who are equally capable can easily find themselves in a stalemate situation, in other words when each player's pieces are immobilized by those of his opponent and vice versa. In this case, the game is a tie.

In earlier forms of the game, moving backward was allowed. Adding this option to the game creates an interesting variant that can be experimented with, keeping in mind, however, that often a stalemate can occur.

THE HOUSE
OF FORTUNE

*A game of chance that has its origins in Nordic medieval times,
and is still a pastime appreciated in Austria and Switzerland.
It is a little of Roulette, a little of the Royal Game of Goose,
with squares that award and penalize the player landing on them.*

Players
Two or more

Game Equipment
- A board with a structure of 1
0 squares, containing Figures
numbered from 2 to 12, except
the number 4 *(Fig. 1)*
- 2 dice, numbered 1 to 6
- Chips

Fig. 1 - A typical playing board.

■ Start & Object of Game

First establish the total number of chips
each player gets to start with and the relative value of each chip. Note that in the
traditional version, all of the chips have
the same value. The object of the game is
to win as many chips from the opponents as possible.

■ The Play

Once all the players are gathered around
the table, the first throws the dice, and
then passes the turn on to the player at
his left, and so on.

According the numbers on the dice,
the player will put a chip in a corresponding square. Every time a player has
his turn, except as described below, he
places a chip, which stays in the square
as a stake until someone wins it.

WINNING THE CHIPS
If a 4 is thrown, no chips are laid down.

If the player ends up on a square with
other chips they are won and one of the
player's own chips is left in its place.

If a 2 is thrown, the player proceeds
to the square of the "lucky pig" which
gives him the right to round up all the
chips present on the table, except for
those on square 7.

If a 7 is thrown, the player proceeds to the square of "matrimony": the chips on this square cannot be won, unless the player ends up on square 12. as described next, or wins the game.

If a 12 is thrown, the player proceeds to the square of the "king", which gives him the right to round up all the chips present on the table, including those in square 7.

END OF THE GAME

Whoever winds up without chips must leave the game.

Whoever is the last to remain playing wins the game. If, once the game is won, there are still chips remaining on the table, these will also go to the winner.

If the game is a long and protracted one, with two or more players whose fortunes (like the chips in hand) are equivalent, it can be decided that the game will finish after a certain time. In this case, once the time has run out, whoever has the most chips in hand wins the game. The winner adds those chips that have remained on the table.

■ Strategy and Variants

As has been previously noted in other games of chance, there are no available strategies in existence that would help in any way: the dice cannot be influenced by intelligence or cleverness!

If players wish to increase this fun characteristic of a game of chance, they can decide to put in the square the same number of chips that correspond to the numbers on the throw of the dice. Be careful, however: this implies that if one ends on square 2 of the "lucky pig", the chips on the table will be rounded up but also that two will be left on square 2. The same thing occurs if a player ends up on 12: all the chips on the table are won, but twelve must be left on the square of the "king."

THE FOX & THE GEESE

*Inspired by hunting, this game of Nordic origin was widespread in Italy
already in Medieval times and, from the second half of the 1400s onward,
became very popular in England, where it was, centuries later,
one of the favorite pastimes of Queen Victoria.*

Players
Two

Game Equipment
- A cross-shaped board crossed with
horizontal, vertical, and diagonal lines
forming 33 intersection points *(Fig. 1)*;
or a board with 33 spaces to take in
the pieces
- 17 pieces representing the geese
- 1 piece representing the fox

■ Start & Object of Game

The luck of the draw determines who
will play the fox and who will play the
geese. In successive games the two roles
will be alternated.

The geese are set up as illustrated in
Figure 2. The fox can be put on any
intersection point among those left
vacant.

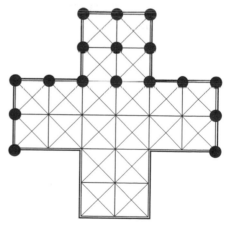

*Fig. 2 - Initial setup of the 17 pieces rep-
resenting the geese.*

For the geese the object of the game is
to immobilize the fox, by surrounding or
cornering it. For the fox the object of the
game is to take at least 12 geese (since,
the remaining 5 would not be enough to
immobilize it).

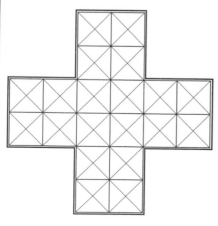

Fig. 1 - The playing board.

■ The Play

The fox has the first move.

The fox can move in any direction, from one intersection point to another adjacent one that is vacant (one per move), horizontally, vertically, or diagonally, forward or backward *(Fig. 3)*.

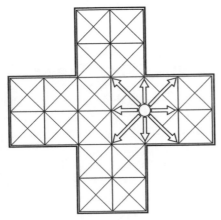

Fig. 3 - Outline of possible movements allowed to the fox.

The geese can move only in forward direction, horizontally, or vertically, but not backward or diagonally (Fig. 4), always one point per turn.

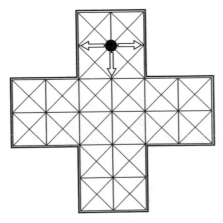

Fig. 4 - Outline of possible movements for the geese.

The fox "eats" a goose by jumping it, if it can land on a vacant adjacent point *(Fig. 5)*.

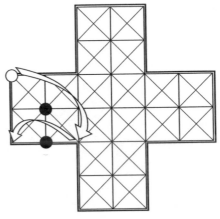

Fig. 5 - The fox eats a goose by jumping it, if it can land on a vacant adjacent point.

A goose that has been eaten has to leave the game.

Multiple leaps are allowed, only if between one jumped goose and another there is a vacant intersection point where the fox can land.

MANDATORY MOVES
The geese cannot jump the fox nor its own companions.

If the fox's only possibility is to make a move or jump that puts it in a difficult position, it is nevertheless compulsory for it to do so (it cannot skip a turn).

The same is true for the geese which, being more numerous, always have greater alternatives.

■ Strategy and Variants

Play either role willingly since both groups, although different in appearance, in reality are equivalent.

In the earlier versions the geese only numbered 13 but could also move diagonally and backward. Try experimenting with this interesting variant that was abandoned in 1600 when the number of geese was increased from 13 to 17.

MANDATORY JUMP

The jump can be made mandatory for the fox which, if it stops from executing it in favor of another move, can be forced by the opponent to retrace its steps and carry it out. Like in other similar situations, it is up to the player with the geese to evaluate on a per case basis whether or not to point out the fox's error to it: perhaps one or two pieces are lost, but it forces the opponent into a less favorable position.

In this case, however, it becomes mandatory to proceed with a multiple leap, once it is initiated.

LUDO

A classical game of race and capture, Ludo derives from Pachisi.
Ludo has its origins in India and was subsequently imported to England.
It is a faster and more simplified version than its oriental ancestor, still widespread
today, especially on the naval ships of the English Royal Navy.

Players
From two to four

Game Equipment
- A board that has a cross-shaped playing area and four Start Squares in the corners *(Fig. 1)*
- 4 sets, each of a different color, of 4 pieces each
- 1 die, numbered from 1 to 6

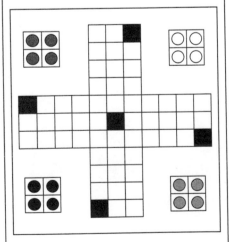

Fig. 1 - The playing board.

■ Start & Object of Game

Each player positions his own four pieces in the Start Square to his left, as shown in Figure 1. The die is thrown in order to determine who begins the play (that is, whoever obtains the highest number of points).

The first player throws the die and, if the points obtained allow him, enters one or two of his pieces into the game. Taking turns, the other players do the same in a clockwise direction.

The object of the game is to move throughout the whole board, capturing and staving back, when possible, the opponents, in order to ultimately bring all of one's own four pieces into the Central (Home) Square.

■ The Play

In order to have the pieces enter the game it is necessary to obtain a score of 1 or 6 on the die. With 1, the player can position a piece on the first square on his lower left.

With 6, he can choose between putting two pieces on that same square or one piece on the sixth house, that is the sixth square along the cross, counting from the Start Square in a clockwise direction *(Fig. 2)*.

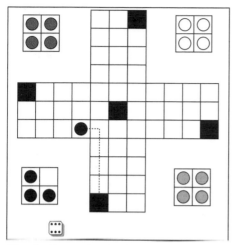

Fig. 2 - Example of possibilities and ways for pieces to enter onto the playing board.

ADVANCING THE PIECES

Successive throws allow the player to advance along the length of the cross one piece at a time, chosen among those in play, for as many squares as is indicated by the number obtained on the die.

Whoever obtains 6 can move, and has automatic right to throw the die again.

After having entered at least one piece in the game, at each throw of the die the player can decide whether or not to advance those pieces already on the playing board or have new pieces enter the game. In any case, in order to have a piece enter the game the player must obtain a 1 or 6.

A player is allowed to have two or more of his own pieces on the same square. However, each of these pieces must move separately, one at a time, in successive turns.

ELIMINATING OPPONENT PIECES

Whoever arrives with his own piece onto a square occupied by the opponent,

sends it back to his Start Square, from which he can enter the game once more if he throws a 1 or 6.

If, however, a square is occupied by two or more pieces, these cannot be attacked and they prevent all opponents from landing on that square.

If a player obtains a score on the die that keeps him from moving his pieces, he skips the turn.

FINAL PHASE

After completing the entire track of the cross, each player begins to move along his central track, until the last square, which makes up part of the Home Square (Fig. 3).

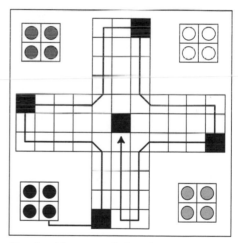

Fig. 3 - After completing the entire track of the cross, each player begins to move along his central track, until the last square, which makes up part of the Central (Home) Square.

The Home Square can be reached only through an exact score. If the score exceeds the number required, then the piece cannot be moved.

If possible, this score can be used to move other pieces, otherwise the turn must be forfeited.

The winner is the player who first manages to get all of his four pieces onto the Home Square.

Strategy

When a player is reaching the end of his track it is good for him to try to protect his own pieces, by placing two or more on the same square, thereby avoiding being sent back to the Start Square. Still, the fun in this game is really in the sudden changes of fortune and the future possibility, always present, of having to begin from scratch just when it seemed as though the end were near . . .

Naturally, in the central track the danger of being eliminated is nonexistent. At this point in the game, players are at the mercy of the throw of the die!

LUDUS DUODECIM SCRIPTORUM

A Latin name whose translation means "the game of the twelve letters,"
and for this reason an ancestor of the Board so much in fashion in ancient Rome,
and which has been considered, in turn, a close relative first of the Royal Board
and later of the very famous Backgammon. The most famous board of Ludus
Duodecim Scriptorum was recovered during archaeological digs in North Africa;
instead of simple letters, it carried the following inscription:

VENARI LAVARI
LUDERE RIDERE
HOC EST VIVERE

The meaning of the sentence says a lot about how much ancient Romans
loved the pleasures of life: "Hunt, bathe, play, laugh: this is living."

Players
Two

Game Equipment
- A scheme of three rows of twelve letters each where each row is made up of two groups of six letters *(Fig. 1)*
- 2 different-colored sets of 15 pieces each
- 3 dice, numbered from 1 to 6

CCCCC —— BBBBB

AAAAAA   AAAAAA

DDDDDD——EEEEEE→

Fig. 1 - The arrow indicates the direction of the game: A-A-B-C-D-E.

Start & Object of Game

Players decide by luck of the draw who goes first. In successive games the players will alternate going first.

The player who opens by throwing the dice puts three tokens on the three letters corresponding to the central row, counting from the left *(Fig. 2)*.

CCCCC   BBBBB
○
A♟♟♟AA   AAAAAA
DDDDDD   EEEEEE

Fig. 2 - In row A, two opponent pieces (or two groups of pieces) can even occupy the same letter. A player reaching the letter A occupied by the opponent puts his own piece on top of the opponent's.

The object of the game is to move through the entire A-A-B-C-D-E scheme with one's own pieces, and have them exit the board.

■ The Play

The dice are thrown by turns.

Only after making all 15 pieces enter the game can the player begin to move through the scheme.

The score on the dice cannot be taken, in whole or part, as the total. In other words: throwing 1, 3, and 4, a piece could be moved, for example, 8 letters, but always separately as 1, 3, or 4, or 3, 4, 1, etc.

The same point is valid if a player intends, for example, to take advantage of the throw by moving one piece 1 and another 7, the latter one only separately as 3 and 4 letters (or vice versa).

It is just like Backgammon.

MORE PIECES ON THE SAME LETTER

A player can have more pieces on the same letters, in which case he can put them on top of each other.

There are no limits to the number of pieces that can be present at the same time on the same letter.

In row A, two opponent pieces (or two groups of pieces) can even occupy the same letter. The player reaching a letter A already occupied by the opponent only has to place his piece on top of the opponent's (Fig. 2).

In the upper row and lower row, opponent pieces can be eliminated if they are individual (as in Backgammon).

In other words: when a player's piece reaches a letter (B, C, D, or E) occupied by one opponent piece, the opponent's piece exits the board and must begin from scratch (Fig. 3).

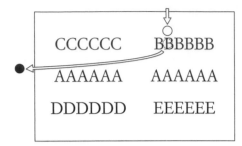

Fig. 3 - When a player's piece reaches a letter (B, C, D or E) occupied by the opponent piece, the piece exits the board and must begin from scratch.

If a player has a piece outside the board, he must make it reenter the game before moving any of his other pieces.

A letter of the upper or lower row that is occupied by one or two of a player's pieces cannot be attacked by the opponent.

USING THE SCORES

If a player is unable to use one or more scores on the dice because all his pieces would then end up on letters occupied by the opponent, he stays put and doesn't move.

If, on the other hand, the dice scores force him to moves that are strategically damaging (such as separating more pieces) then he must nonetheless execute the move.

EXITING FROM THE BOARD

Once reaching row E, the pieces can exit. It is not necessary to have rounded up one's own pieces all in row E in order to begin and make them exit.

To exit, the score must be exact or, in the event that there are no more of one's own pieces on the preceding letters, a score that exceeds it is needed (Fig. 4). Otherwise the points on the dice can be used to advance other pieces, or in the worse case scenario, remain in place. For example, in the situation in Figure 4, Black leaves E4 only with a 4, but can leave E5 with a 5 or 6 if there are no pieces on the preceding letters.

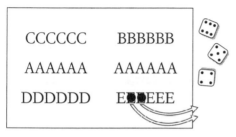

Fig. 4 - To exit, the score must be exact or, in the event that there are no more of one's own pieces on the preceding letters, a score that exceeds it is needed.

The winner is the player who first exits all of his pieces from the board.

▩ Strategy

It is obvious that Ludus Duodecim Scriptorum is a simplified version of Backgammon, with which it has many rules in common.

In particular, there is the rule that in some areas of the board (while in Backgammon this happens in all areas) an individual piece can be attacked by the opponent and made to exit.

The most important advice, then, is not to leave any individual pieces alone on the upper or lower row of the scheme, and to privilege those moves that cover such pieces, rather than advancing pieces that are already in a safe spot.

POSSIBLE MOVES

Playing with three dice certainly expands the possibile moves. It would be rare, then, that a player would not be able to use one or more of the scores obtained.

However, a wide range of possibilities imposes on the player—at every turn—to reason in long and complex ways.

What is imperative is that players do not act out of impulse, but evaluate first all of the alternatives before deciding on how to act.

MANCALA (or WARI)

*A fascinating board game of very ancient Egyptian origins,
Mancala is also known by the name Wari and is still very much
in practice in Africa, where it is also linked to religious rituals.*

Players
Two

Game Equipment
- A rectangular board with rows of 6
holes per side, for a total of
12 holes, in addition to 2 larger
end holes where captured pieces are
placed *(Fig.1)*
- 48 pieces

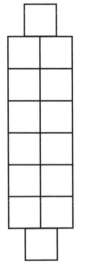

*Fig. 1 - The (vertical) scheme
of the playing board.*

■ Start & Object of Game

The two players sit in front of each
other, next to the long sides of the playing board. The 48 pieces are divided up
into the holes, such that each hole contains 4, as shown in Figure 2.

Players decide by luck of the draw
who goes first.

This player takes any 4 pieces from
any of his holes and divides them up,
one by one, into the next 4 holes, counterclockwise.

In doing this, he can also go to
"invade" the row of his opponent's
holes, as seen in Figure 3, where player
A left the fourth hole from the left and
moved a piece into any one of the following holes, including the first two of
the opponent's row.

The object of the game is to capture
the greatest number of pieces in the
holes of the opponent.

■ The Play

Each one of the players moves, one at a
time, all of his pieces (whatever this
number may be) from one hole to successive ones.

When the last piece moved ends up in
a hole of the opponent's row having only
one or two pieces, then the two or three
ensuing pieces in that hole at the end of

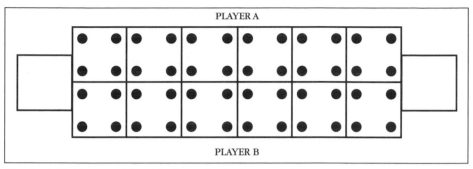

Fig. 2 - Initial layout of the 48 pieces in the holes of the game.

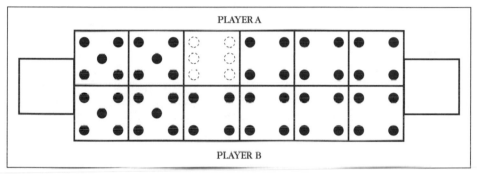

Fig. 3 - First move by player A, who moves 4 pieces.

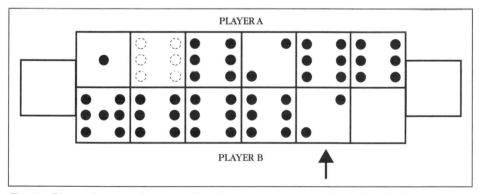

Fig. 4 - Player A moves 6 pieces. The last one ends up on the hole with the arrow: the other two pieces are eliminated.

the move will be "captured" and eliminated from the game (Figs. 4 and 5).

The pieces captured by a player are put in the end hole on his right.

If, once the pieces are captured in one hole, the successive ones—including in the opponent's row—contain two or three pieces, these also are captured in the same turn of the player who executed the first capture.

The holes just left vacant then are jumped and filled on the successive turn.

In other words, when a player, moving the pieces, ends up on a hole that has

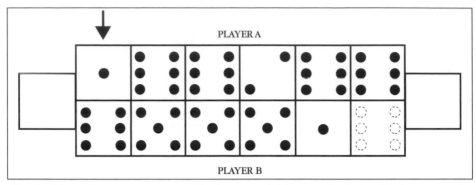

Fig. 5 - Player B moves 6 pieces. The last one finishes on the hole with the arrow: the piece gets eliminated.

just been left vacant (by him or the opponent), he jumps it; and vice versa, on the successive turn, if the opponent's move takes him to the same vacant hole, he must fill it with one of his pieces.

When all the holes in the row of a player are vacant, and it is his turn to play, and that is not possible, then the game is considered finished.

Once the game is finished, the player who has pieces remaining in his holes adds them to the ones put aside in the end hole.

Whoever has the most pieces wins the game.

■ Strategy

Mancala is a complex and fast-paced game that can be learned only with a great deal of practice and which gradually becomes more fascinating. The lay-out of pieces in the opponent's holes must always be observed with attention, especially those holes containing one or two pieces, and which therefore are more vulnerable.

THREATENED HOLES & DEFENSE

Managing to threaten more holes at the same time reduces the defense possibilities of the opponent.

Certainly, the most dangerous situation is when a hole containing one or two pieces is threatened by an opponent who has an equal number of pieces on the holes separating the two.

One possible defense consists in "dismantling" the vulnerable holes: if they contain one or two pieces, it might be opportune to move them in order to avoid an attack; naturally, a hole with two pieces is defended also by adding a third one.

NYOUT

*Of Korean origin, and thousands of years old, Nyout is a typical racing game,
with pieces called "horses" that compete along a circular track.
It owes its popularity to the simplicity of the rules, which make it a pastime
appreciated for its speed, in addition to the possibility of placing bets.*

Players
Two or four in pairs

Game Equipment
- A circular scheme, with twenty
spaces crossed by a cross of 9
spaces: the spaces corresponding to
the ends of the cross and the Central
Space are larger *(Fig. 1)*
- 4 sets of 4 pieces each
- 1 die, numbered from 1 to 6

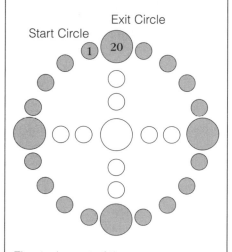

Fig. 1 - Layout of the game.

■ Start & Object of Game

Players decide by luck of the draw who
goes first. The chosen player throws the
die and then enters one of his horses from
the space marked with the number 1 *(Fig.
2)*, moving it counterclockwise exactly as
many spaces as are indicated by the
number on the die.

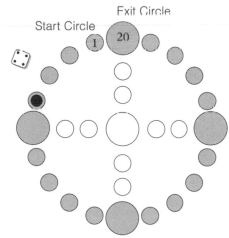

*Fig. 2 - The chosen player throws the
die and enters one of his horses from
the space marked with the number 1,
moving it as many spaces indicated by
the score obtained.*

The object is to move through the circle until space 20, from which one's
horses are allowed to exit.

■ The Play

Before advancing the horses, the player must first enter all of them in the game. More than one of the same player's pieces can be positioned on the space.

TAKING THE OPPONENT'S HORSES

If a player lands on a space already occupied by an opponent horse, the opponent piece must return to the Start Circle. If there is more than one opponent piece, only one piece returns.

Whoever has made an opponent horse return throw the die again.

CHANGE IN DIRECTION

When a player lands on one of the large circles, the end points of the inner cross with an exact number on the throw, he can decide to run through the arms on his next turn, and, once arrived in the center of the cross, direction can be changed 90 degrees *(Fig. 3)*.

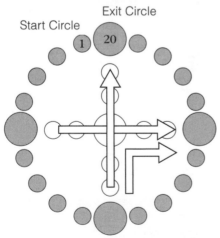

Fig. 3 - Once arrived at one of the end points of the cross, a player can decide to run through the arms, and, once arrived in the center of the cross, direction can be changed 90 degrees.

EXITING FROM THE GAME

A player exits when, on an exact throw, he reaches the Exit Cricle. Otherwise, he goes back the number of points that exceed the number necessary to reach the Exit Circle.

The player who is first to exit all of his horses wins.

PLAYING IN PAIRS

The rules are the same for when there are only two players or four divided into pairs. The only difference is that, once the die is thrown, a player can freely decide on whether or not to move one of his horses or one of his companion's.

■ Strategy

The success of Nyout depends heavily on the throw of the dice. The only strategy, then, is to attack as much as possible: if after a throw you find yourself having to choose between advancing a piece that has gone back or making an opponent piece return, it is no doubt preferable to do the latter, unless you have most of your pieces at the start of the track, where they could be easily attacked by an opponent horse at the moment of its reentry.

SOME VARIANTS

In practice, the number of pieces can vary from 2 to 4. Begin, then, by playing only with 2 and then 3 horses, in order to master the game. Even if Nyout is usually played in two or four, the number of participants can be increased as one wishes.

Another variation: in Korea rather than traditional dice, special wooden rods numbered from 1 to 5 are used. In this way, the game lasts slightly longer, but the strategy doesn't change.

PACHISI

A very ancient game, and precursor of the very vast family of race and capture games, Pachisi has its origins in India. The English spread it throughout the world, including with its numerous and often simplified variants.

Players
Two or four

Game Equipment
- A board in the form of a cross (Fig.1) with 24 squares per arm, three of which the Castles—are marked with an X, and a center of different colors called "Home"
- 4 different-colored sets of 4 pieces each
- 6 cowrie shells, with one side convex and the other side showing an opening

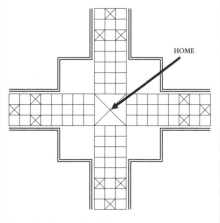

HOME

Fig. 1 - Layout of the game.

■ Start & Object of Game

The players gather their own pieces in the central Home. The object of the game is to move throughout the entire board and return to Home before any of the other opponents.

■ The Play

When playing with four individuals, each player sits in front of his own arm of the board. When playing in pairs, the teams face each other.

When playing with two, each player moves his own pieces and those of a hypothetical companion beside him.

Players decide by luck of the draw who goes first. The game moves in a counterclockwise direction.

POINTS OF THE SHELLS
Every player, on his turn, throws the shells (Fig. 2, on page 76) which, in accordance with the way that they fall, have a particular score.

The points are calculated according to the shells that land open-side up:
- no open-side up: 25 points;
- 1 open-side up: 10 points;
- 2 open-sides up: 2 points;
- 3 open-sides up: 3 points;
- 4 open-sides up: 4 points;

Fig. 2 - 3 open side up = 3 points.

- 5 open-sides up: 5 points;
- 6 open-sides up: 6 points.

For the pieces to enter the game (making them leave Home), the player needs a total of 6, 10, or 25 points.

The pieces are initially moved along the central path. Once they have arrived at the base of the player's own arm along the cross, they continue to move, in a counterclockwise direction, the same number of squares as calculated by the throw.

The trajectory of the game is illustrated in Figure 3.

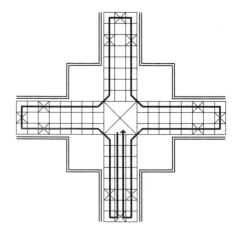

Fig. 3 - Trajectory of game.

ATTACKING OPPONENT PIECES

When a piece arrives in a square occupied by an opponent, the opponent is sent Home. The opponent piece can only leave home again when the throw totals 6, 10, or 25.

The player who sends an opponent piece Home has is given another throw.

The pieces in the Castles, marked with an X, cannot be attacked.

Whoever obtains a score that would lead him to a safe square occupied by an opponent piece, loses a point and stops on the preceding square.

Playing in pairs as a team, a piece can "host" one of his companion's pieces on his square.

The same can be said for the game played between two with hypothetical companions.

When a player ends up on a square occupied by one or more of his pieces, these pieces are gathered and can advance together, thereby becoming immune to attack by equal or lower numbers of gourped opponent pieces (but which must, consequently, stop on the square that immediately precedes, losing a point).

The pieces grouped together can "disband" whenever they wish.

FINAL PHASE

When a piece has completed the round and finds itself on his own central path, it goes back toward Home.

The piece that reaches its own castle in the central path on the exact throw of 25 goes directly Home, without further throws.

In all the other situations, Home must be reached with an exact throw. Otherwise, the player goes back along the central path as many squares as the number that exceeds an exact throw.

A player may, if he wishes, forfeit his turn, if for example a score of 25 would lead him to run back through so many squares that he would end up much farther from Home.

When playing in pairs, a player whose pieces have all gone Home ceases to play. Or, if he wants, he can reenter one or more pieces into the game, if this might prove useful for his companion. Those pieces would necessarily have to repeat the entire circuit.

When playing as four individuals, after the first player has led all his own pieces Home, the three remaining players continue, and then two, so as to establish an order of arrival.

The winner is the player, or pair of players, who leads all of his own pieces Home first.

Strategy

The pieces gathered in a group cannot be attacked except by a larger group; so, whenever possible, it is a good idea to form groups for protection.

It is therefore essential to evaluate all possible moves carefully upon each throw.

In certain cases, the same score can lead to situations that are very different from each other. Thus, one should consider all possible situations.

Forfeiting one's turn can be a good strategy, especially at the end of the game, when perhaps one would distance oneself too much from Home or end up one square away (the 1 is—as is obvious—a score that is impossible to realize with the shells).

PULUC

A popular street game among the indigenous people of Guatemala
—of Mayan origin—Puluc symbolizes the elements
of their millennial traditions: agriculture and war.

Players
Two

Game Equipment
- 10 little wooden sticks or ears of corn
- 4 chips or 4 dice with only two different sides, one white and one black (heads = white; tails = black). The simplest version is played with 4 grains of corn having one of the two sides painted in black
- 2 sets of 5 pieces with a flat surface, just like the ones used to play Checkers, which symbolize the warriors

■ Start & Object of the Game

Arrange the wooden sticks in a shape of a ladder *(Fig. 1)*.

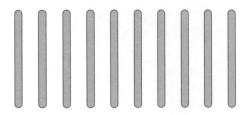

Fig. 1 - Arrangement of the sticks.

The players place themselves at opposite ends of the ladder: the starting points are the respective villages.

Players decide by luck of the draw who goes first. The object of the game is to eliminate all the opposing warriors.

SCORING
The throw of the dice, shown in Figure 2, has the following score:
- Two heads: 2 points
- Three heads: 3 points
- Four heads: 5 points
- Four tails: 4 points

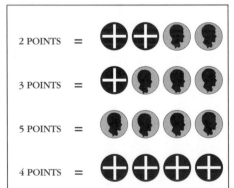

Fig. 2 - The possible scores.

■ The Play

The starting player tosses the dice and, according to the score, places one of his own warriors on the track, between two adjacent wooden sticks, as shown in Figure 3, below.

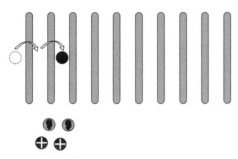

Fig. 3 - Placing a piece in the track.

You play in turns, tossing the dice and letting your warriors enter the game or move forward. A warrior cannot occupy the space already taken by another warrior of his same side.

CAPTURING OPPOSING PIECES

When a warrior advances to a space already taken by an opposing piece, he takes the opponent captive, placing it underneath himself. Once a warrior gets a prisoner, he heads back on the track, trying to get back to his own village, still according to the toss of the dice.

If he gets to his own village, the opposing piece (the prisoner) is eliminated, while the warrior, with the next toss of the dice, can go back and forward on the track, trying to capturer othe opponent warriors.

GETTING OUT OF THE TRACK

Getting out of the track, carrying an opposing warrior, does not require a perfect score of the dice. It is enough to get a score exceeding the number of the spaces between the warrior and the end of the track. For example, in Figure 4, the piece in the third space will get out, eliminating the opponent placed underneath, with a 3, a 4, or a 5.

GROUPS OF PIECES

A warrior who gets to a space already occupied by an opponent who has captured a piece of that warrior's side gets on top of the two and takes them to his own village. If he reaches it, the opponent is eliminated, while the two warriors, at the next turn, can get back on the track one at a time.

A group of pieces placed on top of each other can change possession any number of times during a game, every time, of course, changing direction.

A group of pieces, topped by a warrior, can capture a single enemy piece, just as well as another group led by an opposing piece.

GETTING BACK ON THE TRACK

If a warrior gets on the track and goes along it until the end without capturing any opponent, neither being caught himself, as he gets to the end, he goes back

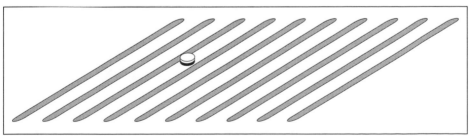

Fig. 4 - This warrior with a prisoner can get back to his village to the left with a score of 3, 4, or 5.

to his own village, from which the following turn he reenters and starts the game again.

The player who first eliminates all the opponent's pieces wins the game.

■ Strategy

Puluc is a simple game but quick and captivating for the endless chasing and the overturning that follow one another. The player who goes second is, at the beginning, the favorite and right away has the chance to catch the piece of the player who played first. For this reason, it is fair to switch who begins every game, or to establish that the player who loses the game gets to start the following one. The outcome of the game is greatly affected by the luck that one has with the dice; nevertheless a little strategy is possible.

At the beginning of the game it is wise to place as many pieces on the track as possible (unless one manages to catch an opponent), considering that a piece that reaches the end of the track has to go back to the starting point.

RINGO

A strategic game of German origin, Ringo is similar to others,
such as Tournament or the Fox and the Geese, for the disparity of the forces
in the field that get evened out by the different possibilities for moving the pieces,
and by the goal of conquering a fortress.

Players
Two

Game Equipment
- A round board *(Fig. 1)* divided into seven concentric circles and eight sectors, for a total of 49 spaces; the round space in the middle, of a different color, is the fortress; one sector of the board is distinguished from the others by its different color, which is neutral; the other sectors alternate spaces of one color and another
- 4 pieces of one color for the defender; 7 pieces of a different color for the attacker

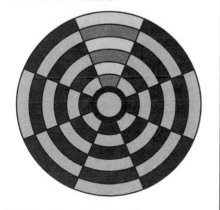

Fig. 1 - The game board.

■ Start & Object of the Game

Arrange the pieces as shown in Figure 2: the defender's around the fortress, the attacker's in the outer circle, leaving the neutral segment free.

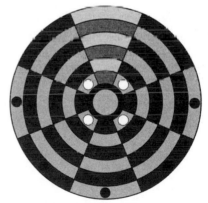

Fig. 2 - Initial setup: the 7 black pieces of the attacker and the 4 white ones of the defender around the fortress.

The object of the game for the attacker is to take over the fortress with at least two pieces. The object of the defender is to prevent the attacker from doing so.

■ The Play

Players decide by luck of the draw who attacks and who defends. For the next game, roles will switch.

The attacker moves first. The attacking pieces can move only one space at a time, either forward, toward the fortress, or sideways *(Fig. 3)*.

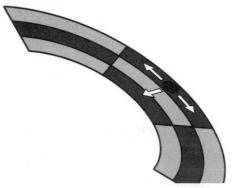

Fig. 3 - Possible moves for the attacking pieces.

The defender's pieces can move one space at a time, forward, sideways, or backward *(Fig.4)*.

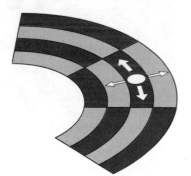

Fig. 4 - Possible moves for the defending pieces.

No one can move diagonally. Moving a piece sideways will keep it in the same circle, while moving it forward or backward, in the same sector.

ELIMINATING OPPOSING PIECES

A piece can take an opposing one by jumping it, moving to an unoccupied space of the same circle (in case of a sideways jump) or the same sector (in case of a forward or backward jump), as shown in Figure 5. Only the defender's pieces can jump backward.

Fig. 5 - A piece can take an opposing one by jumping it, moving to an unoccupied space of the same circle (ia sideways jump) or in the same sector (a forward or backward jump).

It is not compulsory to jump a piece. Multiple jumps are not allowed.

FORTRESS & NEUTRAL SECTOR

The defender's pieces cannot enter the fortress, but by jumping over it, they can take an opponent's piece inside *(Fig. 6)*.

In the neutral sector no one can take his opponent's piece.

The neutral sector, nevertheless, can be the starting or the landing point of a jump in which one takes his opponent's piece located in a space of an adjacent sector or in the fortress.

The attacker cannot have more pieces in the neutral sector than the number of pieces that the defender has on the entire board: for example, if the defender has only two pieces left, the attacker cannot have more than two of his pieces in the neutral sector.

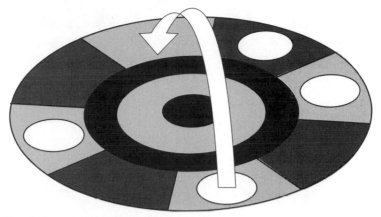

Fig. 6 - *The defender's pieces cannot enter the fortress, but by jumping over it, they can take an opponent's piece from inside of it.*

WINNING THE GAME

The attacker wins by placing 2 pieces inside the fortress.

The defender wins by taking 6 of the attacker's pieces. The defender can also win by blocking the attacker's pieces, preventing him from placing two pieces inside the fortress.

■ Strategy

The defender's pieces face a double danger when placed around the fortress: being jumped and letting an attacker's piece inside the fortress.

Two pieces of the same team, next to each other, defend themselves from sideways attacks; one in front of the other defends from forward or backward attacks. An attacker's piece placed on the circle around the fortress is safe from forward or backward attacks, but not from attacks coming from the side.

It is wise for an attacker who has one piece placed on the last neutral space, adjacent to the fortress, to keep it in that position, completely safe, while trying to reach the fortress with a different one first, leaving the last move to the piece on the neutral space.

CLASSIC SOLITAIRE (or FRENCH SOLITAIRE)

One of the best known solitaires originated in France in the 1700s.
It is claimed to have been created by the mathematician Pelisson to entertain
the Sun King (Louis XIV) during his long travels by horse and carriage.
According to another version of the story, the conceiver of the game was
an aristocratic prisoner of the Bastille, who wanted to kill time. Nevertheless,
it was later exported to England where it became very popular in Victorian parlors.

Players
One

Game Equipment
- A board with 37 spaces (Fig. 1)
- 36 pieces
- Usually, the spaces on the board are little cavities, and the pieces are marbles. Alternatively, the spaces are little holes and the pieces are pegs

```
        ( 1 ) ( 2 ) ( 3 )
     ( 4 ) ( 5 ) ( 6 ) ( 7 ) ( 8 )
 ( 9 ) (10) (11) (12) (13) (14) (15)
 (16) (17) (18) (19) (20) (21) (22)
 (23) (24) (25) (26) (27) (28) (29)
     (30) (31) (32) (33) (34)
        (35) (36) (37)
```

Fig. 1 - Outline of the game board, with the spaces numbered, to simplify the interpretation and the solution of the problems.

▩ Start & Object of the Game

Arrange the pieces in the spaces, leaving the one in the middle free. One must eliminate all the pieces, one after another, until only one piece is left.

▩ The Play

The pieces are eliminated by jumping them with an adjacent one, which has to land in a free space: the piece that has been jumped over is eliminated (*Fig. 2*).

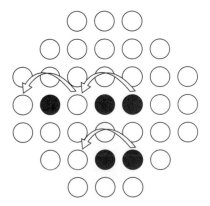

Fig. 2 - The pieces are eliminated by jumping them with an adjacent one, which has to land in a free space. The drawing in the middle shows the execution of a multiple jump.

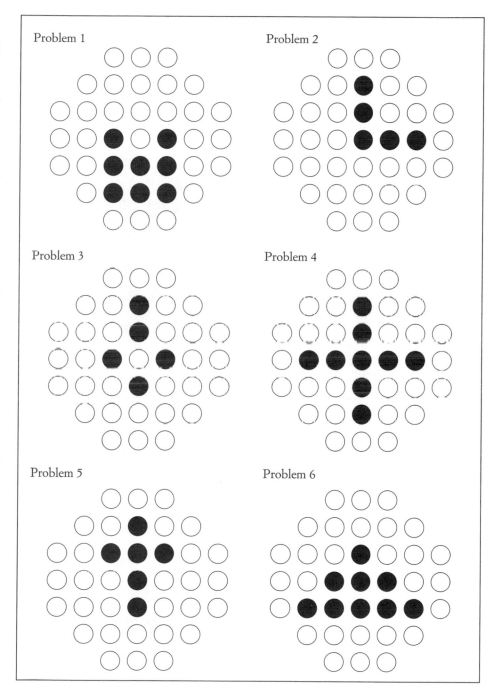

Fig. 3 - To master the rules of the game, it is a good idea to practice with simple schemes: the six problems represented here must be solved with only one piece in the middle at the end of the game (in position 19).

One can move the pieces horizontally or vertically, but not diagonally.

Multiple jumps are allowed only in stages of one space at a time. One can not jump two adjacent pieces unless there is an unoccupied space between them *(Fig. 2, see previous page)*.

▓ Strategy

Classic Solitaire is a mathematical game and as such, can only be solved with reasoning and practice.

It is important not to leave pieces that are isolated from others, making them impossible to jump. To practice, at the beginning, use the six simplified problems represented in Figure 3 (see previous page), ending with only one piece in the middle.

▓ Variations

One can start with a reduced scheme, taking away a few pieces before starting and leaving more unoccupied spaces at the beginning. This implies a larger number of possibilities for the choice of the first move.

Before beginning, one can decide to end the game with more than one piece on the board, rather than only one, displayed in a scheme already planned.

One can also decide to end the game with only one piece on the board, in a space previously decided. For example, leaving the one in the middle or the one opposite the piece taken away at the beginning.

A few examples follow of problems that are fun and instructive to solve, given in increasing difficulty, using the numbering of the spaces shown in Figure 1, that is, from 1 to 37, from left to right, from top to bottom.

▓ Challenges Starting with a Set Scheme

THE OCTAGON

Start as shown in the picture below.

End with only one piece in the middle (space number 19).

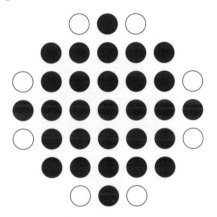

THE HOURGLASS

Start as shown in the picture below.

End with only one piece in the middle (space number 19).

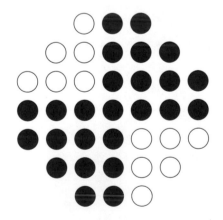

THE CRYSTAL

Start as shown in the picture on the next page.

End with only one piece in the middle (space number 19).

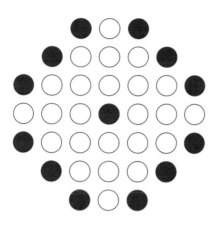

THE SQUARE

This is a particularly sophisticated game.
Start as shown in the picture below.
End with only one piece in the middle
(space number 19).

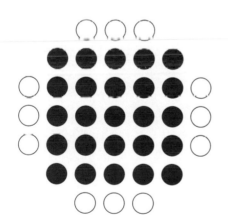

THE PIRATE

This is a game of intermediate difficulty
but greatly satisfying.
To start take away piece number 3.
End with only one piece in space
number 35.

■ Challenges Starting with a Complete Scheme

THE WORLD

This is a problem of intermediate difficulty. Start with only the middle space empty (number 19).
End as shown in the picture below.

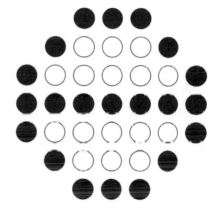

LE TRIOLET

Start with only the middle space empty (number 19).
End as shown in the picture below.

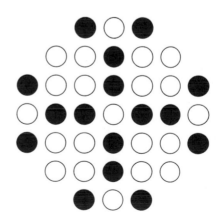

CARD GAMES

TRUMPS

*Trumps has its origins in northern Europe toward the end of the 1500s,
but has become the most popular card game in Italy as "Briscola." Trumps is played
throughout the Italian peninsula, and the Italians have changed the rules
so much to create almost a new game. Trumps is a simple game,
often with unexpected outcomes, especially if played by people
with similar skill and knowledge.*

Players
Two, three, or four (in pairs)

Game Equipment
- A deck of 40 cards (remove the 8, 9, and 10 of every suit in a deck of 52)

■ Start & Object of the Game

Each of the players cuts the pack of cards, showing the one at the bottom: the player who shows the card of lesser value will be the dealer. In the subsequent hands, each player will take turns being the dealer in a counterclockwise rotation.

When playing with four (two pairs), the teammates of each pair will sit facing each other.

With three players, before beginning the game, one of the 2s (it doesn't matter which suit) must be removed from the deck, leaving 39 cards.

The object of the game is to score as many points as possible through tricks.

The dealer, after having shuffled the cards, has a player on his left side cut the deck and then deals three cards to each player in a counterclockwise direction.

ESTABLISHING TRUMP

Once the cards are dealt, the dealer places the first card of the leftover pile faceup in the middle of the table, half covered by the remaining pack: this card is the trump of that specific hand. This card and all the others of the same suit have a greater value than any other card of a different suit. For example a four of trumps (that is, of the same suit of the trump) has a greater value than a King of a different suit (*Fig. 1*).

Fig. 1 - Example of a trick which the trump wins.

■ The Play

The player to the right of the dealer begins the game, placing a card on the table, which he replaces immediately with one from the deck.

The other players must, when possible, play a card of the same suit and then pick a card from the deck, so that during the game every player will always have three cards in their hands.

WINNING A TRICK

A trick is won by the player who has placed the highest valued card of the leading suit (that is, the one played by the first player) or a trump card.

The values of the cards are the followings: Ace, 11 points; three, 10 points; King, 4 points; Queen, 3 points; Jack, 2 points *(Fig. 2)*.

ENDING A HAND

When there are no cards left in the pack (the last one will be the trump), the players of the same team can see each other's cards in to plan a better conclusion of the hand. The player or team who scores 61 or more points wins the hand. If each player or team scores 60 points, the hand is tied and will not count.

The player or team that wins two out of three hands wins; but this rule can be changed, before starting by establishing the number of hands needed to win.

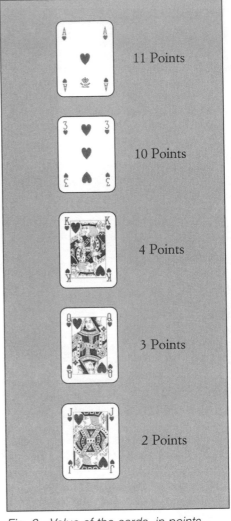

Fig. 2 - Value of the cards in points. All the other cards not listed here have no point value.

■ Strategy

During the first round, the teammates are not allowed to communicate in any way, neither in words nor signs. From the second round on, communication is allowed, but discreetly, and in such a way that the players of one team will not know what cards the opponent holds.

The most common signs in the game of Trumps are: pursed lips for the Ace; twisted mouth for the three; eyes toward the sky for the King; showing the tip of the tongue for the Queen; raise the shoulders for the Jack *(Fig. 3)*.

However, any pair that gets on well together can establish their own signs.

Fig. 3 - The most common signs used to communicate the important cards to each other.

LOADS & TRICKS

Aces and threes, for their value, are called "loads."

It is a good idea, if possible, to avoid laying down a card when neither of the loads of the same suit has been played yet, unless it is sure that both loads are in the hands of the teammate.

During the game it is important to memorize all the cards played, particularly loads and trumps.

When the faceup trump on the table beneath the deck is a load, or even a King, one may decide to lose the second to the last trick on purpose. The losing player or team is guaranteed to get that card with the following pick. When doing so, one must consider whether it is worth it to lose the trick, especially if it contains many points, in spite of getting the loaded trump card as the last pick from the table.

CANASTA

*Canasta means "basket" and it is a South American game.
It comes from Uruguay and became very popular in the United States
in the 1950s and then all over the world. In the United States it is still,
without a doubt, one of the most popular games around.*

Players
Four (two teams)

Game Equipment
- 2 decks of 52 cards plus four jokers

▣ Start & Object of the Game

The players cut the deck of cards: the two with the highest cards (from Ace highest to two lowest, from spades to hearts to diamonds to clubs; a player who holds a joker must cut the deck again) make a team and the other two another team.

The player who cut the highest card shuffles the pack and deals, clockwise, thirteen cards to each player, including himself.

The object of the game is to lay down melds made with the cards that a player has in hand, earning the highest number of points possible.

RULE OF THE RED THREES
The players look at their own cards: if a player has one or two red threes (hearts and diamonds), he lays them down on the table. These cards must be replaced with the same number of cards that are picked from the leftover pack.

The rule of the red threes is also applicable during the game: when one picks a three of hearts or diamonds he must lay it down and exchange it with another card picked from the pack.

The dealer, after having laid down any red threes, uncovers the first card from the pile, starting a new little pile of discarded cards, called the "well." If the card is a red three, a joker or any two (also called a "deuce" which has the same characteristics of a joker), the dealer uncovers another card, and so on, until uncovering an ordinary or "natural" card.

The Play

The player to the left of the dealer begins the game, picking a card from the pack and laying down all the possible melds in his hand (provided he can "open," described below); then, the player discards a card of his choice on the well and passes the play to the player sitting to his left.

In order to "open" (to lay down cards for the first time), a player (that is, one of the two players of the pair) must lay down a meld with a minimum value,

Table A	
Total score so far for a team	Required value for the initial meld to open
Negative	15
0 - 1495	50
1500 - 2995	90
3000 or more	120

according to the total score achieved up to that point in the course of the entire game, as shown in Table A.

Once one opens, either player of a pair can freely lay down melds of any value or add cards to the melds already laid down.

MELDS

A meld is a set of at least three cards of the same value. The melds can be made of only natural cards or between natural cards and jokers or the two's (the deuces). As a matter of fact, the jokers and the twos are called "wild cards," which means a card that can assume any value in order to make a meld.

However, in a meld there cannot be less then two natural cards or more then three wild cards.

The red threes cannot join a meld, and must alwasy be turned faceup on the table as soon as they are drawn.

The black threes (spades and clubs) can be used only in melds when "going out" (see below).

CANASTA

If one combines seven cards of the same value it is called "canasta."

If a canasta is composed of only natural cards, it is called "clean"; if there are wild cards, it is called "dirty." One can attach cards to a canasta, as long but there can never be four wild cards.

PICKING FROM THE WELL

A player can pick the first faceup card from the well, instead of picking one from the pack. The player can do so only if he is going to lay that card down immediately, combining it with two natural cards or with a natural card and a wild card of his own.

A player can also pick the first card from the well when it can be added to one of the melds already laid down by him or by the teammate.

A player who can meld the top card from the well picks up the whole well and with it tries to lay down as many cards as possible. The cards from the well can be laid down if combined with other cards from the well or with cards that the player has already in hand. He can even attach them to any meld already laid down by him or the teammate. The red threes present in the well can also be laid down.

The cards from the well that have not been laid down are kept; then the player discards one card, starting again another well, and passing the turn to the next player.

Table B	
Card	Points for each card in a combination
Joker	50
2	20
Ace	20
8, 9, 10, J, Q, K	10
4, 5, 6, 7	5
Black 3	5

FROZEN WELL

A well is "frozen"for all players when it contains a red three and/or a wild card.

The discarded cards are placed crosswise over the card(s) of the frozen well.

The well can only be "unfrozen" by the player who picks the card from the top and melds it with two of his own cards, as long as they are natural (that is without wild cards). Then the player takes possession of the well, including red threes and wild cards.

The well gets frozen for the next player when the previous players discard is a black three, which cannot be picked up nor combined (unless at closing). The well frozen by a black three gets unfrozen automatically when the next player discards a different card on top of the black three.

The well is frozen for a pair that has not opened.

GOING OUT

A player goes out when he is able to meld all his cards, as long as there is a canasta among the combinations laid down by him or the teammate.

A player "goes out concealed" when he melds all the cards at once before having laid down a meld for the first time. To go out, the player must make at least one canasta, unless one has previously been laid down by the teammate. One can go out by either discarding a card or not.

Usually, but not always, a player asks his teammate for permission to go out. In the case of a negative answer (just as binding as an affirmative one), the player must postpone going out to his next turn. Doing so, the player gives the chance to the teammate to lay down the most possible cards on his turn.

CALCULATING THE SCORE

When a player goes out, the score of the melds laid down by each pair must be calculated. To compute this score, one must subtract the value of the leftover cards in the hands of each pair. The total represents the score for the pair for that round.

Every card in a meld has its specific value, as shown in Table B.

A clean canasta is worth 500 points.

A dirty canasta is worth 300 points.

Going out is worth 100 points.

Going out concealed is worth 200 points.

Red threes are worth 100 points each.

If a pair has all the red threes they double the value, and are worth 800 points altogether.

Careful though! The points of the red threes count in a negative way if, at the moment the opponent pair goes out, the team who has them has not yet opened—laid down any melds.

The couple that first reaches 5000 points wins the game.

■ Strategy

Notice that the value given to going out is not very high. In fact, at the end of a round, the couple that has not gone out may have scored highest if they have laid down melds of more value.

Ask your teammate for permission to go out so that he is not left with cards of high value which will be counted against your total score. Keep in mind that asking the teammate for permission to go out works also as a warning for other pair who will then try to lay down as much as possible in their turn. So, in certain cases (for example, when the teammate has very few cards left and the opposing players have many), one may skip asking permission and go out, surprising everybody.

COCINCINA

Cocincina, similar to the classic Scopa, or Sweep, (which shares some of its rules), is curiously played with two decks of forty cards which are not distributed equally but . . . in "chunks."

Players
Two

Game Equipment
- Two decks of 40 cards each (remove the 8s, 9s and 10s from decks of 52).

■ Start & Object of the Game

The players cut the deck; the one with the highest card is dealer. Consider that the cards have nominal value; that is, the Ace is worth 1, the two is worth 2 and so on until the seven, then the Jack is worth 8, the Queen 9 and the King 10.

The dealer shuffles the two decks together. Then, the dealer picks the first card from the deck which he places face up on the table. Then the dealer cuts the deck in two packs, trying to make them more or less the same size.

The opponent chooses one of the two packs. Both keep their pack of cards facedown on the table in front of them.

The object of the game is to make "sweeps," or tricks, to earn points.

■ The Play

The opponent starts the game, uncovering the first card from the top of his

pack: if the card is of the same value as the card already faceup on the table, the player gets both of them in a sweep. If the cards have different values they are both left on the table, next to each other.

The other player (who dealt) then uncovers a card, with which he can:
● make a sweep by getting both the cards from the table if, for example, he uncovers a 7 and on the table there is a 4 and a 3 *(Fig. 1);*

Fig. 1 - The 7 gets the 4 and the 3.

● get one of the two cards from the table which corresponds to value of the card he uncovered;
● leave his card on the table next to the other two if the card does not have the value of either of the other two.

The two players proceed in turn according to these rules until they run out of cards from their packs.

If the dealer runs out of cards before the other player, the hand is over; however, if the other player runs out of cards first, the dealer may still uncover a card.

COVERED & UNCOVERED SWEEPS

One can score only with sweeps, of two types: covered and uncovered.

● The covered sweeps are those made with Jacks, Queens, Kings, or Aces of different suits but the same value.

● The uncovered sweeps are those made of cards of the same value and suit, or those made of cards of different suits, including also the last card played.

During the play, the covered sweeps of Jack, Queen, King, or Ace are placed, as in the traditional game "Sweep," face-up and perpendicular to the pack, toward the middle of the table *(Fig. 2)*.

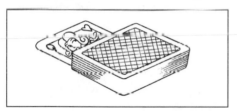

Fig. 2 - Placement of a covered sweep.

The uncovered sweeps are placed in the same way, at the opposite side of the pack, toward the player *(Fig. 3)*.

CALCULATING THE SCORE

Once the cards have run out, the score is tabulated:

● the covered sweeps from 2 to 7 do not count;

● the covered sweeps of Jacks, Queens, Kings, or Aces are worth 1 point;

● the uncovered sweeps of Aces are worth 2 points;

● the uncovered sweeps with a 2 of clubs is worth 3 points;

Fig. 3 - The 2 of clubs is an uncovered sweep and as such it is directed toward the player.

● the uncovered sweeps with Jacks are worth 4 points;

● the uncovered sweeps with Queens are worth 5 points;

● the uncovered sweeps with Kings are worth 6 points;

● the uncovered sweeps from the 2 (other than the 2 of clubs) to the 7 are worth face value; that is the 2 is worth 2, the 3 is worth 3 and so on.

The winner is the player who, at the end of the hand, scores the most points.

▉ Strategy

Success at Cocincina depends mostly on the luck of the draw. Nevertheless, it is possible to apply some reasoning when there are several cards on the table that can give the player more than one possibility to make a trick. In that case, one would prefer to get the cards that would not give the opponent the chance to make a sweep of good value.

For example, if on the table there is a Queen (which is worth 9), a 4 and a 5, and the next player uncovers a Queen, it is better if that player gets the single card (the Queen) rather than the other two, which together are worth 9. Doing so, one avoids leaving the opponent the chance to do a sweep with the Queen.

FROG

*A classic game of tricks, very popular, with different names,
all over Europe. It is played in quick hands, in which two players
form an alliance against the third player.*

Players
Three

Game Equipment
- A deck of 36 cards: 6s, 7s, 8s, 9s,
10s, Jacks, Queens, Kings, and Aces
of all four suits.

▮ Start & Object of the Game

The players each cut the deck to decide
the dealer. The dealer is the one who
cuts the highest card (Ace is high).

The dealer gives 11 cards to each
player, including himself, in a counterclockwise direction. The last three cards,
left covered, constitute the "widow."

Object of the game is to make the
highest "bid" (see below) and fulfill it,
scoring at least 60 points. The object of
the players whose bids are topped isto
impede the "high bidder's" success.

▮ The Play

Starting with the player on the left of the
dealer, the players have the chance to
pass or to make a bid. Every bid must be
higher than the preceding one.

The player who makes the highest bid
is the "high bidder" for that specific
hand.

The other two players try to stop the
high bidder from achieving his bid.

There are three possible bids:
- "frog" is the bid to achieve as many
tricks as possible, with hearts as
"trump" (leading suit), changing three
cards with the widow;
- "chico" is the bid to achieve as many
tricks as possible with any trump the
high bidder calls (except for hearts);
- "grand," the most challenging, is the
bid to achieve as many tricks as possible
with hearts as trump.

In the cases of chico and grand, the
widow cards do not take part in the
game, but they will be counted in favor
of the high bidder at the end of the
hand; in the case of frog, the cards that
the declarant discards in place of the
widow are counted in his favor at the
end of the hand.

VALUE OF THE CARDS
The value of the cards *(Fig. 1)* is:
- 11 points for the Ace;
- 10 points for the 10;
- 4 points for the King;
- 3 points for the Queen;
- 2 points for the Jack.

For the outcome of the score, only the
cards gotten with the tricks of the high

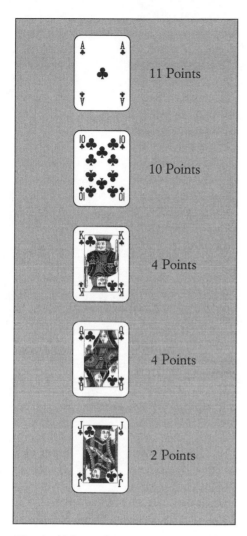

11 Points

10 Points

4 Points

4 Points

2 Points

Fig. 1 - Values of the cards expressed in points.

bidder count, plus the three of the widow, or in the case of a "frog" bid, the three discarded.

WINNING THE TRICK

The technique of winning a trick is the usual for this type of game. That is, in turns, first the high bidder and then the other players in a counterclockwise order, place a card on the table. The trick is won by the player who places on the table a trump (or in case of more than one trump on the table, the highest one), or the highest card of the suit of the first card played. The player who wins a trick starts the play in the following round.

KEEPING SCORE

A high bidder who declared frog when the hand is over writes down the corresponding score of the cards gotten with tricks.

A high bidder who declared chico counts the points of the cards gotten with the tricks and then doubles those points.

Finally, a high bidder who declared grand multiples by four the points of the cards gotten with the tricks.

The high bidder wins the hand if he scores 60 points or more. In this case, each opponent loses half of his points exceeding 60 (if there are any), which are then given to the high bidder.

The high bidder loses if he scores less then 60 points. In this case he loses as many points as there are left to reach 60, of which he gives half to one player and half to the other.

Usually, the game ends after a certain number of hands, decided by the players at the beginning of the game.

The player who has scored the most points at the end wins the game.

▉ Strategy

As in all the other games of tricks, it is a good idea to play the strong cards when one is reasonably sure not to be taken by surprise by the opponent.

Be also aware of the fact that if you are the high bidder the other two play together to make you lose.

KING

*A very famous game of tricks with a precise scheme of playing
which during the game forces the players to change their strategies all along.
Of course, the fun is all here.*

Players
Four

Game Equipment
- A deck of 52 cards

■ Start & Object of the Game

The players cut the deck to choose the dealer. The player who gets the highest card is the dealer.

The dealer turns a card over to establishes trump. The trump card is put on the bottom of the deck. He deals 13 cards to each player, including himself, in a clockwise direction.

The player on the left of the dealer starts the game; for subsequent rounds, the player who won the last trick starts.

Object of the game is to fulfill the "decrees" of the different hands, earning as many points as possible.

■ The Play

The cards have face value, and the Ace is the highest. A complete game is made of ten different hands, each of them having a specific "decree" and a specific strategy to play.

"TAKE NO" HANDS

The first six hands are "not to take," which means that the players do not want to win the tricks, as they count in a negative way.

The first hand decrees "take no tricks": so, for every trick taken, the players score 2 negative points.

The second hand decrees "take no hearts": so, for every card of hearts taken, the players score 2 negative points.

The third hand decrees "take no Kings and no Jacks": so, for every King and for every Jack taken, the players score 6 negative points.

The forth hand decrees "take no Queens": so, for every Queen taken, the players score 10 negative points.

The fifth hand decrees "take no King of hearts": so, the player who takes it scores 40 negative points.

The sixth hand decrees "do not take the last trick": so, the player who takes it scores 20 negative points.

TAKE" HANDS

From the seventh hand on, the decree change from "take no" to "take"; so the strategy changes, which means that the players try to win the tricks.

Every hand, the suit of trump (leading suit) is the suit of the last card of the deck, which goes to the dealer, after he has shown it to the other players.

The player who plays the highest card of the same suit of the first card played (every round changes) wins the trick. If a trump is laid down, the trick is won by the player who plays the highest trump.

For every trick won, a player scores 4 positive points.

PLAY THE SAME SUIT

In all ten hands, one must follow suitof the card played first in a specific round. It is not compulsory to try to win a trick, in case one has the card to do so.

If a player cannot follow suit, he can play any other card including a trump (in which case there is a good chance of winning the trick).

The player who can can follow suit does not do it, if he gets caught, gets 2 negative points.

The player who wins a trick starts the following round.

SCORING

At the end of every hand, the players count separately the negative and the positive points.

At the end of the ten hands, the total and final score is calculated.

The player who totaled the highest score wins the game.

■ Strategy

Every hand, one must adjust to the new decree. During the "take no" hands, one would try to give the other players the "heavy" cards, that is the ones that are worth more points.

During the "take" hands, of course, one must pay particular attention to the value of the cards, to avoid wasting them too soon.

During the first hand ("take no tricks") a player would give away high valued cards when he does not have the leading suit on that specific round.

It is this continuous changing of strategy that makes King an enjoyable and never monotonous game.

A VARIATION

The position of the dealer is favorable during the first round of a hand or during the hands with trumps, considering that at least one trump (the last card of the deck) always goes to the dealer.

The game can be limited to ten hands, managed by only one dealer, or one can play four sets of ten hands: in this case the game is longer, but doing so, every player has the chance—very enjoyable—to be the dealer.

RAMINO

Very famous and played around the world, Ramino is a derivation of an Anglo-Saxon game. Ramino belongs to the Rummy family, described next in this volume.

Players
From two to six

Game Equipment
- Two decks of 52 cards

■ Start & Object of the Game

The players cut the deck to decide the dealer. The one with the highest card is the dealer (Ace is low).

The dealer shuffles the two decks together, then gives ten cards to each player including himself, one at a time in a clockwise direction. Then, the dealer places the leftover pack of cards in the middle of the table and turns over the top card, starting a pack for the discarded cards, also called the "well."

The player on the left of the dealer starts the game.

The object of the game is to lay down melds of cards, trying to finish the hand holding the least amount of points.

The Play

Every player, in turn, picks a card, either from the facedown pack or from the well. Then, if possible, he lays down one or more melds. At the end of his turn, the player discards a card.

The player who picks from the well cannot discard, in the same turn, the card that he has just picked.

If the pack of cards runs out, the well is turned facedown; the first card turned faceup starts a new well.

MELDS

The melds must be made with a minimum of three cards, of the same value or in a straight in which the cards have the same suit *(Figs. 1 and 2)*.

Fig. 1 - Example of a meld: three of a kind.

In order to attach a card to another meld that is already on the table, one must have already laid down a meld himself.

Fig. 2 - Example of a straight: at least three cards in sequence and of the same suit.

GOING OUT

The player who first lays down all his cards, in melds and/or attaching to other melds already on the table, ends the hand by going out. If the player is left with one card, he can discard it. To go out it is not compulsory to discard.

The player who goes out concealed, that is, with all the cards still in his hands, he is able to combine all the cards without having laid down any card previously, accomplishes Ramino.

To accomplish Ramino one may not add cards to the melds already laid down by the other players.

When a player goes out, the others count the points of the cards they have left in their hands; an Ace is worth 1, the two is worth 2 and so on; Jacks, Queens, and Kings are worth 10.

SCORING, GOING OVER & REENTERING

The player who accomplishes Ramino earns 10 points, which he can subtract from his score. The player who exceeds 101 points "goes over." That player can reenter the game by taking a score to match the score of the player who has the next highest number of points.

For example, playing in three:
- player 1 has 57 points
- player 2 has 87 points
- player 3 goes over 101 points. Player 3 reenters the game with 87 points.

If the players are playing for money, the player who goes over must pay a penalty that all of the payers have decided together at the beginning of the game.

Any player who manages to force all the other players to go over 101 points at the same time wins the game

▮ Strategy

At the beginning of a hand it is a good idea to discard the cards that would be useless toward the combinations that one has in mind to meld.

Toward the end of the hand, it is better to discard the cards that are worth more points, in case they would be left over in the hands and so be counted as that many points against you. Getting rid of high cards is especially worth it if there is a player who appears to be planning to go out.

RUMMY

This is the patriarch of those types of games in which it is necessary lay down combinations of cards in order to close. Rummy is of American origin and with its numerous variations it is certain to be the most played in the world.

Players
From two to six

Game Equipment
- A deck of 52 cards

Start & Object of the Game

The players cut the deck of cards to establish the dealer. This privilege goes to the player who gets the lowest card, from the Ace (lowest) to the King.

The dealer shuffles the cards and lets any player cut the deck, then he deals one card at a time to each player, including himself, in a clockwise direction: each player receives ten cards if the game is played by two people only, seven cards if the game is played by three or four people and six cards if there are five or six players.

The leftover pack of cards is placed, facedown, in the middle of the table: it is called the "heel" and the players pick the cards from it.

The first card of the heel is uncovered, starting the pile of the discarded cards.

The object of the game is to lay down the cards, making all the possible melds.

The Play

The player on the left of the dealer starts the game, picking a card either from the heel or from the pile of discards (which at that point has only one card). Then, that player can lay down a meld(s), if he has any and desires to do so, and finally discard any card other than the one he has just picked.

The melds can be made by three or more cards of the same value or of the same suit in a straight *(Figs. 1 and 2.)*

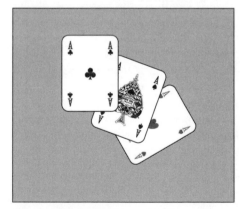

Fig. 1 - Example of a meld: three of a kind.

After a player has laid down at least one meld, for that player it is possible to add cards to the other melds already on the table, those of his own or of any other player.

Fig. 2 - Example of a straight: at least three cards in sequence and of the same suit.

If the heel runs out of cards before any of the players manages to go out, the pile of the discards is turned over, without shuffling. Doing so, a new heel is started and the first card gets uncovered to start a new pile of discards.

GOING OUT

One goes out by laying down all of his cards in melds. To close it is not necessary to discard.

One makes "Rummy" by laying down all his cards in one single shot, with or without a discard, without having laid down before and without attaching any card to other melds laid down by others.

When a player goes out he earns a score equal to the value of the cards left over in the hands of the other players. Consider that the Jack, Queen, and King are worth 10 points.

A player who makes Rummy is rewarded by doubling the score.

When playing in three or more, once one person goes out, the player on the left of the dealer is the new dealer.

When playing in two, the player that goes out is the new dealer.

The player who first reaches a pre-established total score wins the game (for example: 100 when playing in two, 200 when playing in three or four, 300 when playing in five or six).

■ Strategy

As in similar games, at the beginning of a hand it is wise to discard only the cards that seem like they will not fit in any meld, while at the end it is better to discard the cards with higher value.

Don't be obstinate trying to make Rummy, especially if one or more player does not have many cards left. The points that you might earn from it (a player with few cards left presumably has few points) would not be worth the cost if another player goes out.

FORTY FLUSH

*A variation of the game Rummy, played and appreciated
especially in Italy, where it is the standard game
for reunions of friends and family.*

Players
Two to four

Game Equipment
- Two decks of 52 cards
(more, in the "easier" variant
of the game, four jokers)

■ Start & Object of the Game

Cut the deck of cards to decide who will
deal. The dealer shuffles and distributes
the cards (10 to 13 per person) clockwise to each player, including himself.
Then he places the remaining stack in
the center of the table, facedown, and
turns the first card faceup, which starts
the pile of discarded cards or "the well."
The player to the left of the dealer
begins the game.

The aim of the game is to put down
melds, aiming to be left holding the least
points in his hand.

■ The Play

Each player, when it is his turn, turns a
card over from the facedown deck. At
the end of his turn, he discards a card in
the well.

To begin the game, it is necessary to
put down one or more melds of the
cards, whose total value should reach or
exceed 40 points—values as in Rummy
(Fig. 1). If it is not possible to open, discard a card and continue the game.

Before anyone has opened, no one is
allowed to pick from the discarded
cards, so that a previously picked card
does not reenter into the opening.

Whoever picks from the well cannot,
in the same turn, discard the same card
that was picked.

If the covered deck runs out, the well
gets turned upside down, then the first
card is turned over.

MELDS & JOKERS

The melds must consist of at least three
cards, of the same value or suit as a flush.
The joker can be used as any value.

When a joker is melded it can be
assigned and named by the player, as
whatever card it is substituting for.

GOING OUT

The first player to meld and discard all
his cards goes out, ending the hand. To
go out it is necessary to discard.

When a player goses out, the others
count the value of the cards remaining in
their hands.

Whoever manages to go out by meld-
ing all his cards at the same time he dis-

Fig. 1: Example of melds to open; together they are worth exactly 40 points.

cards his last card without having put down any melds previously that is, he goes out concealed—scores 10 points for the hand and is the winner.

▦ Strategy

As in Rummy, in the first hands of the game, it is good to discard the deuce and any useless cards until a desired meld is thought of. In this sense, useless cards are those that do not give immediate possibilities of melds, especially those adjoining cards that are discarded by the other players.

Near the end of the hand it is good, instead, to discard cards that, remaining in the hand, would have a higher score, especially when one of the opponents seems about to go out.

SWEEP (or SCOPA)

Dates from the 15th century and could be defined as the Italian national game.
Simple rules, quick development, the gift of ability and memory
makes Sweep (or Scopa) a favorite pastime, easy to learn
but not so easy to play, stimulating, and engaging.

Players
Two

Game Equipment
- A deck of 40 cards (remove the 8, 9, and 10 of every suit in a deck of 52) for a Neopolitan or Lombardian deck

Start & Object of the Game

Decide who will deal by cutting the cards: whoever has the highest card is the dealer. Rank the cards by nominal value from the Ace (one) to the seven; the Jack is worth eight, the Queen nine, and the King ten.

The dealer shuffles the cards and asks his opponent to cut, and then distributes three cards, one at a time, to both of them. Then he places four cards from the deck faceup on the table, putting the remaining cards beside the four faceup cards.

The object is to accumulate the most possible cards and sweeps, winning points.

The Play

The suits of the Neapolitan cards are coins, cups, swords, and batons; those of the Lombardian cards are the usual diamonds, hearts, spades, and clubs.

One can play in the same way with both types of decks.

The opponent begins by putting one of his cards on the table.

This card may be matched with one of the four cards on the table, both must be equal in value *(Fig. 1);* or in the absence of such a card, two or more

Fig. 1 - Example of matched cards.

Fig. 2 - Example of matched cards; a three and a five match the Jack (8).

cards can add up to and be matched with one of the four cards on the table *(Fig. 2).*

If the player cannot make a match with any of the four cards, he must put down one of his cards on the table and simply leave it there.

TO SWEEP
When a player is able to play a card of equal value to one of the cards on the table or is able to play two or more cards equal to one of the cards on the table, he "sweeps," that is he takes all of the

cards, except if he is the dealer playing the last card of the deck. In that case, the dealer indicates the "sweep" by placing the matched card faceup, under the facedown deck, perpendicular to the deck *(Fig. 3).*

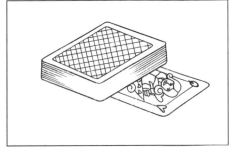

Fig. 3 - The position of the sweep (scopa).

SUCCESSIVE DISTRIBUTIONS OF CARDS
At the end of a round the dealer distributes three more cards to the players, without reshuffling the cards, and turns over four new cards for the next round.

The hand ends when the dealer plays the last card of the last deal. If this card matches one of the four cards on the table, the dealer is awarded the cards, otherwise the remaining cards on the table go to the opponent.

COUNTING THE POINTS
At the end of a hand, count the points:
● 1 point for every sweep
● 1 point for the "most cards," which goes to the player who has accumulated at least 21 cards.
● 1 point for "golds," which goes to the player who has accumulated at least 6 heart cards (when the Neapolitan cards are used) or 6 diamond cards (in the case of the Lombard cards).
● 1 point to whoever has the "beautiful sevens," which are the sevens of hearts and of diamonds;

• 1 point for the "prime," which goes to the player who has a total value higher than eighty-one, the so-called premium points of four cards of different suits: twenty-one for the eight, eighteen for the six, sixteen for the Ace, fifteen for the five, fourteen for the four, thirteen for the three, twelve for the two, and ten for the Jack *(Fig. 4)*.

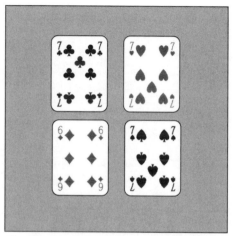

Fig. 4 - Example of the "premium" that is worth eighty-one points.

At the end of a hand the deal passes to the other player. The game is won by the first who reaches eleven points or, by the players' choice (if established at the beginning of the game) the one who reaches sixteen or twenty-one.

■ Strategy

It is fundamental in the game of Sweep to attempt to keep track and remember the cards played in order to know exactly what to do at the end of a hand. A device to make this easier is to remember the "scattered" or "odd" cards. If, for example, a seven takes a three and a four, these three cards will be "scattered." Hand by hand is how the game moves ahead, the scattered cards will appear again and, at the end, you can know what cards your opponent is holding. Turning to the previous example, if a five takes a two or three, the three will equal itself, but the two and five become odd when added. At the end of the hand, if the two and the five are not drawn, and not in your hand, they must be in your opponent's hand.

HINDERING THE OPPONENT'S SWEEPS

Keeping in mind the "scattered" cards also helps to prevent the opponent's sweeps.

For example, assume that, after a four has been exchanged with another, the third is drawn together with a two from a six. At this point there is only one four in the turn, odds. If you have it in your hand, you can play it after the opponent has made a sweep, being sure that your opponent will not be able to take it with another sweep. Then, you can leave it on the table and take all the cards that the opponent has put down, if you can, always certain that the opponent will not sweep, but will "dance" around your four odds.

Naturally, it is also good to keep track of the cards of value that pass with each hand: seven and six (for the premium), "beautiful sevens," and golds.

FIFTEEN SWEEP

*Fifteen Sweep is a variant of traditional Itlaian Sweep
(or Scopa) that is popular predominantly
with experts of calculating odd cards.*

Players
Two

Game Equipment
- A deck of 40 cards (remove the 8, 9,
and 10 of every suit in a deck of 52)

▧ Start & Object of the Game

Decide who should deal by cutting the
cards: whoever has the highest card is
the dealer. Keep in mind that the cards
should have nominal values from the
Ace (one) to the seven; the Jack is worth
eight, the Queen is worth nine, and the
King ten.

The dealer shuffles the cards, asks the
opponent to cut them and distributes
them three to each of them. Then, he
draws four cards from the remainder of
the deck, putting them on the table and
setting aside the remainder of the deck
for the successive distributions.

▧ The Play

The dealer's opponent begins, putting
one of his cards on the table.

In contrast to the traditional game of
Sweep (where, a card or cards are
matched with another card of the same
value), in this variant one card takes
another card (or two or more) if the sum
of the played card plus the taken cards is
equal to fifteen. For example, with a 5
one can take a King, that is worth 10
(5 +10 = 15), otherwise a six and a four
(5 + 6 + 4 = 15), as shown in Figure 1.

Fig. 1 - Examples of drawn cards:
with a 5 one can take a King, that is
worth 10 (5 + 10 = 15) or a 6 and a 4
(5 + 6 + 4 = 15).

If the player has no card that can take
any other cards (add up to 15), he must
play a card, which then simply remains
on the table.

Each player takes any matched cards into his hand, hiding them from his opponent.

When a player plays a card that, added to one or more of the cards on the table, equals 15, the player takes all the cards and makes "Fifteen Sweep."

At the end of a round, the dealer distributes three more cards to each of them, without reshuffling the deck, and turns over the four new cards to start the next round.

THE END OF THE HAND & CALCULATING POINTS

The hand ends when the dealer plays the last card of the last deal. If this card also takes one of the face up cards present on the table, the dealer is awarded all of them, otherwise the remaining cards on the table go to the opponent.

To end a hand, count the points, the same as in traditional Sweep (sweeps, golds, beautiful sevens, premium, and the most cards).

At the end of a hand, the deal passes to the other player.

The winner is the first player who,after many hands, reaches eleven points, sixteen, or twenty-one points.

■ Strategy

The difficulty, as mentioned earlier, is in counting the odds, since every sweep hides the cards that were in play.

Whoever is more able to keep track will certainly have more of a chance than his opponent will.

It is not easy to foresee the sweeps, which happen generally in greater numbers for the game of Fifteen Sweep than in traditional Sweep.

It can also be played in fours, singles or pairs; in this last case, getting along with the partner is fundamental.

SCIENTIFIC SWEEP

Scientific Sweep is a variation of traditional Sweep (or Scopa); just as popular and widely played in all circles and inns of beautiful town villages. The main difference between "easy" Sweep and that of Scientific Sweep, is this, it is a "Sweep of the Ace"; four players, in pairs, will make the game much more "colorful," because of the heated discussions between friends.

Players
Four, in pairs

Game Equipment
- A deck of 40 cards (remove the 8, 9, and 10 of every suit in a deck of 52)

■ Start & Object of the Game

To form the pairs, everyone draws a card (the one with the highest card becomes partner with the player who holds the lowest card) or, more often, you play with a chosen partner: Scientific Sweep or "Sweep of the Ace," in fact, requires harmony between the partners.

Always decide who deals by luck of the draw (usually whoever has the lowest card).

The dealer shuffles the cards, asks the player on his left to cut the cards, and deals them, counterclockwise, ten to each player, three cards at a time, turn of the last single card faceup in the final round. The dealer then places four cards faceup on the table.

The player to the right of the dealer begins. Like in Sweep, the object of the game is to have more cards than your pair of opponents, accumulating points.

■ The Play

The rules of Scientific Sweep are the same as those of traditional Sweep (Scopa), with some additions (see below).

The first player of a pair plays one card and keeps it faceup, in front of him: the cards of the teammate are also added to this to form a pile.

At the end of each hand, count the points, using the scoring got Sweep.

In "Sweep of the Ace" the important rule is that an Ace takes all the face up cards on the board, but without needing to make a sweep: the act of putting down an Ace is called "cutting."

SWEEP OF THE ACE & NAPOLA
In "Sweep of the Ace" there exists also an additional system for scoring points, that of the "Napola" *(Fig. 1)*. The Napola is given to the pair that has at

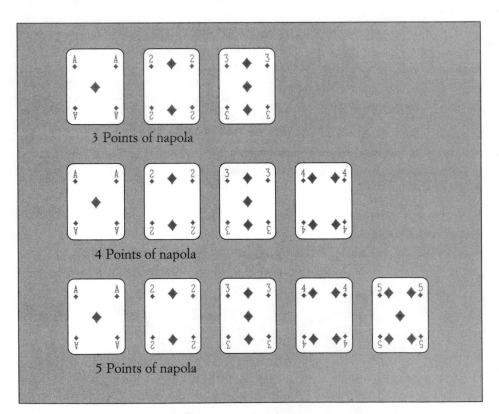

3 Points of napola

4 Points of napola

5 Points of napola

Fig. 1 - The first sequence is the minimum of napola and is worth 3 points. The second is worth 4 points, the third is worth 5 points and so on.

least an Ace, the two, and three of the golds (hearts or diamonds). This case wins three points; every gold in sequence added to the first three earns a player an extra point; thus, 4 points for whoever has an Ace, two, three, and four; five to whomever adds the five, and so on; a pair that takes all the golds up to a King makes a "Napolitan" and the pair wins the game.

Strategy

More than in two player Flush, in Scientific Flush and Ace Flush it helps to remember the discarded cards, not only to hinder the opponents' game and to benefit from them in the team, but also to single out which card has been played already, and after the opponent makes a flush, to hinder him from making another.

BEING IN HARMONY WITH A PARTNER

Being in harmony with your partner is fundamental; so that each may guess the other's cards, divide the play, and respond to the other's moves: this only come with experience, but getting along with your partner is equally important.

The player who opens the game must try to put down a card that is part of a pari in his hand, to block the opponent's sweep. The teammate of the first player has to "respond to him" by putting down, if he has it, the same card as his partner put down in the opening.

The player under threat by an opponent's sweep who plays card from three of a kind has a good chance that the opponent will not sweep; however, if this happens, it takes away from the partner any chance to respond. For this reason, playing a card from one of three is not always the right choice.

THREES
(or TERZIGLIO)

A close relative of Three-Seven (Tressette), Threes (Terziglio) is played predominantly in northern Italy, in particular in Lombardy. The rules are similar all in all to that of its "big brother," however, Threes is limited to a fixed number of players, namely, three.

Players
Three

Game Equipment
- A deck of 40 cards
(remove the 8, 9, and 10
of every suit in a deck of 52)

■ Start & Object of the Game

Cut the deck to decide the dealer, whoever turns over the lowest card deals.

The dealer distributes 12 cards to each player in packets of four, counterclockwise. The remaining four cards are placed, facedown, at the center of the table and they are considered the "mountain" or *monte*.

The object is, for a player, to gain for himself at least 6 points.

■ The Play

The player to the right of the dealer opens the game and in the case of a good hand, announces the "Call" specifying a card that serves to strengthen his game that he has in hand (for example: "I call the King of hearts"). If one of the other two players has the card (it is not hidden in the "mountain"), the possessor must give it to the caller of that card.

If the first player to the right of the dealer does not have a good hand worthy of an opening call, he can pass. If all three players pass, the hand ends.

The player who opens takes the mountain deck. At this point he has 17 cards in hand or in the case that the called card is found in the mountain, 16. From these the player chooses the 12 that seem the best, eventually restores a card of his choice to the player who gave him the called card and discards the 4 or 3 remaining cards, face up, on the table.

The player, who opens the round, plays alone from this moment against the other two. His first move will be to initiate the first trick by putting down any one of his cards.

The other players have to respond to the suit if possible.

The trick goes to the one who plays the highest card of the opening suit. The value of the cards is, in decreasing order: three, two, Ace, King, Queen, Jack, seven, six, five, and four. Whoever wins the trick starts the next one.

The pile of cards won in the trcik is positioned in front of the player who won the trick.

The two players playing against the player who opened cannot communicate with each other with signs or words, except in the two cases, when one "knocks" and when one "flies." A play-er who declares a "knock" invites his the other to win the round with his best card, and to start a successive one with a card of the same suit (when it is possible). The player who declares a "fly" communicates to his partner that the card that he put down is the only one of that suit in his possession.

NEAPOLITAN

The player who is holding an Ace, two, and three of the same suit, or 3 Aces, 3 twos, or 3 threes (Fig. 1) declares a "Neapolitan" (specifying which cards and which suits) and is awarded three points.

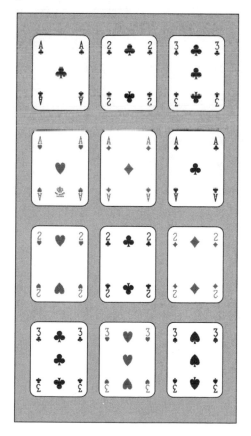

Fig. 1 Combinations of Neapolitan: whoever charges it gains 3 points.

This procedure is called a "charge." An undeclared charge does not get points.

COUNTING THE POINTS

Count the points at the end of a hand:
- Each Ace is worth 1 point
- Two, three, Jacks, Queens, and Kings are called figures: every three figures are assigned a point *(Fig. 2)*.

Fig. 2 Three figures equal a point.

Whoever opened wins the hand if he has at least 6 points total.

Otherwise he loses and pays a stake, agreed upon at the beginning of the game, to his opponents.

■ Strategy

The player who opens should call a card with a high value for winning a trick: three, two, Ace, King, Queen, Jack.

Whoever opens has the best chance of planning a strategy for the game, but the opponents can unite their forces to hinder him.

When a player has a strong hand of the same suit it is good to start with the highest card. If one can win the trick, it is good idea to insist on this suit in order to try to scrape together the most figures possible.

One's score is raised by his capacity to guess his opponents' hands, whether one is alone or playing with the a "partner" against the opening player.

THREE-SEVEN (or TRESSETTE)

Along with Sweep (Scopa) and Trumps, Three-Seven (Tressette) is without a doubt a favorite pastime of passionate card players in Italy. Some think it originated in Naples, others in Spain; in any case, it definitely originated in the Mediterranean region. It is a fast game, easy to learn even for a child, and still passionate and fun.

Players
Two or four, in pairs

Game Equipment
- A deck of 40 cards (remove the 8, 9, and 10 of every suit in a deck of 52)

▪ Start & Object of the Game

If there are four players, they must form groups of two pairs. Players decide by luck of the draw who goes first (the player who draws the highest card pairs up with the one with the lowest card) or, more often, it is simply played with an already chosen partner. Cut the deck to decide who will deal, whoever draws the lowest card is the dealer.

When there are four players, draw only two cards, one per pair.

The dealer distributes 10 cards, five at a time, to each player counterclockwise.

When there are two players, when finished with the first ten cards the dealer distributes another set of ten cards.

The object of the game is to gain the highest number of tricks and points based on the cards won.

▪ The Play

The player to the right of the dealer opens the game, giving way to the first round by playing any one of his cards. The other players must follow suit, if possible.

The winning card is the highest card of the opening suit.

The value of the cards in decreasing order is: three, two, Ace, King, Queen, Jack, seven, six, five, four.

Whoever wins the trck, starts the next one.

The pile of cards won from in the trick is palced in front of the player who won the trick.

DECLARATIONS

When there are four players, partners are not permitted to communicate with each other through signs or words except in two situations: when one "knocks" and when one "flies."

The player who declares "knock" invites his partner to win the round with his best card, initiating the next one with a card of the same suit (when possible).

The player who declares a "fly" communicates to his partner that the card, which he just put down, is the only one of the suit that he possesses.

Players must declare any point-making combinations they have immediately after the first trick. An undeclared combination does not receive any points.

The player who has an Ace, two and three of the same suit, or 3 Aces, 3 twos or 3 threes, declares a "Neapolitan" (specifying which cards and which suits) and is awarded three points *(Fig. 1)*. This procedure is called a "charge."

Fig. 2 Combination of three Figures: worth 1 point.

None of the other cards are worth anything at the end and, therefore, are called "discards."

The winner or winning team is the one who gets 21 or 31 points first, as agreed at the start.

■ Strategy

In a game with four players, it is fundamental to remember all the cards and all the charges passed in order to be in harmony with one's partner.

If a player has a strong hand of the same suits, it is good to begin with the highest card of that suit.

If one wins the trick, it is good to insist on that suit and try to get as many figures as possible.

Since partners cannot communicate, except to declare "fly" or "knock," each can only guess the other's hand.

A discarded card could indicate that the partner does not have strong cards of that suit. In such a case the partner will not play that suit, at least since it is not very strong, or does not give certainty of winning the round, without the help of the partner.

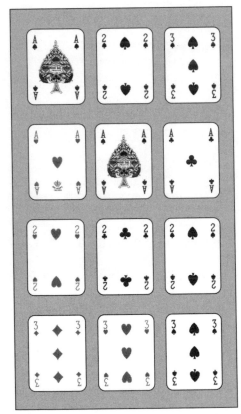

Fig.1 Combinations of Neapolitan: all are worth 3 points.

COUNTING THE POINTS

Count the points at the end of a hand:
- Every Ace is worth 1 point
- Two, three, Jacks, Queens, and Kings are worth a figure: every three figures are assigned a point *(Fig. 2)*.

Not to Take Three-Seven

This is a fun variant that is based on the same rule as Three-Seven (where a player follows suit and wins a round when he puts down the highest card), expect that the winner of the round is the one who has the least points.

The round can therefore end equally at 21 or at 31 points, but in such a case whoever gets those points loses.

Otherwise one can decide to play a certain number of hands at the end of which whoever has gained the least number of points wins.

Naturally, whoever has a strong hand of a particular suit, will try to make his opponent's cards run out, beginning the play with his lowest card; this way he loses the tricks and by remaining the only one who has high cards of that suit, he will not use them to start the trick, but to cut those of the opponents, when it is not possible to follow their suits.

Three-Seven with the Dead

Another variation is played in threes: two in a pair against the dealer. The dealer distributes the cards, face up, clockwise from the first opponent, to a hypothetical imagined partner of the dealer, to the second opponent and finally to himself. The game develops with the same rules as Three-Seven, except that it is, as was said, with faceup cards, making it unnecessary for two partners to communicate with the declarations of "knock" and "fly." The dealer plays with his cards when it is his turn and with the cards in front of him when it is his imaginary partner's turn.

WHIST

Whist is the forerunner of numerous family card games,
the most famous and popular of this type of game is probably Bridge.
Whist is a game with simple rules yet difficult to play well.

Players
Four, in pairs

Game Equipment
- A deck of 52 cards

■ Start & Object of the Game

Cut the deck to decide who will deal; the player with the highest card, from the Ace to the King is the dealer. Be aware, however, that during the game the Ace will not be the lowest card but the highest, worth more than the King.

The players sit around the table, in positions that are traditionally named according to cardinal poles: north and south against east and west.

The dealer distributes the cards clockwise, 13 cards to each player. Turn the last card of the deck face up (that should be his thirteenth card) to establish the trump suit forthe hand.

The object of the game is to win tricks, and so win the hand.

■ The Play

The suit of the first played card determines the suit of each trick.

The player to the left of the dealer plays the first card faceup in the center of the table, followed by the player to his left, who can put down any one of his cards.

Each one must, if possible, follow suit. Whoever does not have a card of the same suit as the first card played could put down any card.

If a player could, but does not follow suit, he can correct himself on his last turn in a round, changing the card on the board.

The partner of any player who does not follow suit can warn him of an eventual mistake which could then be corrected, but always before the end of the round.

CHALLENGING
At the time that the trick has been played by everyone, but before the beginning of the next one, partners could propose proving that one of the two opponents has not followed suit, even when he was able to do so. In this case, a "challenge" is declared.

If it is effective, the challenged pair who is guilty of the revoking has to pay 2 points to their opponents.

WINNING A ROUND
The winner of the trick is the one who plays the higher trump, or in the case of

a round without trump, the one who plays the highest suit of the opening card. Whoever wins a round starts the next one, playing any card.

CALLING

Any player who accidentally turns one of his cards face up without intending to play it, must then leave it face up on the board until one of the other players "calls" him to play it. Following the call, one is required to play the card; this never involves a challenge.

WINNING A HAND

The hand ends when the players have finished all 13 tricks have been played.

In the United States, the hand that wins receives 7 points, keeping in mind that the first six tricks are not counted. For the successive tricks calculate a point for a trick, and in the case of an "unmasked" challenge, give 2 points to your opponents. The pair that achieves or exceeds 7 points wins by the difference of points between them and their opponents.

In English Whist, the hand wins with 5 points, keeping in mind that the first six tricks do not get counted. A point is awarded for each of the successive tricks; also 4 points are awarded if a player is dealt all of the four "honors" (Jack, Queen, King, and Ace) of trump, and 3 points are awarded for three hon-ors; to win the game it is necessary, however, to have won at least one hand in the last deal of the cards. If both the pairs have 5 points total (or the same number of points), the winner is the one who has totaled these points without honors. In the case of the challenge, the pair who has committed the revoke gives 3 of its points to the opponents who have not yet scored, 2 points if the opponents have already scored 1 or 2 points, and 1 point if the opponents have 3 or 4 points.

THE RUBBER

A "rubber" is a round made up of three hands: if a pair wins the first two out of three, the third is not played and the pair is awarded 2 extra points.

The winner of the round is one who at the end of the rubber has scored more points.

■ Strategy

Good team spirit between partners comes from an informed use of the high cards, and in the English version, honor is the winning weapon of Whist or any other game of rounds.

Be aware that with the challenge, a pair uselessly loses points (at the moment that the points go to the opponents, they are deducted from the revoking pair's own points).

GAMES OF CHANCE

TO THE POINT

*Card games of chance come from American Black Jack
or from Italy's Seven and a Half and do not require any ability,
but simply a thirst for risk, and naturally, fortune!*

Players
Two or more

Game Equipment
- A deck of 52 cards
- Chips

■ Start & Object of the Game

Before beginning the game the players must agree on a limit for the maximum bet that can be made, and, obviously, they must also establish the minimum bet that can be placed.

Then proceed by cutting the deck to establish which player is in charge of the bank. This goes to the player who picks the highest card, from the 2 to the Ace.

At this point the players, excluding the player in charge of the bank, take turns to bet "in the dark" before seeing and receiving their cards by placing their intended bets, ranging from the maximum and minimum established bets.

The bank distributes 3 cards facedown to each betting player.

The object of the game is to have more points than the bank.

■ The Play

Each player looks at his cards and adds his points.

After adding the points, only three cards count, those of the same suit.

If all three cards are different, the points for this hand equal the value of the highest card.

The Ace is worth 11, the face cards 10, the other cards have nominal values.

If, for example, a player receives a 2 of clubs, a Queen of spades, and a Jack of clubs, the total is 12, if the sum of the Jack and the 2 are both of the same suit *(Fig. 1)*.

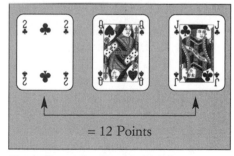

= 12 Points

Fig. 1- Example of a combination.

After all the players take turns to turn their cards and declare their obtained points, the bank pays the player who has more points than the bank and takes points away from whoever has the least points.

If, instead, a player receives an Ace of diamonds, a King of spades, and a 5 of hearts of three different suits *(Fig. 2)*, the points of the highest card of the three is counted, here, the Ace (11 points).

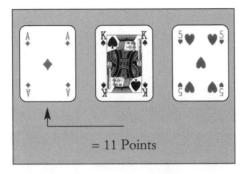

= 11 Points

Fig. 2 - Example of a combination.

THE GAME WITH THE BANK

When the bank and the player have an equal number of points with the same number (one, two, three) of cards, the player collects the points.

If, for example a player has 10 points with the 3 and 7 of clubs and the bank makes 10 with the 4 and 6 of hearts, the hands are equal *(Fig. 3)*.

When the points equal but with a different number of cards, the winner (the bank or the player) is the one who has obtained points using more cards.

If, for example, the bank makes an 11 with the 2, 3, and 6 of diamonds and a player also makes 11 with a 5 and a 6 of spades, the bank naturally wins *(Fig. 4)*.

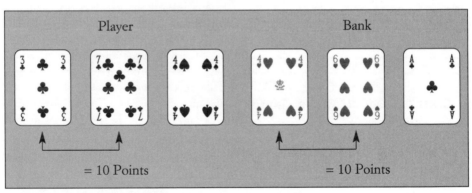

Fig.3 - The hand is equal to the bank.

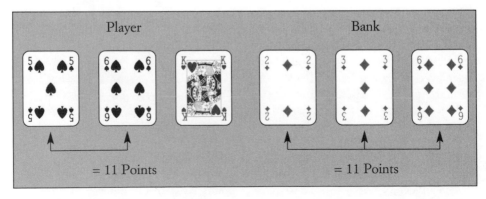

Fig. 4 - The bank wins.

▌ Strategy

Evidently, there is no way to influence the game in one's favor.

One can nevertheless increase his chances by deciding to also make bets after the distribution of the cards.

In such a case, as in the game of poker, the initial bets are an "invitation" to play; then after having seen the cards, each player will be able to choose to pass, leaving the game, or to increase the starting bet.

The bank obviously must first agree to accept this increase.

From hand to hand, it is a good rule of play to pass the bank from one player to another player, especially if there are many players, to equally divide the possibility of losing or winning.

BANGO

*A fast game of chance, Bango is fun and extremely easy to learn
and consists of the elimination of cards based on those turned by the dealer,
similar to Bingo, in which a player covers the numbers of cards
based on the chips drawn.*

Players
From three to ten

Game Equipment
- Two decks of 52 cards
- Chips

The players, including the dealer, place an equal number of chips on the table.

The dealer distributes, from his deck, five cards faceup, one at a time, to each player and to himself. The rest of the cards from the first deck are no longer needed and are put aside.

The object of the game is to eliminate all of one's cards before the opponents are able to get rid of theirs.

■ Start & Object of the Game

Players take turns drawing one card from one of the two decks. Whoever draws an Ace will be the first dealer.

The dealer shuffles one of the two decks of cards and the player to his leftt shuffles the other deck. Then the player to the right cuts each of the decks.

■ The Play

The dealer takes the second deck and deals the top card faceup on the table, staing its rank and suit.

The player (including the dealer) who has the card of the same suit and of the same value as that of the card turned by the dealer turns it over facedown.

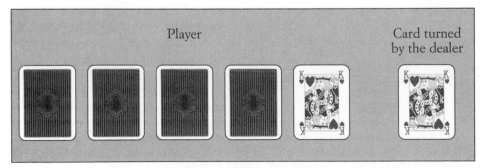

Player   Card turned
                                          by the dealer

Fig. 1 - The player declares "Bango."

The player that turns his last card declares "Bango" *(Fig. 1)*.

The dealer verifies the accuracy of the declaration by comparing the cards of the player with his own turned ones.

If the declaration of Bango is correct, the player in question wins the hand.

If it is not, the player pays a stake (equivalent to the initial one) as a penalty and is disqualified from the game.

At the end of a hand, the deal passes to the player on the left of the previous dealer.

■ Strategy

Bango is a game of pure chance. So, it is good to set a time limit before beginning to play, or a maximum number of hands. Otherwise, the game can go on forever.

BEZIQUE

*This French game had noted popularity in the higher Alps,
especially in the second half of the 1800s. It is also
a forerunner of a series of analytical chance games, the most famous
of which is the American game Pinochle.*

Players
Two

Game Equipment
- Two decks of 52 cards
without the 2, 3, 4, 5, 6,
for a total of 64 cards

■ Start & Object of the Game

Cut the deck to decide the dealer, whoever draws the highest card in the following order: Ace, 10, King, Queen,
Jack, 9, 8, and 7.

The dealer distributes eight cards,
one at a time, to his opponents and to
himself.

The dealer then turns the first card at
the top of the deck to determine the
trump of the hand.

The remaining cards are placed facedown to create the "well" or "stock"
from which the players in turn draw.

The object of the game is to make
winning combinations or declarations
and get the cards that contain "trump"
card-points.

■ The Play

The opponent of the dealer opens the
game, turning over any of his cards.

He then draws from the deck, in
order to always have 8 cards in hand.

The dealer responds with any card,
then draws from the deck.

The winning draw is the card higher
than the opening suit of the game, otherwise known as trump.

Whoever wins the draw may make a
declaration according to the combinations indicated below. To make a declaration, a player must use the necessary
cards from those already drawn.

Whoever gets a combination, indicates the corresponding points and positions the cards faceup to display the
combinations in front to him.

COMBINATIONS
The winning combinations *(Fig. 1)* are:
● The common marriage—King and
Queen of the same suit, 20 points;
● The royal marriage—King and
Queen of the heart, 40 points;
● Bezique—Queen of spades and Jack
of diamonds, 40 points;
● Four Jacks—40 points
● Four Queens—60 points
● Four Kings—80 points
● Four Aces—100 points

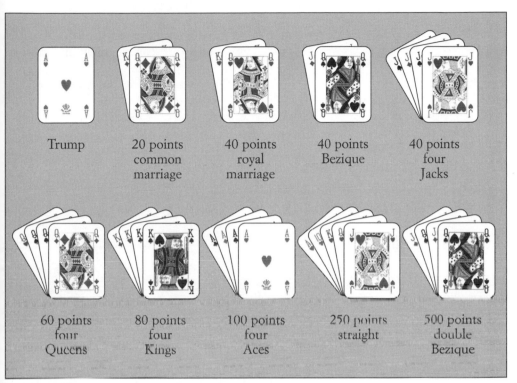

Trump | 20 points common marriage | 40 points royal marriage | 40 points Bezique | 40 points four Jacks

60 points four Queens | 80 points four Kings | 100 points four Aces | 250 points straight | 500 points double Bezique

Fig. 1 - Diplays of the possible winning combinations.

● The straight—(ace, 10, King, Queen, Jacks) only of the suit of hearts, 250 points
● Double Bezique—two Queens of spades and two Jacks of diamonds, 500 points.

The cards of a combination can begin to replace another, provided that they are not similar. For example, a Queen of spades that is part of the common marriage cannot be part of different cards, but it can be part of the four Queens, or of the straight, etc.

DRAWING FROM THE DECK

The player who wins a round opens the next one, drawing directly from the well. He draws the previous winning card from the deck. The opponent takes the trump.

FOLLOWING SUIT

Once the well is exhausted—the last eight tricks—a player must follow suit when he is able. If he revokes, that is, does not follow suit, or does not take a trick when able, he forfeits all eight tricks.

POINTS

All the cards played are scored, along with the Brisques, which are every ten and Ace taken in a trick. Brisques count ten points each, and every trump is worth ten points.

The winner is the first player who gets 1000 or 2000 points (according to what has been agreed by the players at the start of the game).

The loser must pay a preestablished stake for each point of difference between what he has totaled against what the toatl of the winning opponent.

Strategy

Although at first the rules seem complicated, Bezique is an easy and fast game that comes in many variations and happily combines the classic games of draw with those of combinations and also with those of chance.

Be careful: the inexperienced player will do better if he makes a lower bet, otherwise he risks losing much.

BOSTON

A close relative of Whist, Boston is a game of bids, tricks, and chance, with bets that can have extremely interesting amounts . . .

Players
Four

Game Equipment
Two dooks of 52 cards
- Chips

The Start & Object of the Game

Cut the deck to establish the dealer. He will be the one who picks the lowest card from the Ace to the King.

Each player pays 10 chips, placing them on the table.

The dealer shuffles and cuts the deck and distributes all the cards, clockwise, to the players.

Distribute the cards three at a time, except on the last go-around, when you distribute one at a time.

The player who sits in front of the dealer cuts the second deck.

The first card on top of the smaller deck gets turned up: it denotes the "preference suit."

Then the other suit of the same color (red or black) will be the "color suit."

The object is to declare a bid at the beginning of a hand and fulfill that bid.

The Play

Each player, excluding the player to the left of the dealer, can make a declaration or pass.

It is possible to make several declarations if each value exceeds the preceding one: "Boston," in which the declarations of five winning hands with one of the simple suits (neither "preference" nor "color") such as Ace of hearts; six tricks; seven tricks; "little misery," where 12 tricks playing without Ace of hearts after each player, including the declarer, has discarded a covered card; eight tricks; nine tricks; "grand misery," where declarations to lose each trick, playing without Ace of hearts; ten tricks; eleven tricks; "little spread," where declarations of losing twelve tricks, playing without Ace of hearts and with an uncovered hand; "grand spread," where declarations to lose all the tricks playing without Ace of hearts with an uncovered hand; "grand slam," declaration of winning all 13 tricks.

If all the players pass, they pay ten chips into the pool and the hand is void.

ANNOUNCING TRUMP
The player who has made the highest declaration, after all of the bids have been accepted, can announce the suit that he can choose freely for trump. In

the case that two players want to make the same declaration, the higher one will be the one with the preferred suit, then the one with the suit of color, finally the one with a simple suit, hearts and then diamonds, or clubs and then spades. Misery and spread bids do not have trumps.

WINNING THE ROUND

The player to the left of the dealer opens the round, turning over any one of his cards.

The other players must respond to the suit if possible.

If a player can respond to the suit but does not, he "revokes," and loses the hand, paying 40 chips into the pool.

The winner of the trick is the one who plays the highest card of the opening suit of that round, or who, not being able to respond, has played the highest trump *(Figs. 1 and 2)*.

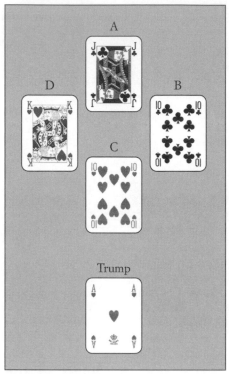

Fig. 2 - D wins the trick.

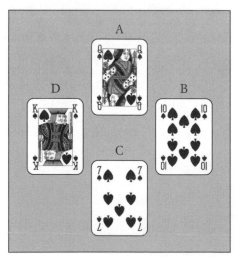

Fig. 1 - D wins the trick.

CONCLUSION

If a player fulfills his declared bid, he receives chips from each player; if his declared bid was to make seven tricks or more, he also receives the chips that are in the pool.

If the declarant does not fulfil his bid, he must pay chips to the other players and double into the pool.

For misery and spread bids, the declarant receives from each player or pays each player the following chips: 20 for the little misery; 40 for grand misery; 80 for the little spread; 160 for the grand spread.

Other bids, wins and losses, are paid according to Tables A and B.

At the end of a hand the deck passes to the player to the left of the previous dealer.

The game could end at that time or after all the players have been dealer for a preestablished number of times.

Table A

Tricks bid	5	6	7	8	9	10	11	12	13
Payment	10	15	20	25	35	45	65	105	170

Table B

Number put in for (failed tricks)

Tricks bid	1	2	3	4	5	6	7	8	9	10	11	12	13	Tricks bid
						Payment								
5	10	20	30	40	50									5
6	15	25	35	45	55	65								6
7	20	30	40	50	60	70	80							7
8	25	35	45	55	70	85	100	115						8
9	35	45	55	65	80	95	110	125	140					9
10	45	55	70	80	95	110	125	140	155	170				10
11	70	80	95	110	125	140	155	170	185	200	220			11
12	120	130	145	160	180	200	220	240	260	280	300	320		12
13	180	200	220	240	260	280	300	320	340	360	390	420	450	13

▪ Strategy

Do not forget that the object of the game is, for the declarant, to fulfill his bid, and to hinder others from doing so.

Managing the pool for a Boston game could make things considerably more pleasant. To distribute the wins in a more equal fashion in the course of the game one can adopt a maximum of 250 chips; when the pool exceeds 250 chips the excess is removed and put aside for the next pool, keeping in mind that the next pool should also not exceed 250.

FAN TAN

Similar to classical roulette, Fan Tan is originally from China.
Well suited for families, it is based exclusively on good luck,
but the bank is not particularly advantaged.
This is why it is no longer played in casinos.

Players
Two or more

Game Equipment
- A set of 52 cards
- A jolly joker with numbers in the corners, as shown in the Figure 1
- Chips of a different color for every player

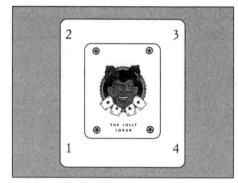

Fig. 1 - The jolly joker.

Start & Object of Game

Players draw cards from the deck, in order to see who is going to have the bank. The bank will be held by the person who draws the highest card, from Ace high to 2.

The special "jolly joker" is placed in the middle of the table *(Fig. 1)*. Players decide upon what the highest bet can be.

All players except the banker make bets as desrcibed below. The player at the left of the banker shuffles the cards. The banker cuts the deck and starts counting the section of cards by fours.

The object of the game is to guess how nearly the cards in the section cut by the dealer will be divisible by four.

■ The Play

The jolly joker has corners that are numbered from 1 to 4, as shown in Figure 1.

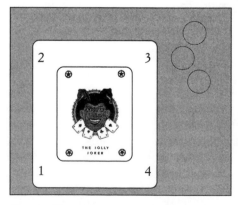

Fig. 2 - The chips placed by the corner with the number 3 show that the player is betting on 3.

A player who places his chips next to one of the corners of the joker *(Fig. 2)* is betting on that number.

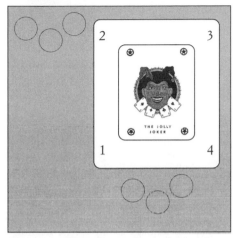

Figure 3 - When a player is placing the chips on a side of the joker, he is betting on the two numbers in the adjacent corners.

A player who places his chips on one side of the joker *(Fig. 3)* is betting on both numbers of that side's corners.

Each player can make more than one bet, but none of the bets should be higher than the limit established at the beginning of the game.

CUTTING THE DECK OF CARDS

The banker must cut the deck to separate a certain number of cards, around a third of the deck, from the rest.

He then must count out those cards four at a time.

If the number of cards he set aside is a multiple of four, then 4 is the winning number.

If the number of cards is not a multiple of four, and the left overs of one, two, or three cards, then that number wins.

If, for example, the banker happens to cut 36 cards, then 4 is the winning number. If he cuts 35, 3 is the winning number. If he the section he cuts is 34, 2 is the winning number. If the cut is33 cards, 1 is the winning number.

PAYING THE POINTS

The bank takes all the losing bets. It pays three times the amount for the winning bets that were placed on the corners, and twice the amount for the winning bets that were placed on the sides.

The bank will be passed on to the next player, when it has lost all its money, or it can pass to the next player every game, or after a preestablished number of games.

▓ Strategy

There is no strategy; the game is based only on luck. In order to be fair, you should make sure that all players are bankers at some point, although this is no guarantee for winning.

PHARAOH II

This is a simplified version of the Pharaoh played in casinos.
It is fast-paced, captivating, well suited for family gatherings or for playing
among friends: naturally, everything depends on luck and on the stakes.

Players
Five

Game Equipment
- Two decks of 52 cards
- Chips

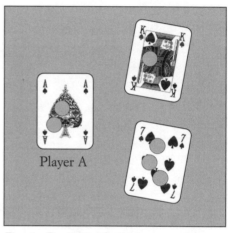

Player A

Fig. 1 - Example of a bet.

■ Start & Object of Game

Cards are drawn to see who is going to be the bank. The bank goes to the player who gets the highest card, from 2 to Ace high.

Players agree upon what the stakes should be for each player, and upon the maximum bet.

The bank gets one of the decks of cards. The other deck will be divided among the players who play against the bank: each player will get a complete set of cards, from the Ace to the King.

The players, and also the bank, make bets, putting on the table one or more of their cards, and placing the chips that they wish to play on top of the card. This will be done in such a way that the total of each player does not exceed the limit of the maximum bet *(Fig. 1)*.

The object of the game is to guess, hand by hand, which cards the bank will lay on the table.

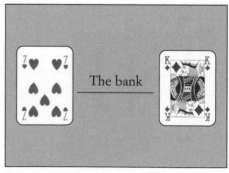

The bank

Fig. 2 - Player A loses with the 7 and wins with the King.

■ The Play

With each deal, the bank will put two cards on the table. The first one it will place to its left, the second one it will place to its right *(Fig. 2)*.

The players who have bet on a card equal in value to the one to the left of the banker lose the bet.

The players who have bet on a card equal in value to the one to the right of the bank, win the bet. Winners win as many chips as they have placed on the winning card. If the card is not only identical in value but also in suit, the loss or the win is doubled.

When the bank has finished its deck of cards, the bank will be taken over by the player to the left.

■ Strategy

Although the game mainly relies on pure chance, this game is full of surprises, and players with a good eye and memory are at an advantage.

Actually, if you can keep track and lremember the cards, you can avoid betting on a card that has already been laid on the table by the dealer, and you can instead bet on a card that he has not yet revealed.

GIN RUMMY

*This type of Rummy belongs to the Rummy family
and had great success in America in the early 1900s
when it was extremely popular as a game of chance in saloons.*

Players
Two

Game Equipment
- Two decks of 52 cards

Start & Object of Game

The two players draw cards in order to find out who will be dealer. This will be the one who draws the highest value, keeping in mind that the Ace is worth 1 and the Jacks, Queens, and Kings are worth 10.

The dealer shuffles the cards of one deck, the opponent cuts the cards, and the dealer deals, one by one, ten cards to each.

Meanwhile, the other player shuffles the second deck of cards and sets it aside for the next game, in which he will be the dealer.

The dealer lays the twenty-first card faceup on the table, next to the rest of the deck (facedown), and starts to build a pile of discards.

The object of the game is to meld the cards you have in hand into combinations and to "go out" before the opponent does, thus gaining points.

The Play

The opponent has the opportunity to take the card that has been laid faceup on the table. If he doesn't take it, then the dealer can take it himself. If the dealer does not want the card either, then his opponent draws a card fromf the deck.

After drawing a card, one must discard. The card drawn from the pile of discards cannot itself be discarded in the same hand.

THE "GIN" COMBINATIONS & GOING OUT
The combinations are made up of at least three cards in sequence or of equal value *(Fig. 1)*.

Fig. 1 - Examples of combinations.

You can go out in more than one way. The most advantageous way to go out is to "make gin." This happens when a player manages to combine all the ten cards he has, with the possible exception of one, which can be discarded (but this is not mandatory). In this case the player announces that he has made gin, then lays his cards on the table to show them to his opponent, who in turn must lay his cards on the table so the points can be counted. The player who made gin wins the points corresponding to his opponent's deadwood, that is, just the points of the opponent's cards that are not included in any combination.

KNOCKING

The second way of going outing is called "knocking." This is possible when one has a certain number of combinations and some discards, whose total value is no more than 10 points *(Fig. 2)*.

divides his cards in combinations and unwanted cards. He also has the possibility to attach cards to the combinations of his opponent.

After this process is over, the points of the cards of each player are calculated. If the person who "knocks" has a lower number of points of the unwanted cards than his opponent, then he has won the hand. Otherwise the hand is won by the opponent.

KEEPING TRACK OF POINTS

Naturally, at the end of each hand the points of each player are written down. Also, one needs to write down "bonus" points, such as extra points for the person who made "gin" (25 points) or to the player who, after the opponent "knocks" actually had a better hand (25 points). When there are only two cards left in the deck of cards, they cannot be drawn.

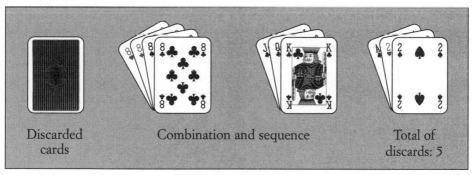

Discarded cards   Combination and sequence   Total of discards: 5

Fig. 2 - The second way of going outing is "knocking." This is possible when one has a certain number of combinations and some discarded cards, whose total value is no more than 10 points.

In this situation, the player draws from the deck of cards, knocks on the table, places one card facedown and shows his hand, combinations and unwanted cards, to the opponent.

The opponent also shows his cards, but without drawing a new card. He also

A game is over when one of the two players reaches 100 points, excluding bonus points. When a game is over, the bonus points are added to the points of each player: the one who has the most points gets a further bonus of 100 points and wins as many points as is the difference between the two totals. The player who manages to reach or exceed 100 points without his opponent ever having won a hand doubles the total of his points, including the bonuses.

■ Strategy

Like all the games of the Rummy family, Gin Rummy can be very exciting, especially if players place bets (which is customary). However, in order to make the game captivating, one must have the courage to risk.

On the whole, knocking is a comfortable way of going out, especially if the hand is dragging on, however, doing it too often can take away from the suspense of the game.

Since there are only two players it is easy to develop an intuition for the game of the opponent.

Try as much as possible not to give the opponent any assistance.

For instance, if you realize that the opponent is trying to make a combination of fours, try, if you can, not to discard any fours . . .

MICHIGAN

The name allows us to guess that this game is originally from the United States. It is a game of chance. This probably contributes to its spread across the ocean and to the rest of the world.

Players
Three to eight

Game Equipment
- A deck of 52 cards
- An Ace, a King, a Queen and a Jack, each one of a different suit. These extra cards need to be taken from a different deck
- Chips

■ Start & Object of Game

The extra cards, also called the "boodle" cards, are arranged at the middle of the table, to form what is called the "pack" *(Fig. 1)*. Each player must place a chip on every card of the pack.

The dealer is chosen by each player drawing a card. The person who drew the card with the highest value, from the 2 to the Ace, will be the dealer.

The dealer deals the cards in clockwise direction, one by one, facedown, to all the players including himself. He will also deal cards to the "widow," an extra hand placed at his left. If the number of cards left to deal is less than the number of players plus the widow, then the dealer will place the leftover cards facedown on the table.

Before the game begins, the dealer will look at his cards. If he wants to, he is allowed to exchange his cards with the widow's. If he forfeits this opportunity, then the widow's cards will be offered to the players each time that one of them wants to buy them. The potential buyer places his cards facedown on the table in the place of the widow's and takes the widow's cards.

Fig. 1 - Initial arrangement of the game.

The player to the left of the dealer starts the game by announcing the value and suit of his lowest card (or one of his lowest cards) and by placing that card faceup on the table.

The object of the game is to put forth sequences of cards, to announce them and uncover them, and to win chips.

■ The Play

After the first player has his card face-down, that player (the same or another) continues with the next card in the sequence. This player uncovers his card and puts it in front of himself *(Fig. 2)*.

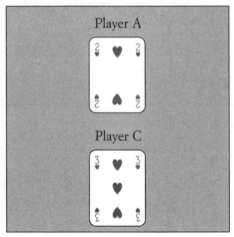

Fig. 2 - Player B does not have the card immediately in sequence, so it is player C's turn.

As the game progresses, each player will have his own cards in front.

The individual piles of cards cannot be consulted to check which cards have been placed on the table up to that point.

Also, neither the widow's cards nor the hand of cards exchanged for it at the beginning can be viewed by the players during the course of the game.

The sequence carries on until the Ace is reached, or until the moment when nobody has the card needed to continue.

WINNING THE CHIPS

When a player announces a Jack, Queen, King, or Ace corresponding in value and in suit to one of the cards in the "pack," then that player wins all the chips that have been placed on that card of the pack.

STOPPED PLAY

When a sequence is interrupted or has been completed, the game is "stopped." The new sequence will be initiated by the player who has stopped the former sequence with an Ace or with any card if no player has the next card in the sequence.

If, after finishing a hand, there are still chips left on some of the cards in the boodle pack, those chips will stay there for the next hand.

At the beginning of each hand, each player antes a chip on each one of the cards in the boodle pack.

FINISHING THE HAND

A hand finishes when one of the players runs out of cards, or when none of the players has the next card in a sequence.

In the first case, when a player runs out of cards, the other players each pay him a chip for every card they still have.

In the second case, when all the players are blocked, the player wins who has the least number of cards left. The other players each pay him as many chips as the difference between their number of cards left and his number of cards left.

When a hand is finished the players must not only count their cards but also uncover them. If a player has not used a card that could have contributed to the sequence, then he will pay a penalty of one chip to each of the other players. If that card could have enabled another player to win one of the bets of the boodle pack, then the player who refused to play that card must pay the latter the equivalent of the lost bet.

If two or more players have the same number of cards left, and all of them are blocked, then the others must pay a chip for each excess card, and those chips will be divided equally among the players with the lowest number of cards left. If a player does not have enough chips to ante the initial bet of a new hand, then that player is out of the game.

THE END OF THE GAME

If all the players except one are out of the game, then that player wins the game and collects all the chips left on the cards of the boodle pack.

The players could also decide to end the game after a certain period of time or after a certain number of hands. In this case, the winner will be the player (or the players) who has the most chips. The chips left on the boodle pack will be collected by the winner or divided among the winners.

■ Strategy

Even though it is forbidden to look at the cards of the widow or even at one's own pile of facedown cards, except the one just laid on the table, these cards have been seen at some point, and it is worth making an effort to remember them in order to avoid betting on an Ace or on another winning card of a sequence that has already been irretrievably stopped.

Of course, the more the game advances, the higher the bets. This is why it is best to decide at the beginning of the game what will be the limit of time to play or the number of hands.

NAPOLEON

*Like Boston, Napoleon is a game from the family of Whist.
It is a capture game, like Bridge, but also of chance,
and owes its name to the fact that the bold Declarant
can adorn himself with the title of the great French leader.*

Players
Two to six

Game Equipment
- A deck of 52 cards
- Chips

■ Start & Object of Game

The chips are distributed, with an equal number given to each player.

The player who draws the card with the highest value will be the dealer (the Ace is high).

The dealer deals 5 cards to each player including himself. The cards are given one by one, in clockwise order.

The object of the game is to win the bid for tricks that one makes at the beginning of each hand.

■ The Play

Starting with the player to the left of the dealer, each player can pass, or can declare his tricks for that round: two, three, four, or five ("Napoleon"), which is the maximum.

The player who announces five captures says "Napoleon."

Each announcement must be greater than the previous one.

After Napoleon has been announced, a player can still call "Wellington," which is also five tricks, however, the bet is double the one of Napoleon.

After Wellington has been called, a player can still declare "Bluecher," five captures with the bet three times that of Napoleon.

Players can also announce that they are not going to make any tricks. In order to do this they have to announce "Misery." One can only announce Misery after a bid of "three" has been declared and before any player has declared the next greater bid of "four."

DETERMINING THE TRUMP

The player who announced the highest bid of tricks to win, the "Declarant," begins the game, uncovering one of his cards. The suit of that card will determine the trump of the hand.

If the player who opens the round has announced "Misery," the round will be played without a trump.

The other players must, when it is their turn, follow the suit, each of them playing one of their cards which is of the same suit.

A player who cannot follow suit can play any of his cards.

WINNING A TRICK

The trick is won by whoever has the card of the highest value, or by the player who, unable to follow suit, puts down a trump, even if the trump is of lesser numerical value compared with the other cards on the table *(Figs. 1 and 2)*. However, the trump must be higher than other potential trumps.

The player who wins a trick will begin the next hand.

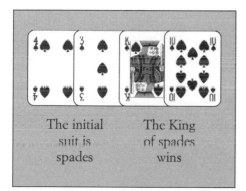

| The initial suit is spades | The King of spades wins |

Fig. 1 - Example of a "game" of four cards.

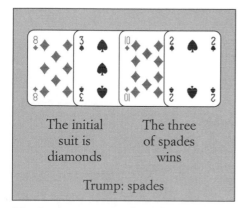

| The initial suit is diamonds | The three of spades wins |

Trump: spades

Fig. 2 - An example of another "game" of four cards.

WINNING A HAND

The Declarant wins the hand and earns chips if he completes the number of tricks that he declared in his bid at the beginning.

Otherwise, he loses and must pay the appropriate points in chips to each of his opponents.

The following numbers of chips will be paid by the other players to the Declarant if his bid is completed:

● 2 for a bid of 2
● 3 for a bid of 3
● 3 for a bid of Misery
● 4 for a bid of 4
● 10 for a bid of Napoleon
● 20 for a bid of Wellington
● 30 for a a bid of Bluecher

If the Declarant does not complete his tricks, and so loses his bid, he will pay the following number of chips to each of the other players:

● 2 to a player who bid 2
● 3 to a player who bid 3
● 3 to a player who bid Misery
● 5 to a player who bid Napoleon
● 10 to a player who bid Wellington
● 15 to a player who bid Bluecher

Once a hand is over, the deck of cards goes to the player to the left of the former dealer.

The player who does not have enough chips to pay the highest bid of the hand, or to pay for his defeat if he was the Declarant, will go out of the game.

THE END OF THE GAME

The game can end after all the players have been dealers, or at a set time established at the beginning of the game.

The player who has won the most chips is the winner. Of course, if a player leaves all his opponents without chips or with not enough chips to continue playing, he ends the game and wins.

Strategy

The Declarant must try to complete the tricks of his bids, and naturally the other players, including those who passed, must try to stop him from achieving his goal. This is also one of the objects of the game, since if the Declarant does not fulfill his bid, he loses chips to the other players.

Obviously, if in a hand there is a Wellington and a Bluecher, there is more than one player convinced that he can make five tricks. However, this is not possible, since there are only five tricks, so only one player can win all five. Who will this be?

Naturally, the most warlike player, but also the one who is the wisest when making his bid.

POPE JOAN

An Anglo-Saxon game of cards and chance, this is the result
of combining two other games: Commit and Matrimony.
Surely, a significant part of its popularity is due to the fact that
one can win significant amounts, since a bet that has not been won
will stay on as a bet for the next round.

Players
Three or more

Gamo Equipmont
 Λ dock of 52 cards, from which
the 8 of diamonds is removed
- A paper square divided into 4 areas:
the central ones correspond to the
Ace, Jack, Queen and King; the
outside areas correspond to Pope
Joan, Intrigue, Game, and Matrimony
(Fig. 1)
- Chips

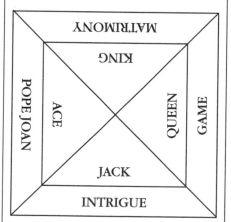

Fig. 1 - The game square.

■ Start & Object of the Game

Once the bet has been agreed upon, the
chips are distributed, all of which must
have the same value.

Cards are drawn to see who will be
the dealer.

The dealer deals the cards to each
of the players, including himself, in
clockwise order, one by one and facedown; each time he gives a card to himself, he also puts another card facedown
on the table.

When the cards left to deal are less
than the number of players, the dealer
places these cards on the facedown pile,
except the last card which he places on
top, faceup.

For example, let's assume there are
three players. After giving 12 cards to
each (48 total, taking into account the
covered pile), the dealer still has 3 cards
left. He will place two, facedown on the
covered pile, and the third one on top of
the pile, faceup.

The object of the game is to play all
the cards, and by doing this, to win
chips.

TRUMP & THE ARRANGEMENT OF THE CHIPS
The faceup card on top of the pile indicates the suit of the trump.

All the players must place the following number of chips on the paper square: 4 each on Pope Joan, 2 each on Matrimony, 2 on Intrigue, and one in each of the other sections.

■ The Play

The nine of diamonds is Pope Joan. If the faceup card on top of the pile is the Pope Joan, then the dealer wins all the chips placed on the paper square in the section of the Pope Joan and in the section of the Game, or, as an alternative, all the chips on the paper square. The hand is closed. *(Fig. 2)*.

THE INTRODUCTION OF THE SEQUENCES
The player to the left of the dealer opens the game by playing any card, placing it faceup in the center of the table, and declaring it, for example: "2 of hearts."

The player that has the next card in increasing order (in our example, the 3 of hearts), plays it by placing it on top of the previous one, and declaring it.

The game like this until no player can continue the sequence. This can happen in two ways: either the sequence has been completed, arriving at the King, or the card that would be next is hidden in the covered pile. At this point, the completed sequence is turned facedown.

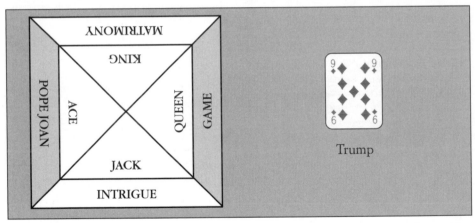

Fig. 2 - If the faceup card (the trump) is Pope Joan, then the dealer wins all the chips in the section of Pope Joan, or, as an alternative, all the chips on the paper square; the hand is closed.

In this case, in the next hand, the new dealer will be the player to the left of the dealer.

The chips that have not been won at the end of a hand remain on the paper square for the next hand.

If the trump is an Ace or a Jack, Queen or King, the dealer wins all the chips that were placed on the corresponding section, but the play of the hand continues.

The player who has played the last card of a sequence gets ot start the next sequence.

WINNING THE CHIPS
The player who, during the sequence, plays the 9 of diamonds (Pope Joan) or an Ace, Jack, Queen, or King in the suit of the trump, wins the chips that were placed on the corresponding section of the paper square.

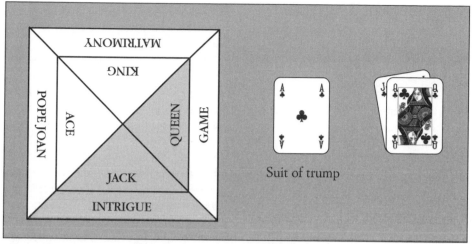

Fig. 3 - The player who plays the Jack and Queen of trump in sequence wins the chips placed on the corresponding sections and also the chips placed on Intrigue.

If a player plays the Jack and Queen of the suit of the trump in sequence, he wins the chips placed on the corresponding sections and also the chips placed on Intrigue. *(Fig. 3)*.

corresponding fields, also the chips placed on Matrimony. *(Fig. 4)*.

One can win only if the card is played correctly in the sequence. Whoever has a "winning" card left in hand at the end of

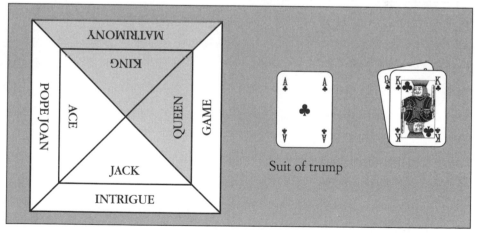

Fig. 4 - The player who plays the Queen and the King of the suit of the trump, in sequence, wins, other than the chips placed on the corresponding fields, also the chips placed on Matrimony.

The player who plays the Queen and the King of the trymp suit, in sequence, wins, other than the chips placed on the

the game gets no chips for that card. The pile of facedown cards cannot be viewed by anyone.

CLOSING & BEGINNING A NEW HAND

The player has no more cards wins all the chips placed on the field called Game and thereby closes the hand. The other players must give a chip for each card they still have to the player who closed the hand. The player who has Pope Joan does not need to pay.

In the next hand, the dealer will be the person seated to the left of the previous dealer.

At the beginning of each new hand, chips are placed on the paper square, according to the distribution rules explained at the beginning; naturally, the chips that have not been won will also be left on the paper square. This is why, with every new hand, the bet will increase significantly.

If at the beginning of hand, a player does not have enough chips to place on the paper square, he leaves the game.

THE ROUND

A round finishes after all players have been dealers.

At the end of a round, the chips left on the paper square will be divided among the players by choosing a trump and then collecting each player's cards and redistributing them, one by one, faceup. The player who gets Pope Joan, the Ace, Jack, Queen, or King of the suit of the trump will receive the chips on the corresponding field. The chips on Intrigue will be divided between the player who has the Queen and the player who has the Jack, and those on Matrimony will be divided between the player who has the King and the one who has the Queen.

If a player leaves all opponents without enough chips to start a new hand, then he wins not only the round but also all the chips left on the paper square.

POKER

Without doubt, Poker is the most widely spread card game of chance.
It is equally loved by Americans and Europeans. It can result in the loss
or gain of tremendous fortunes, as the previous century's gold-diggers
and the members of the international jet-set well know.
These people have made poker a "disease." Naturally, without arriving
at such excesses, this game can be a captivating and fun pastime.
It is not rare that, within groups of friends, there is a habit of the weekly
poker-night. By always playing among themselves, the members of a group,
winning and losing now and then, end up in the long run breaking even.
However, they will have passed many enjoyable evenings together.
The type of Poker illustrated in these pages is considered Draw Poker,
the most widespread and played throughout Europe.

Players
From two to six

Game Equipment
- A deck of 52 cards
- Chips, usually of various colors
that are agreed upon to represent
values of cash

■ Start & Object of the Game

Cards are drawn to decide who will be
the dealer. This will be the player who
draws the highest card.

Players must decide how many chips
each player will get, and what the minimum and the maximum bets will be.

Rules and variants will be established,
the length of the round, and so on.

The order of play and where each
player sits is decided by drawing cards:
The dealer gives one card to each player,
including himself. The player who has
the highest card can choose where to sit,
after that it follows in order of the value
of their cards. The last person to sit will
be the one who has drawn the card with
the lowest value. This person will sit in
the last empty chair.

All the players can, if they wish, shuffle the cards. The last person to shuffle
the cards will be the dealer. The player at
the right of the dealer will cut the cards.

Players put down a "chip," or a minimum bet in the pot. An alternative is
that only the dealer puts down a chip.

The dealer deals five cards to each
player, including himself. This will be
done one by one, in clockwise order.
The object of the game is to get the best
hand, or "point," by beating the hands
of the other players and thereby winning
the pot with the bets.

◼ The Play

Once the cards have been dealt, each player will look at his cards. The object of the game is to get winning hands, or points. These are the points, from the highest to the lowest:

● "Royal flush" or "straight flush" is five cards of the same suit, in sequence *(Fig. 1)*. The royal flush is topped by an Ace. A straight flush is any other, and it loses to a higher straight flush or a royal flush.

Straight flush

Fig. 1.

● "Four of a kind" is four cards that are equal in value *(Fig. 2)*; the highest four of a kind is that of the Aces.

Four of a kind

Fig. 2.

● "Full house" is three cards of the same value, and a pair of cards of the same value *(Fig. 3)*; if two players have a full house, the highest set of 3 wins.

● "Flush" is five cards of the same suit, not in sequence *(Fig. 4)*.

● "Straight" is five cards in sequence, but of different suits *(Fig. 5)*.

● "Three of a kind" is three cards of the same value *(Fig. 6)*.

● "Two Pair" is two pairs of cards of the same value *(Fig. 7)*; in the case of two pair, the highest card is taken into account (in our example it is two pair with a pair of Aces); if two players have two pair, the player with the highest value wins; if the two pair are of the same value, then the minor pairs are taken into account; if the lower pairs are the same, one looks at the value of the 5th card.

Full house

Fig. 3.

Flush

Fig. 4.

Straight

Fig. 5.

Three of a kind

Fig. 6.

Two pair

Fig. 7.

● "Pair" is two cards of equal value (*Fig. 8*).

Pair

Fig. 8.

THE OPENING

Starting from the person seated at the left of the dealer, each player has the opportunity of "opening": The player who has a pair of Jacks or better will open. He does not need to show his hand, but if he wins this can be demanded of him.

If none of the players can open, the hand is void: the chips will be left in the pot for the next hand; the deck of cards will be passed to the player on the left of the previous dealer. In order to open in this new hand, one needs to have a pair of Queens at least.

BETS & RAISING

The player who opens makes a bet, based on the cards he has.

The other players can:

● "Fold," which means leaving play without putting more chips in the pot;

● "Call," which means putting the same number of chips in the pot as the player who opened, and thereby staying, that is, continuing to play;

● "Raise," which means putting down more chips than the player who has opened the game. In this case the other players, in order to continue playing, must add chips or they must fold.

After a raise one can raise again, thereby making the bet even higher.

CHANGING CARDS

After the first phase of opening has been completed, after all raises and counter raises, the players who are still in play can exchange some of their cards, from one to four.

The player who does not wish to exchange any cards says he will "stand pat."

The players who do want to change their cards should place them facedown in front of themselves. The cards that have been put down will not be seen by anybody. An exception to this is when the person who opened wins. In this case, as mentioned earlier, at the end of the hand the other players can ask him to reveal the opening pair.

The dealer will give each player, in clockwise order, as many cards as the player has put down.

If the dealer finishes the deck before he has been able to fulfill the exchange requests of all the players, he will then collect the cards that have been placed down by the players to be exchanged, will shuffle them, and will use them to complete the exchange. In this case, if the player who has opened has put down his opening pair, he must warn the other players who can decide that they want to see the opening pair before the dealer collects the cards.

FINAL PHASE

After the exchange of cards, the next player to speak is the one who opened. After all players have spoken, and after all players left in the game have accepted the raises or counter raises, then the cards are revealed. The player who has placed the highest bet after the others have accepted, must show his hand. If no player can beat it, that player receives the whole pot. Otherwise the pot goes to whichever player has accomplished and shown the best hand.

CONTINUING THE GAME

The game goes on until the time that has been agreed upon at the beginning. At that point, a few hands will still be played, equal to the number of players, so that every player will be a dealer.

After the game is over, the wins and losses are tallied.

■ Strategy & Variations

The bluff is the essence of poker. Never let the others suspect what your hand is. But this is not all. You must appear very sure of yourself, even when you have a weak hand, and you must seem hesitant when you have a strong hand. The poker player must be gifted with a certain amount of common sense and intuition in order to anticipate the opponent's game, to know when to stop betting, and when to raise the bet. This subtle psychology is surely what makes poker so fascinating, even if for years one plays with the same three of four friends.

BLIND & OVERBLIND

A version that makes the risk element even stronger (and makes the game even more fun), is the one of the "blind": the player who speaks first can, before having seen his cards, make a bet that is equal to the whole pot. The blind can be followed by the overblind. The player who comes directly after, can, without looking at his cards, raise the bet. The other players, if they want to stay in the game, must match the bet or fold.

SEVEN & A HALF

*An Italian version of American Black Jack,
Seven and a Half is not played in casinos. It is, however,
very popular in circles of friends and for family gatherings.
It is fun not only to play this game but also to watch
and maybe even bet on the winning hands of the players.*

Players
Two or more

Game Equipment
- A deck of 40 cards (a poker deck
minus the 8s, 9s, and 10s)

■ Start & Object of Game

The cards will be dealt in order to decide who the dealer will be. This will be the person who has the King of diamonds. The dealer establishes the maximum bet, shuffles the cards, and asks the player to his right to cut the cards. Then the dealer deals a card facedown to each of the players, including himself.

The object of the game is to beat the bank and to make, with one's own cards, seven and a half points, or as close to this number as possible.

■ The Play

The are worth their number fromAce (1) to 7. The Jack, Queen, and King are each worth half a point. The players look at their covered card and make bets.

The dealer does not bet. The players each take turns playing. The person sitting at the left of the dealer starts.

The player who, as his first card, gets a four or a three, can, when his turn comes up, ask to exchange his card. He will show the card and receive another card, facedown.

If the new card is once again a four or a three, the player once again has the opportunity of changing it.

STAYING OR CALLING
Each player, at his turn, can decide whether he wants to "stay," and in that case, having only his one card to play, or to "call."

The player who calls, receives a card facedown from the dealer. The values of the two cards, the covered one and the facedown one, will be added. The player then can choose to "stay" or to call another card, trying to reach the total of seven and a half.

The player who calls a card and receives a four or a three, facedown, can no longer exchange them: Only the dealt card can be exchanged, and only before calling another card.

The player who exceeds seven and a half must leave the game, pays his bet to the dealer, and gives up his hand.

The player who, after having called the first card, makes seven and a half, declares "seven and a half amble" and shows his cards *(Fig. 1)*.

Fig. 1 - Seven and a half amble.

In all other cases, when a player decides to "stay," or when he gets seven and a half with three or more cards, he does not need to declare or show his points until the end of the hand.

The dealer plays last. Just like the other players, he can stay, call a card, make seven and a half, or seven and a half amble, or also go out.

SETTLING THE ACCOUNTS

At this point the accounts need to be settled. The dealer must pay each player whose points are higher than his own, and takes the bets of those whose points are lower than his own.

The player whose points are equal to those of the dealer withdraws his bet and then they are even.

Seven and a half amble wins double the bet, but only if the dealer has not also achieved a seven and a half amble, or if the dealer has not made seven and a half with three or more cards.

If the dealer goes out of the game, he must pay all the players, except for those who have already gone out.

The player who makes seven and a half amble becomes the new dealer. If the dealer has also made seven and a half amble, then he remains the dealer.

A NEW HAND

Once a hand is finished, the dealer gathers the cards from the table, puts them aside, and deals from the left overs. If those cards are not enough, then he also takes the cards from the previous hands, shuffles them, and deals them.

The winner is the player who, after a preestablished amount of time, has won the most hands.

■ Strategy

It is important to look at the cards that the players are calling. If, for example, many Jacks, Queens, Kings, and low numbers have already been dealt and if you have a five, it is probably better to stay. The player who calls many cards, most likely holds a Jack, Queen, King, an Ace, or a two.

If you don't like to take chances and you have a seven or a six, it is probably wisest to stay. Even if you have a five you should probably stay.

THE RULE OF THE KING OF DIAMONDS

In this version the King of diamonds can function as a trump and have any value desired. A King of diamonds, with any other face card can, in this case, make a seven and a half amble. *(Fig. 2)*.

Fig. 2 - Seven and a half with the King of Diamonds.

Players must agree whether or not to adopt this rule before starting the game.

TERESINA

An Italian version of Poker for players who are definitely skilled (or maybe just courageous), this game allows bets, pots, and even more plentiful wins. During a Poker night between friends, the game could be revitalized with a few hands of Teresina, which is faster and more fun.

Players
From two to five

Game Equipment
- A deck of 32 cards, actually just 7s, 8s, 9s, 10s, Jacks, Queens, Kings, and Aces for all 4 suits
- Chips

■ Start & Object of Game

Whoever draws the highest card, from the 7 to Ace, in the order hearts, diamonds, clubs, spades, is dealer.

Players agree on how many chips each player gets and what the minimum and the maximum bet should be.

Rules should be agreed on. The players also need to decide on the length of the game, and so on.

Players draw cards to decide their seats. The dealer gives a card to every player, including himself. The player with the highest card can choose where he wants to sit. The others choose when their turn comes, according to the value of their cards. The last person to sit is the one who has the lowest card. This person will sit in the last empty seat.

All players can, if they wish, shuffle the deck of cards. The last person to shuffle them will be the dealer. He will ask the player sitting at his right to cut the cards.

All players must put a "chip," or minimum bet, into the pot. One version is where only the dealer puts down a chip. The dealer deals a card facedown to each player, including himself, in clockwise order. Then he will deal a card faceup for each player *(Fig. 1 on page 164)*.

The object of the game is to get the best hand (or "point") by beating the hands of the other players, thus winning the pot with the chips.

■ The Play

The game is played following the rules and the combinations of poker. The player who opens, or who speaks first, is the one who has the faceup card with the highest value. If two players have faceup cards of equal value, the one who is first to the left of the dealer will open.

BETS & RAISING

Whoever speaks first has two possibilities:
● "Leaving" the game, in which case he will turn over the faceup card and will set both his cards aside. Naturally, by doing so, he will lose his chip;

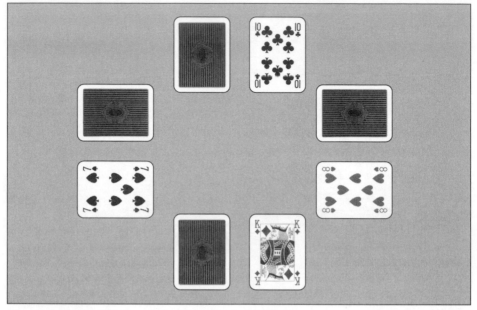

Fig. 1 - Initial distribution of the cards for four players.

- "Opening" by placing the chips that he is willing to bet into the pot.

The other players can, in their turn:

- "Leave";
- "Stay," in which case they must put in the pot the same amount of chips as the player who has opened;
- "Raise" or "counter raise," just as in poker.

After raises and counter raises, all the other players must declare if they want to stay (in which case they must add to the pot to match the new bet), or if they want to leave.

The dealer will deal a new card, face-up. The next player to speak will be the one who has the two faceup cards of highest value. To the possibilities above another is added. Players now have the right to say "parole." This means that they are not making a declaration and they limit themselves to accepting some-body else's hand.

If all players say parole, the game goes on, and the dealer will deal the next card.

SECOND & CONSECUTIVE HANDS

Once the declarations and bets for the second hand of cards have been com-pleted, the dealer will deal a third card faceup. The player who has the highest faceup hand speaks first.

After the declarations and the bets for the third hand have been completed, the dealer will deal cards for the fourth and last time. Now all players have four face-up cards, and one facedown. As in poker, one plays by showing the cards.

SHOWING THE CARDS

After all declarations and bets have been completed in the last hand, the player who has made the highest bet will let the other players see the fifth card, which up to that point has been facedown.

After that, all players will show their cards one by one.

The player who has the highest combination wins, following the rules of poker.

In any phase of the game, if all players except one leave, the remaining player wins the pot, and does not have to show the facedown card.

■ Strategy

In Teresina also there is the art of bluffing. The facedown card cna be insignificant, or, on the contrary, be extremely influential. The player must be able to not make the others suspect the truth.

Since one bets four times in one hand, with raises and counter raises, the stakes in Teresina can become high. This is why it is good to agree at the start on the maximum bet, as well as the minimum bet and the duration of the game.

DECLARING STRAIGHTS & FLUSH

In one version of the game, after the distribution of the fourth and last faceup card, any player who has a straight or a flush formed by their cards must declare and show it. *(Figs. 2 and 3)*.

This does not necessarily lead to winning the hand, because there could be a straight flush which beats the flush or a full house which beats the normal straight.

But this limits the loss to those players who, doubting the regularity of the game, would place high bets, assuming that others are bluffing.

Naturally, on the other hand, even the most unfortunate players could make the player with the declared straight believe that they have a full house—even if they don't have it. This way they would force the player with the straight to leave, and they would win the pot with a simple double pair!

Fig. 2 - A version according to which, after the distribution of the fourth and last faceup card, the players who have a straight declare and show it.

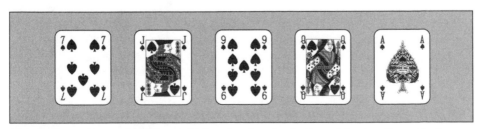

Fig. 3 - A version according to which, after the distribution of the fourth and last faceup card, the players who have a flush declare and show it.

TONTINA

Tontina is one of the games in which one can adopt the saying: "the more the merrier." It is well suited for family gatherings or for evenings among friends. It is a fast-paced, fun game, and one can play it with low or high bets, depending on the company, or on one's own propensity to risk.

Players
Two or more

Game Equipment
- A deck of 52 cards
- Chips

■ Start & Object of Game

The chips are divided among the players, 15 or 30 to each player, all chips being of the same value.

The dealer is chosen by drawing cards.

Each player antes 3 chips in the pot.

The dealer gives a faceup card to each player, including himself, in clockwise order.

The object of the game is to win chips on the basis of the cards received in each hand.

■ The Play

Chips are won or lost depending on the card one has just received.

The player who has a King, a Queen, or a Jack takes from the pot 3, 2, or one chip, respectively *(Fig. 1)*.

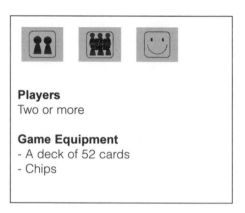

Wins	Wins	Wins
3 chips	2 chips	1 chip

Fig. 1

The player who gets an Ace, a 2, or a 3 pays the player to his left 1, 2, or 3 chips, respectively *(Fig 2)*.

Pays	Pays	Pays
1 chip	2 chips	3 chips

Fig. 2

The player who gets one of the remaining odd number cards (i.e., 5, 7 or 9), puts 1 chip into the pot *(Fig. 3)*.

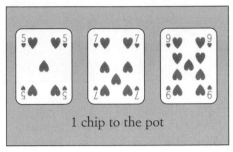

1 chip to the pot

Fig. 3

The player who gets one of the remaining even number cards except the 10 puts 2 chips into the pot **(Fig. 4)**.

2 chips to the pot

Fig. 4

The player who gets a 10 does not have to pay anything, but also does not win anything. Also, the player to his right does not owe him anything.

SUCCESSIVE HANDS & THE ROUND
Once a hand is over, the cards that have been played aree set aside. In the next hand the remaining cards are used. After the second, the cards that have been set aside are shuffled and dealt again.

From hand to hand, the role of dealer will pass from the previous dealer to the person to his left.

The round finishes after a set time, or, alternatively, after all players have been dealers.

At the end of a round, the player who has the highest number of chips, will also win the remaining chips in the pot. If there are two or more players who all have the same amount of chips which is also the highest number of chips, the chips in the pot will be divided among them.

■ Strategy

In Tontina there is no strategy that can give one player any advantage; there is only chance. Being the dealer also has an impact. In order to increase the chance, players could decide at a certain point in the round (when a considerable bet would be in the pot) to play a hand betting "blind," which means betting before distributing the cards.

In this case, each player antes three chips to the pot, then also puts down a certain number of chips as a bet (however, this must be within the scope of the preestablished minimum and maximum), before receiving a card.

Depending on whether the card he receives is a winning or a losing card, the player will either receive or pay one, two, or three times the bet he made.

WHISKEY POKER

*Among the many versions of poker, this one, invented in the saloons
of the Old West, adds more of the element of chance for the players
and offers the possibility of making rather large bets.*

Players
From two to five

Game Equipment
- A deck of 32 cards, (use the 7s, 8s, 9s, 10s, Jacks, Queens, Kings and Aces in all four suits)
- Chips

■ Start & Object of Game

Cards are drawn in order to decide the dealer. This is the person who draws the highest card, from the 7 to the Ace.

The dealer deals five cards facedown to each player, including himself, and then places down hand of 5 cards faceup, which is available to all players.

The object is to complete winning combinations with one's own cards.

■ The Play

The game is played according to the rules of poker: the same combinations, the same possibilities for speaking, raising, counter raising, and showing cards. The extra option this game gives to players is that of using the faceup cards on the table. Players have this possibility after the first distribution of cards, and

after the first bets are made, before asking the dealer to change cards.

At this point in the game, each player can, if he chooses, exchange one or even all of his cards (which he placed facedown and which no other player can ask to see, except in order to check on the opening, at the end of a hand), with the cards that are faceup on the table.

If, in this phase, a player declares that he is served, the other players after him have the right to change only one card with one of the faceup cards.

Once this phase is over, the game proceeds to normal exchange (if a player has already declared himself served, he cannot, at this point, ask to exchange cards), and the hand goes one like a traditional poker hand, in which the player wins who has the highest combination.

■ Strategy

Whiskey poker is, like Teresina, a version of poker at a high level, and this is why it has been adapted to more skilled players. This is because, while changing one's cards with the cards on the table, one gives the other players the possibility of guessing one's game. The player who has the opportunity to choose first among all the five cards is favored, and so this is why it is very important that all players get to be dealers.

ZIG-ZAG

A game of chance for an unlimited number of players,
which, just like Tontina, is based on the cards that each player gets by chance,
determining who wins and who loses chips.

Players
Two or more

Game Equipment
- A deck or two (if there are more than five players) of 52 cards
- Chips

Start & Object of Game

Players decide on the number of chips that each will receiveat the start. All of the chips are of the same value. Also, players decide on the minimum and the maximum bet.

The deck of cards is cut in order to decide the dealer. This will be the player who draws the highest card, from the 2 to the Ace (Ace is high).

Each player antes a predetermined number of chips in the pot, for example, the double of the minimum bet.

The dealer deals the cards, one by one, facedown, to all the players, making facedown piles.

When the cards the dealer has left are insufficient to deal evenly among all the players, these cards will be set aside.

The object of the game is to win the chips that are in the pot according to the cards one has.

The Play

The players are not allowed to look at the cards they have received.

Once all cards have been dealt, each player will make a bet, placing the number of chips he chooses to wager in front of his pile of cards.

Each player keeps his facedown pile in front of himself, and, at his turn, uncovers the first card. According to the value of this card, the player wins—and takes the amount of his bet from the pot—or loses, and payss his bet into the pot instead.

If the card that the player uncovers is an Ace, the player loses, and must deposit into the pot double the amount he has bet.

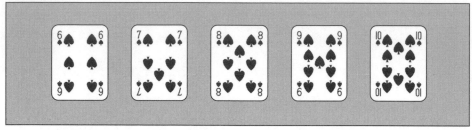

Fig. 1 - The player takes back his bet.

If the card is a 2, 3, 4, or a 5, the player loses and deposits into the pot as many chips as he has bet. If the card is a 6, 7 8, 9, 10, the player takes chips equal to his bet from the pot *(Fig. 1)*.

If the card is a Jack, a Queen, or a King, the player wins double his bet *(Fig. 2)*.

Fig. 2 - The player wins double his bet.

SUCCESSIVE HANDS & BETS

Once the first round of uncovering cards is finished, new bets are made, and new cards uncovered. This goes on until the

piles are finished. Once the cards are finished, all cards are gathered and shuffled, and the person to the left of the first dealer becomes the new dealer.

Chips are placed in the pot again, new cards are dealt, and the game restarts.

A round is finished after all players have been dealers.

The chips left in the pot will be given to the player who has won the most chips (if two or more players have won the same amount, then the pot will be divided in equal shares). An alternative would be to divide the pot among all players.

▓ Strategy

In this game, luck is everything.

However, towards the end of a hand, a player can guess whether there are still winning figures remaining, and he can adjust his bets accordingly.

SOLITAIRE GAMES

CORNERS

This is a simple but captivating solitaire which requires the player, traditionally, to form the four color sequences: hearts, diamonds, clubs, and spades.

Players
One

Game Equipment
- A deck of 52 cards

▧ Start & Object of the Game

The cards are shuffled, and, keeping the deck facedown, the first nine cards are drawn, and, not looking at them, they are then placed on the table, making 3 columns of 3 cards each.

At the four corners of this "square" there should be four cards of different suits. If this is not so, then the cards will be collected, the deck shuffled again, and the same arrangement repeated.

The aim of the game is to put all the cards of each suit in sequence on top of the cards of the corners.

▧ The Play

The sequences must start with the four cards of the corners. If, for example, these cards are the 3 of hearts, 5 of diamonds, King of clubs and Ace of spades,

one will look among the cards that are not in the corners for the 4 of hearts, the 6 of diamonds, the Ace of clubs, and the 2 of spades.

The possible holes in the arrangement will be filled in with cards taken from the pile that is still facedown.

The pile of cards will be placed facedown outside of the arrangement, and cards will be drawn one by one: those which can continue a sequence will be placed on top of the piles in the corners.

For each card in a corner, one must check whether the following card in the sequence is present in the arrangement.

When a sequence reaches the Ace, it will be continued with the 2.

One can draw three times out of the facedown pile. The game has been successful if, after three drawings, all the sequences in the corners have been finished.

▧ Strategy

Being successful in the game depends entirely on luck.

In order to avoid making and remaking the arrangement with new cards, one can choose four cards by chance, one for each suit, and place them in the corners; after that, the deck is shuffled, the arrangement is completed and one begins to play.

ACE IN COMMAND

This is a sequence solitaire, with a fixed starting point (actually starting from the Ace down). It is played with a classic Poker deck.

Players
One

Game Equipment
- A deck of 32 cards, from the Ace to the 7

Start & Object of the Game

First you must shuffle the deck. You must keep the deck face-down in front of you. You must draw the first two cards in such a manner that you can only see the second one *(Fig. 1)*, putting aside the rest of the deck.

The aim of the game is to complete the four sequences of hearts, spades, clubs and diamonds, in decreasing order, from the Ace to the 7.

Fig. 1 - Position of opening the deck of remaining cards.

The Play

Out of every pair of cards you can only play the second one (actually the one on the top of the deck of remaining cards). If this card is an Ace, then it will be placed on the table, and it will be the start of its sequence.

After an Ace has been found, you need to look for its King: if the King is the second card of a pair, then you can place it on top of the Ace of the same suit.

From pair to pair you find more cards, which, one by one, will take their place within their sequence.

When a card on top of the deck of remaining cards is taken and put into a sequence, it liberates another card, which can, in turn, be used in a sequence, and so on.

After all cards have been used, you can turn the deck of remaining cards upside down, and, without shuffling it, once again start drawing pairs of cards.

The game is successful if you can complete the sequences after turning the deck upside down twelve times.

Strategy

There is no trick for winning this solitaire, which, like many similar pastimes, is based only on the arrangement of cards within the initial deck.

BLOCK

This is a rather complex solitaire which takes a long time and must be played with two decks of 52 cards, forming sequences from the Ace to the King.

Players
One

Game Equipment
- Two decks of 52 cards

Start & Object of the Game

The two decks are shuffled together. After that you make a row of 12 cards, as shown in Figure 1.

From this row you remove potential Aces, which are placed beyond the row. *(Fig. 2).* These will be the main cards on which you will build ascending sequences (with 2, 3 and so on, up to the King, in the four suits).

The Play

If Aces have already been removed from the first row, and if in the first row there are 2s, 3s, and so on, these cards will be placed on top of the corresponding Aces. The holes will be filled with cards from the facedown pile.

Fig. 1 - Initial position of the cards.

Fig. 2 - Potential Aces will be taken out of the row, and placed beyond. These Aces constitute the main cards, on which ascending sequences are built (continued with 2, 3, and so on, the last card in a sequence being the King) in all four suits.

Fig. 3 - If none of the cards of the first line can enter the sequences that have already been started, you should check whether two or more cards can form a descending sequence. In that case, those cards will be placed on top of each other naturally filling in the potential holes.

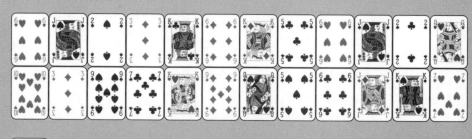

Fig. 4 - When the first line (and the potential descending sequences) is blocked (actually, when none of the free cards can be placed in any of the existing sequences), one will make a second row of 12 cards, which will be taken out of the facedown deck.

If, at any point of the game, an Ace is drawn from the deck, it does not go into the line, but becomes a main card.

If none of the cards of the first line can enter the sequences that have already been started, you should check whether two or more cards can form a descending sequence. In that case, those cards will be placed on top of each other (Fig. 3), naturally filling in the potential holes.

Only the cards that have not yet been blocked by another card can be taken from their place in the line, and placed in a sequence.

BLOCKED LINE

The first line (and the potential descending sequences) is effectively blocked when none of the free cards can be placed in any of the existing sequences. When the line is blcoked int his way, the player makes a second row of 12 cards, which will be taken out of the facedown deck (Fig. 4).

The player continues the game in the same manner according to the rules that have been outlined above by building ascending sequences on top of the main cards, and descending sequences on top of the lines (rows).

Each time a row is blocked, you must make another row.

Each hole within a row must be immediately filled using a card from the facedown deck.

The game is successful if, once the deck of cards is exhausted, the full sequences on top of the Aces have been completed.

■ Strategy

As the game goes on, several lines and sequences will be made. You must control these so that entire descending sequences do not wind up going to waste, which, in a single change, would make a nice contribution to an ascending sequence.

QUEENS & KINGS

This solitaire is played on two fronts, with the Queens, who generate sequences of mixed suits in descending order on one side, and the Kings, from whom ascending sequences based on color will be built on the other. The final setup should be to have the Queens on one side and the Kings on the other side.

Players
One

Game Equipment
- Two decks of 52 cards

■ Start & Object of the Game

Eight Queens will be removed from the decks. They will be arranged as shown in Figure 1, in two lines of 4.

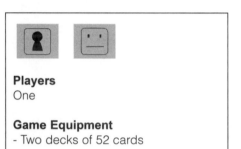

Fig. 1 - Beginning of the game.

The other cards are shuffled. The deck is placed face-down and the cards are uncovered one by one. The object is to complete eight ascending sequences, from the King to the Jack, next to the Queens which must stay alone.

■ The Play

When you uncover a card and get a King, it is placed to the right of the Queens. After all the Kings are out (they must be arranged in two lines of four cards each), you will have an arrangement as shown in Figure 2.

Uncovering the cards, place on top of the Queens those cards that follow in sequence, in descending order, paying no attention to the suits. For example, on the Queen of spades you can place the Jack of hearts, the 10 of diamonds, and so on. On top of the Kings you can only build sequences of the same suit, and only in ascending order, A, 2, 3, and so on up to the Jacks *(Fig. 3)*.

On top of the Kings you can only build sequences of the same suit, and only in ascending order, Ace, 2, 3, and so on up to the Jacks *(Fig. 3)*.

DISPLACEMENTS

When one of the cards of the sequences on the left (the Queens) can enter one of the sequences on the right (the Kings), this card will be displaced. After the displacement you can also liberate a card which also finds its place in a color-sequence.

In this case, naturally, the card will pass from the left to the right.

Fig. 2 - When you uncover a card and get a King, it will be placed to the right of the Queens. After all the Kings are out (they must be arranged in two lines of four cards each), you will have an arrangement.

Fig. 3 - Uncovering the cards, place on top of the Queens those cards that follow in sequence, in descending order, paying no attention to the suits. For example, on the Queen of spades you can place the Jack of hearts, the 10 of diamonds, and so on. On top of the Kings you can only build sequences of the same suit, and only in ascending order, A, 2, 3, and so on up to the Jacks.

Once the deck is exhausted, a player cannot turn the deck over and start again.

This solitaire is won if, at the end, you have the Queens alone on the left, and the sequences, completed with the Jacks, on the right.

■ Strategy

When making the mixed sequences you have the choice of placing a card on top of a card of the same suit or on top of one of a different suit. The first solution is always in your best interest.

Let's assume that, for example, you could place a ten of hearts on top of a Jack of hearts or on top of a Jack of spades. If you place it on top of the Jack of hearts, you can, when one of the color-sequences of hearts reaches the nine, with only one movement conclude the sequence with the ten and the Jack taken from the left.

GARGANTUA

This solitaire requires making alternate sequences of black and red.
Also, if a card is being moved, all the cards on top of it must follow it,
since they are tied to it.

Players
One

Game Equipment
- Two decks of 52 cards

■ Start & Object of the Game

The two decks of cards are shuffled.
After that you will form new little piles
of one card faceup and one card facedown on top of a third faceup card, and
so on, until you have eight face-down
cards, with one faceup on top *(Fig. 1)*.

If at this point, like in any other stage
of the game you will come across an Ace,
you must place it outside of the arrangement *(Fig. 1)*.

The aim of the game is to complete
ascending sequences beginning with the
Aces (which are followed by the 2s, the
3s, and so on, until the King.)

■ The Play

Prepare nine little piles to begin with,
and, once you have removed the Aces
from the arrangement, you will begin
drawing the remaining cards from the
pile, keeping them facedown in front of
yourself.

Under the little piles you form
descending sequences of different suits,

Fig. 1 - Arrangement for the beginning of the game.

as long as you respect the alternation of red and black. This way, under a seven of clubs you can make a sequence that contains the 6 of hearts, the 5 of spades, and so on. These sequences need to be put in line (not one on top of each other), in such a way that you can see all the cards they contain.

MOVING THE SEQUENCES

If a descending sequence needs a card that is present in another sequence, the latter sequence will be moved entirely on top of the card of the highest value and of different color. At any moment you can take the last card of a sequence or a card drawn from the pile and place it on the corresponding color sequence.

When, moving one card or a line of cards, you make a hole in the original arrangement of eight cards, this will immediately be filled with a King, and any cards that are on top of it.

Once you have drawn all cards from the deck, you turn the deck around and start drawing again.

After the second drawings the game has reached its end: if you completed 8 ascending sequences on top of the Aces, the game has been successful.

■ Strategy

In the mixed sequences, if you have the choice between placing a card on top of a card of the same suit or on top of one of a different suit, choose the same suit.

Let's say that, for example, you could place a ten of hearts on top of a Jack of hearts or on top of a Jack of spades: when placing it on top of the Jack of hearts, you can, when one of the color sequences of hearts reaches the nine, add the ten and the Jack taken from the sequence on the left to it in a single movement.

HIERARCHY

*This is a very simple solitaire, suitable even as a pastime for children,
who need to know only the value of the card
in order to place them in a correct sequence.*

Players
One

Game Equipment
- A deck of 52 cards

Start & Object of the Game

The deck is prepared by removing, for
each suit, the cards from 2 to 6. This way
you will get a deck of 32 cards, from the
7 to the Ace, for all the four suits.

The cards are shuffled, and the first
fifteen are placed faceup on the table.

The aim of the game is to get a complete sequence of eight cards.

The Play

The sequence, or hierarchy, is formed
by 7, 8, 9, 10, Jack, Queen, King, and
Ace *(Fig. 1)*.

The hierarchy can be made up of
cards of different suits *(Fig. 1)*.

The game is won when you form the
hierarchy using only cards taken from
the fifteen placed on the table.

Strategy

The game is won only through luck and
involves no particular skill. In order to
help ensure the success of the game, you
can, after you have put the first fifteen
cards on the table, place aside three
facedown cards. These three cards can
be reserved for use as your last resort if
you cannot form the hierarchy from the
first fifteen cards.

*Fig. 1 - This is an example of a sequence, or a hierarchy. As you can see,
the hierarchy may be formed by cards of different suits.*

THE CLOCK

This is a potentially difficult solitaire, but it is also fast-paced and captivating.
You might want to repeat it over and over again just for pleasure. It owes its name
to the starting arrangement, which represents the face of a clock.

Players
One

Game Equipment
- A deck of 52 cards

▨ Start & Object of the Game

The cards are divided in 13 facedown piles, of four cards each *(Fig. 1)*.

The aim of the game is to form piles of cards of the same value on the corresponding hours, keeping in mind that the Jacks are the hour 11, the Queens are the hour 12, and the Kings are important since they make up the central pile of the clock arrangement.

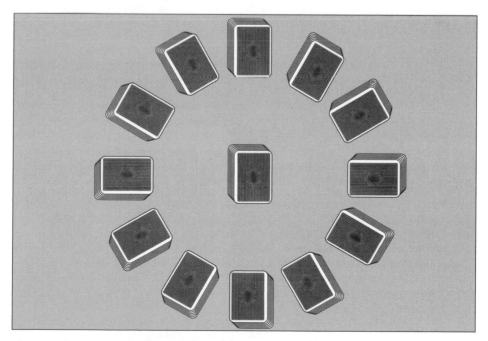

Fig. 1 - Arrangement for the opening of the game.

■ The Play

Draw the first card from the central pile of the clock, and place it, faceup on top of the corresponding facedown pile.

If, for example, the card you have drawn from the center pile is a 6, place it upon the 6 o'clock pile; then draw the card that was previously on top of that pile, and place it, in turn, on top of the appropriate pile. This is how to travel from pile to pile.

When you draw a card which has already been placed on top of the appropriate pile, (from example a 3 on the 3 o'clock pile), place it underneath its pile and proceed to draw the top facedown card.

The Kings will remain in the central pile, and when the last King is found before having completed all the hours, the game is over.

The game is won when you have formed 12 piles with hour cards on top, and the pile of Kings in the center.

■ Strategy

The success of the game depends on the order in which the Kings appear, interrupting the exchanges by remaining in the middle. When you have found the fourth King, naturally the game is over (even if this was not the last card to be drawn), and this is what makes the game suspenseful.

THE RULE OF KINGS

The rule of Kings allows one of the Kings to make an exception and, instead of being placed in the center, it can be substituted for one of the facedown hour cards. However, this rule can be applied only once during the game.

When you use the rule of Kings, it is better to substitute it for the last card in a pile that already has three uncovered cards: In this case, there will be little probability of drawing that one and only card which would cause the King to be drawn. Although you can never tell . . .

LUCAS

*This is a fairly complex game of sequences that can be very interesting
and captivating. It requires two complete decks of cards from which
you draw only once, making the game very difficult to finish.
When this happens, though, you will have great satisfaction.*

Players
One

Game Equipment
- Two decks of 52 cards each

▦ Start & Object of the Game

Remove the 8 Aces from the deck and
arrange them in a line.

The remaining cards are shuffled.
After that you make 3 lines of 13 cards
each *(Fig. 1)*. The rest of the deck will
remain facedown.

The aim of the game is to complete,
on top of the Aces, 8 ascending sequences, up to the King.

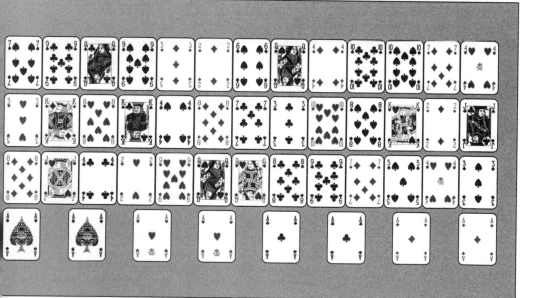

Fig. 1 - Arrangement for the opening of the game.

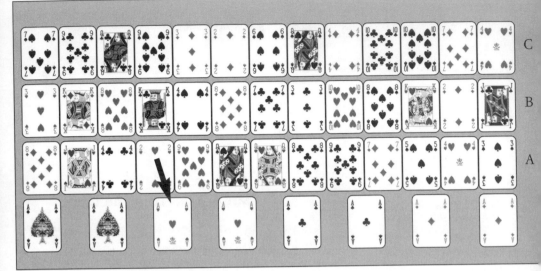

Fig. 2 - First phase of the game: First of all you will check the first line (the one that is marked with an Ace). If in this line there are 2s(and after that 3s, 4s, and so on), you should take them and place them on top of the Aces of the same suit, thus starting the sequence.

■ The Play

First check the first line (the one that is marked with an Ace in Figure 2). If in this line there are 2s (and after that 3s, 4s, and so on), take them and place them on top of the Aces of the same suit, thus starting the sequence.

When you take a card out of line A, the cards in the column of line B and C will automatically descend one space. After this, the next available card will be the one found in line B.

The hole in line C after having moved the cards down one space will be filled with the card on top of the deck of face-down cards.

DRAWING FROM THE DECK

After you have exhausted the possibilities in the original arrangement, you may begin drawing cards from the facedown deck, thus building a pile of discarded cards, which will be placed faceup. The card on top of the deck of discarded cards may be placed on top one of the sequences until it is covered up by another discarded card.

The solitaire is successful when, after having finished drawing from the deck, all 8 sequences have been completed from the Ace to the King.

■ Strategy

The success of the game relies greatly on the order of the cards, and, actually, on pure luck. However you can apply some strategy.

This happens when, in line A, there are two cards of equal value and suit, and you must choose which one to use in a sequence. It is obvious, then, that it is best to move the card that will liberate a card that will either quickly or immediately find its place in a sequence.

WINDMILL

The original arrangement of this solitaire is similar to a star,
flower, or the sails of a windmill, which is how the game got its name.
This is a solitaire that you must finish during the first round,
since you are not allowed to use the deck again.

Players
One

Game Equipment
- Two decks of 52 cards

■ Start & Object of the Game

Remove an Ace and 4 Kings from one of
the decks, arranging them as in Figure 1.

The decks of cards are shuffled. Take
the first 8 cards and arrange them clockwise on the sides of the central Ace, as
shown in Figure 2, on page 188.

The deck containing the rest of the
cards is kept facedown.

The aim of the game is to complete
sequences, even of mixed suit, in ascending order on top of the Ace (actually,
2, 3, and so on, until you reach the
King), and descending sequences on top
of the Kings (queen, Jack, 10, and so on,
until you reach the Ace).

■ The Play

Check the two "sails" of your arrangement, looking for 2s (then 3s, 4s, and so
on), and you place them in sequence on

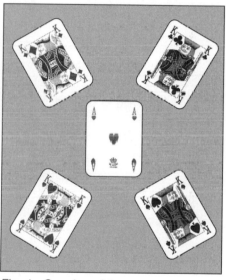

Fig. 1 - Opening of the game.

top of the central Ace. At the same time
you also look for Queens (then Jacks,
10s and so on), and you place them in
sequence on top of the Kings.

Naturally, each card taken away from
one of the sails will immediately be
replaced with the first card of the facedown deck.

DRAWING FROM THE DECK
After taking all possible cards from the
arms, start drawing cards from the facedown deck, making a pile of discarded
cards, which are placed faceup.

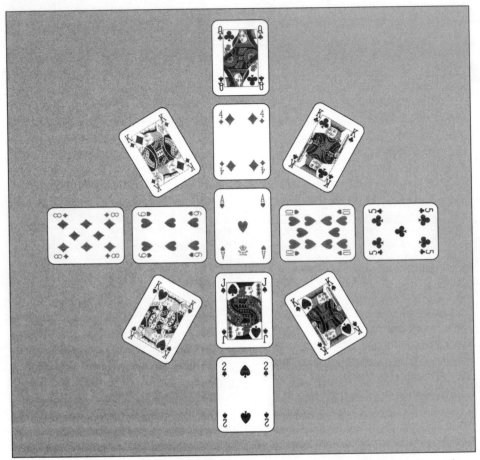

Fig. 2 - The next move after the original arrangement is to take the first eight cards and to arrange them in clockwise order, as shown in the above Figure.

The card on the top of the discards can enter a sequence until it is covered with another discarded card.

Plcae the card on the central sequence even if it can be placed on the diagonal sequence.

When you have completed in one round the sequences on top of the Aces and the Kings the game is won.

Strategy

Windmill appears simpler than other games because it does not require building sequences using cards of the same suit. However, it depends on the luck and the precision of the player, who must not skip putting all the cards that can be used into the sequences.

PARALLEL

Parallel is a classic solitaire game of double sequences, ascending and descending. At the center of the parallel lines, which gives this game its name, lines of auxiliary cards are formed which, when they are more than two, cannot be used unless they are free.

Players
One

Game Equipment
- Two decks of 52 cards

■ Start & Object of the Game

Remove the four Kings and the four Aces from one of the decks and place them in two parallel lines at a good distance apart, as shown in Figure 1.

Shuffle the rest of the cards of the two decks and, keeping the deck face-down, remove the first ten cards and form a line as shown in Figure 2, on page 190.

The object is to form ascending sequences, all of the same suit, on top of the Aces (with 2, 3, 4, and so on, up to the King), and descending sequences on top of the Kings (with Queens, Jacks, 10s, and so on up to the Aces).

■ The Play

Check the first line to see if there are any cards that can enter a sequence. A card that has been placed on one of the par-

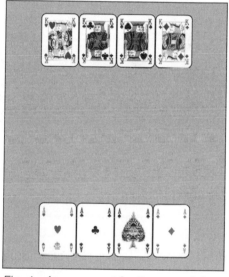

Fig. 1 - Arrangement for the start of the game.

allel lines will be replaced with the first card from the facedown deck.

Once you have completed all possible moves in the first line, immediately proceed to the second line. As soon as you remove the cards that you will place in the sequences you must replace them.

After you have completed all possible moves in the second line, create a third line. At this point, the cards of the second line, blocked upwards and downwards by the first and third lines can no longer be used.

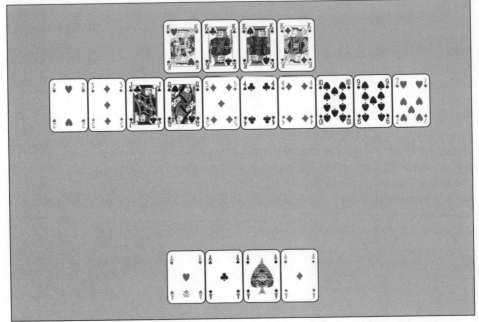

Fig. 2 - Second phase of the game: shuffle the rest of the cards of the two decks and, keeping the deck face-down, remove the first ten cards and form a line.

FREEING THE CARDS

If you remove a card from the first or the third line before replacing it, check if the card above or below (the card of the second line) can also enter a sequence. If this is so, this card is replaced, starting with the center line.

As the number of lines increases (four, five, and so on), you can use only the cards of the first and last line, as well as possible freed cards, for sequences.

When all sequences are completed, and the deck exhausted, the game is won.

■ Strategy

A good deal of luck and a quick eye are the ingredients of success in Parallel.

A player's doubt comes when a card can enter either an ascending sequence or a descending sequence. In this case, the decision is made by considering the possibilities you have in continuing the sequence of your choice.

This case requires special attention since this decision can determine the success or the failure of the game.

PRISON

Successfully completing this solitaire game depends on freeing certain cards which are blocked in the lines or even locked up in prison, as the title suggests.

Players
One

Game Equipment
- Two decks of 52 cards

▦ Start & Object of the Game

Remove the cards from 2 to 6 for each suit from one of the decks. This deck will then have 32 cards, from the 7 to the Ace for all four suits.

The cards are shuffled, and the first four cards are placed on the board, face-up. The other cards will be kept in the facedown deck.

If one of the four cards is an Ace, it is placed at the top to eventually form a line of cards, and it is replaced with the first card from the deck.

Below the line of Aces and potential sequences there must always be a line of four cards, or four sequences as the game proceeds, as in Figure 1.

The object of the game is to build complete sequences for each suit on top of the Aces, with 7, 8, 9, 10, Jack, Queen, and King.

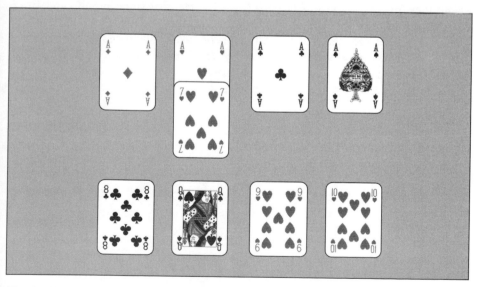

Fig. 1 - Arrangement for the opening of the game.

The Play

From the first line remove and then replace any potential Aces.

After the Aces, remove and replace the 7s (then the 8s, 9s, and so on) which are placed on top of the Aces.

Also, on top of the first line you can build descending sequences in alternate colors. Let's assume that in the first line you have a Queen of hearts. On top of it you could place a Jack of clubs, then a ten of hearts, and so on, one on top of the other, half covering each other.

THE PRISON

Once the possibilities offered by the first line have been exhausted, draw the first card from the facedown deck. If this card is an Ace, place it in the line above. If it is a card belonging to a sequence on top of the Aces or on top of the cards in the first line, place it in that sequence. Otherwise it is placed to the side of the arrangement, in "prison."

As more and more cards are put in prison, they are placed on top of each other, half covering each other.

The last card of a sequence or the last card in prison can at any moment be inserted into one of the sequences on top of the Aces, freeing the next card.

Naturally you can place an entire sequence on top of another one, if the bottom card can be inserted on top of another sequence.

In this way you free a space in the first line. It is then replaced with the first card from the facedown deck.

DRAWING THE PRISON

Once the deck is finished, the prison is shuffled, turned around, and the cards are drawn one by one, placing them, whenever possible, in the mixed sequences, sequences on top of the Aces, or sending them back to prison.

The game is won if, after having finished drawing the cards from the prison, the four sequences on top of the Aces have been completed.

Strategy

Before drawing a card, one must carefully evaluate the possibilities offered by the mixed sequences, and the moves that permit liberating useful cards.

The fact that you can only draw from the deck once, and only once from the prison, makes any omission inexcusable.

This is especially true for the cards in prison, which, once covered up by another card, are blocked.

SUNDIAL

*This game owes its name to its configuration, which resembles the face
of a sundial, where the 11 and 12 are the Jacks and the Queens, respectively,
and the Kings occupy the center of the face.*

Players
One

Game Equipment
- A deck of 52 cards

■ Start & Object of the Game

Draw the first card from the facedown
deck: its suit is the suit of the first round
of the clock. The card is placed at the
appropriate time in the sundial.

The Jack and Queen are at 11 and 12
o'clock; the King goes at the center.
Drawing one card at a time, fill in the
first round of the face in the opening
suit, including the center *(Fig. 1)*.

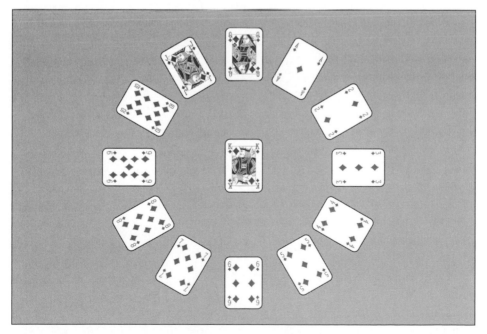

Fig. 1 - Opening arrangement after having completed the first round of the face.

Naturally the object of the game is to complete four sundails, on top of each other, in alternating colors.

■ The Play

On top of each card that has already been placed in the quadrant (even when the round has not yet been completed), you can place another card of the same value but different color. once you encounter it.

For example, on the 6 of diamonds you can place the 6 of clubs, on top of which you could place the 6 of hearts, and conclude the pile with the 6 of spades.

THE DISCARD PILE

The cards that do not enter the sundial form a faceup pile of discards.

The card on at the top of the discards can be used until it is covered by another card. Also, by using the card on the top of the pile of discards, you free the card immediately beneath.

Once the facedown deck is finished, you turn over the discard pile and begin drawing again.

At the end of the second draw you should have already completed, on top of every hour of the quadrant as well as in the center, the piles of four cards of the same value in alternating colors.

■ Strategy

The particularity of this game is not forming sequences but piles of cards equal in value.

Success depends on luck, and naturally on not omitting any move.

QUADRILLE

This solitaire is reminiscent of the dance with the same name and—
when you win—shows the ladies (queens) surrounded by gentlemen
(jacks and Kings), in the shape of a star or a flower.

Players
One

Game Equipment
- A deck of 52 cards

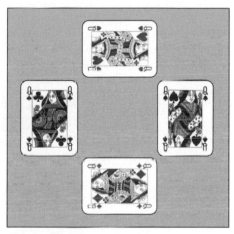

Fig. 1 - The first point of the game.

■ Start & Object of the Game

Draw cards and placing them in a face-up pile of discards until you come across each Queen, placing them as in Figure 1.

Once you have finished arranging the Queens, draw cards from the deck looking for 5s and 6s, which are arranged as in Figure 2 on page 196.

Now the game begins. The object is to form ascending sequences up to the Jacks on top of the 6s, and descending sequences up to the Kings on top of the 5s, using cards of the same suit.

■ The Play

Once the original arrangement has been completed, continue drawing cards. If it is possible, place the cards in one of the sequences, otherwise place them in the discard pile. The top discard can be used until it is covered up by another card. Once the deck of facedown cards

is used up, the discard pile is turned over. After drawing from the deck three times, the sequences should be completed. If the game has been successful you will have the four Queens in the center, surrounded by Kings and Jacks as shown in Figure 3 on page 196.

■ Strategy

The success of Quadrille depends only on the order of the cards within the deck, actually only on luck, just as in the dance with the same name—it often happens that more gentlemen are circling the same lady in the hope of dancing with her.

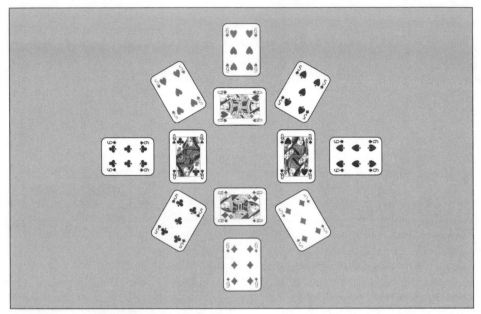

Fig. 2 - The second point of the game.

Fig. 3 - The final point of the game: In the center you will have the four Queens, surrounded by Kings and Jacks.

KING

This is a complex solitaire of mixed sequences which is played with two decks of cards, and which, like other similar pastimes, follows the rules of forming provisory sequences on top of what are considered to be auxiliary cards, from which to take, when possible, the right cards for the main sequences.

Players
One

Game Equipment
- Two decks of 52 cards

■ Start & Object of the Game

Remove the eight Aces from the decks and arrange them as shown in Figure 1 in two vertical lines of four cards each, in the form of a rectangle.

Shuffle the remaining cards. After that place the deck face-down on the board and take the first 8 cards and arrange them in two lines next to the lines of the Aces, as shown in Figure 2 on page 198.

The object of the game is to complete the eight mixed ascending sequences from the Ace to the King, paying no attention to the suits.

■ The Play

Arrange outside lines of cards and then check if one of the cards can be placed, according to its value, on top of one of the Aces in the central lines.

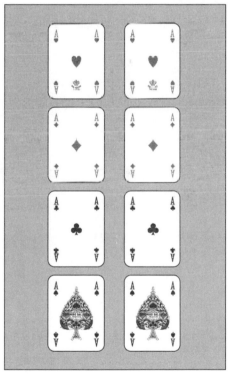

Fig. 1 - Arrangement for the opening of the game.

For every card that goes in the central sequences, you must fill the void with the first card of the uncovered deck.

When the possibilities of moving cards from the first two lines have been exhausted, arrange another two lines, one on the right and one on the left.

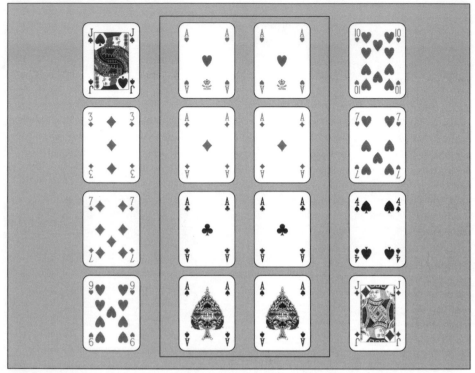

Fig. 2 - The arrangement immediately following the opening arrangement.

When a card is palces in a third line (and of the following ones) the cards of the preceding lines are blocked.

Also, when you place an outer card on top of the central sequences, before replacing it with a card from the face-down deck, you can also play that next card form the deck.

SECOND PHASE

When all the cards of the main deck have been arranged on the board, the cards of the last two external lines can be moved as you please, without following the rule of the block.

However, from the third exterior line to the center, you must wait for cards to be freed before being able to place them in the sequences.

If in this phase of the game you exhaust an entire horizontal line, you can fill the gap with any of the external cards in the other lines.

When all of the cards have been played and the central sequences have been completed, showing the eight Kings, then the game is won.

■ Strategy

Be careful attention, because, in order not to miss the possibility of continuing a sequence, you must keep in mind the rule that once a is card placed in a new outer line it block the preceding cards, sometimes until the end of the game, bringing about an unsuccessful ending to the solitaire.

QUEENS
AT A CONGRESS

This is a long and well-developed but interesting and fun solitaire of sequences in alternating colors that uses two complete decks of cards.

Players
One

Game Equipment
- Two decks of 52 cards

■ Start & Object of the Game

Arrange the eight Kings as shown in Figure 1 in two lines of four cards each, forming a rectangle.

Shuffle the remaining cards and arrange the first ten cards in two lines beneath the Kings *(Fig. 1)*.

The facedown deck is placed on the board and cards are drawn one by one.

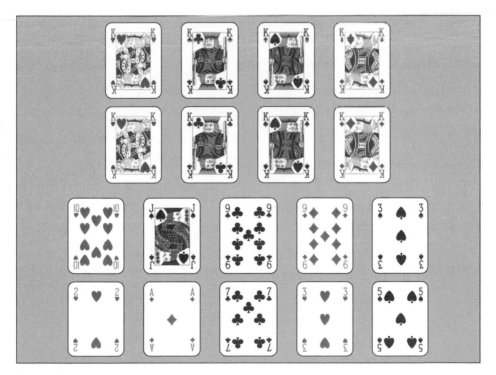

Fig. 1 - Arrangement for the opening of the game.

The object is to complete eight ascending sequences on top of the Kings of the central rectangle (King, Ace, 2, 3, and so on), ending with the 8 Queens.

◼ The Play

The cards of the facedown deck are drawn, one by one, trying to place them in sequences.

A card can go into the ascending sequence on top of a King if it is of the correct value and of the same suit as the sequence.

Otherwise it can be placed in a descending sequence on top of one of the 10 cards beneath the Kings, if it is of the correct value but of a different suit or color. A descending sequence can be formed by a 10 of hearts, a 9 of spades, an 8 of diamonds, a 7 of clubs, a 6 of spades, and so on.

The cards that cannot enter any ascending or descending sequence are placed one on top of each other, forming a faceup pile of discarded cards. The first card of this pile may be used in a sequence if preceding maneuvers make such a move possible. However, once a card has been covered by another one it can no longer be used.

MOVING THE CARDS

The card on top of a descending sequence may be placed on top of an ascending sequence.

In this case the card is moved from the mixed sequence to the sequence of its suit, thus freeing another card in the descending sequence.

When a descending sequence has been exhausted, the space that has become empty will be filled with the first card from the discards.

Once the facedown deck is finished, the pile of discards is turned over, and, without shuffling, cards are drawn from it one by one.

The solitaire is won when, once you have finished the second round of draws, the 8 sequences, finishing with the 8 Queens are completed on top of the Kings.

◼ Strategy

For each card you draw you must take into account each possibility; actually you must carefully consider whether the card can be placed on top of one of the ascending or descending sequences. Once you have placed this card you must next check whether the card on top of the pile of discards can be taken and used, and then the next one from the discard pile.

After that you must check the descending sequences and see if any cards can be moved on top of the ascending sequences. You must take into account that, also in this case, each moved card frees another one.

Finally, if there are any holes in the lines of descending sequences you must fill them one by one with cards from the discard pile. Only after having executed all these moves can you be sure to have exhausted all possibilities and thus you can draw another card from the facedown deck.

ROUGE ET NOIR

This is a pastime based on double sequences: auxiliary sequences
are based on double colors, and main sequences are based on suit.
This game gives the player, on several occasions, the possibility of choosing.
However, winning depends also on the moves that are made during the solitaire.

Players
One

Game Equipment
- Two decks of 52 cards

Start & Object of the Game

Remove the eight Aces from the decks and arrange them in a line of alternating colors as shown in Figure 1.

Shuffle the remaining cards keeping the deck facedown, and place the first eight cards in an auxiliary line, underneath the Aces *(Fig. 2 on page 202)*.

The object of the game is to complete all eight required ascending sequences from the Ace up to the King.

The Play

To start the sequences, check the auxiliary line: if there are any 2s (and then also 3s, 4s, and so on), place them on top of the Aces of the same suit.

The empty spaces in the auxiliary line are filled with the first card from the facedown deck.

Draw the cards one by one: the cards that cannot be placed on top of the Aces can possibly be placed on top of one of the auxiliary cards to form descending sequences (from the King to the 2) in alternating colors by placing cards halfway on top of each other.

The cards that cannot be placed in the descending or ascending sequences will be placed faceup to form a pile of rejected cards.

The last card in a mixed sequence can be taken and used if it belongs in one of the main sequences, this way also freeing the preceding card.

Fig. 1 - Arrangement for the beginning of the game.

Fig. 2 - Arrangement of the game immediately following the opening.

If an entire mixed sequence is placed on top of a main sequence, the free space is filled with the first card of the facedown deck.

UNBLOCKING THE PILE OF DISCARDS

If, after one or more moves, you find you can use the first card on the pile of discards, the card immediately below the useful card is freed for play.

A card in the pile of discards, as well as a card in the mixed sequences, is blocked by the card on top of it.

Once you have finished the facedown deck, you can turn over the discard pile and, without mixing it, you can continue to draw cards one by one.

If at the end of the second round of draws the main sequences have been completed, then the game is won.

■ Strategy

If, when drawing a card, you realize that it can be placed either in an auxiliary or main sequence, you must choose to place it in the main sequence, in order to avoid blocking the game.

It is important that once you draw a card you carefully analyze all possibilities (at least 16, counting main and auxiliary sequences), in order not to risk blocking a card which could have been used in a sequence.

NAPOLEON'S SOLITAIRE

Napoleon, one of the most famous and beloved historical figures,
has been credited with the creation of several solitaires, clearly because he had
a predilection for these games of cards, maybe to make time go by during his exile,
or maybe because they are a good exercise in strategy, which is an important
leadership skill. Among the many versions, this one is the most manageable.
This is surely the world's most famous solitaire!

Players
One

Game Equipment
- A deck of 52 cards

■ Start & Object of the Game

Shuffle the deck and then arrange all the cards in order to form two regiments of four lines with five cards each, and then a fifth and last line of only four cards. As you proceed in the arrangement, as you find the Aces, place them in a central line that separates the two regiments, forming the opening arrangement, as shown in Figure 1 on page 204. The object of the game is to complete 4 ascending sequences, from the Ace to the King, in the central line.

■ The Play

First, check the outer cards in order to see if they may be placed, according to sequence and suit, on top of the central

Aces (first 2, then 3 and so on). If there are such cards, place them where they belong, freeing the preceding cards.

Outer cards can also be used in partial sequences on top of other outer cards, for example, an outer 5 of hearts can be placed either on top of a 6 or on top of a 4 if both are outer hearts. If you free an entire line of five, or, in the case of the last line, of four cards, you can, at this point, fill the empty space with an entire sequence placed on top of one of the other outer cards. The game is won when the four ascending sequences on the central Aces have been completed.

■ Strategy

There is no facedown deck nor a pile of rejected cards from which to draw several times. Everything depends on how you decide to move the cards. This is why, before deciding to move it is wise to carefully study the initial configuration in order to determine what the most opportune movements are.

As the game proceeds, cards are moved, liberating other cards. This is very important for the success of the game, because otherwise the game would become blocked.

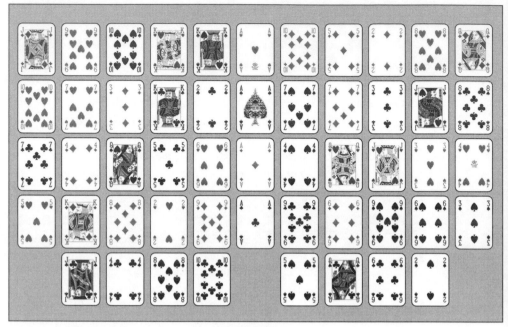

Fig. 1 - Arrangement for the opening of the game.

When you fill a line that has remained empty with the cards of a sequence, it is good to place them in such a way that the cards with the lowest values are on the outside, so that you can move all the cards as a "block," at the opportune moment, onto the appropriate main sequence and thus win the game.

ELEVEN I

This is a fast-paced pastime based on adding cards from the opening configuration with cards drawn from the facedown pile, eliminating them in pairs until you exhaust the main deck.

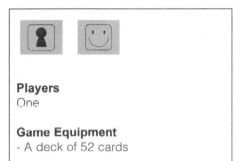

Players
One

Game Equipment
- A deck of 52 cards

Start & Object of the Game

Shuffle the deck and keep it facedown, arranging the first nine cards in three lines, as shown in Figure 1.

The object of the game is to eliminate pairs of cards whose sum is eleven, until the facedown deck is exhausted.

The Play

In order to be eliminated the two cards must add up to eleven, wihtout regard to suit or position within the arrangement.

The Jacks, Queens, and Kings each are worth 11 points and will be eliminated one by one. The eliminated cards are immediately replaced with cards from the facedown deck.

When it is no longer possible to eliminate any card out of the arrangement, the first card from the facedown deck is drawn: if it is a Jack, Queen, or King,

eliminate it and draw the next card; otherwise check if the card can be added to another card from the board, and if so those two cards are eliminated together.

If the drawn card cannot help eliminate any other card, the game is over.

Strategy

This solitaire depends only and exclusively on luck, and there is no other way of winning it. However, it is original and fast-paced.

You can also play it with more than one player, perhaps betting on the success of each individual solitaire: the player wins who finishes the deck, or, who, once the game is blocked manages to finish with the smallest number of facedown cards.

Fig. 1 - Opening of the game.

ELEVEN II

Like the previous game, this solitaire is based on the sum of pairs of cards,
which, rather than being eliminated, are covered by other cards, taken
from the facedown deck, in order to form a final arrangement of only face cards.

Players
One

Game Equipment
- A deck of 52 cards

■ Start & Object of the Game

Remove the 12 face cards from the deck and place them beneath the other cards (which have previously been shuffled), thus forming one facedown deck.

Arrange the first twelve cards on the board, in four lines of twelve cards each.

The object of the game is to cover all the cards of the arrangement with the face cards that have been placed at the bottom of the deck.

■ The Play

When two cards of the arrangement, without regard to suit or position, add up to eleven they are covered with the first two cards of the deck, faceup.

In this way, little piles are formed: the card on top each pile can be added to any other card on top of the arrangement, if that card is not covered.

Each time a card has been covered, it is eliminated.

DRAWING THE FACE CARDS
Proceed by covering the cards in this manner. At a certain point you will begin to draw the face cards, which cannot be summed and thus cannot be covered.

If the face cards are placed two by two on top of the little piles of the arrangement until they cover it entirely, the game is won.

■ Strategy

In this solitaire, as in the previous one, luck is all that matters. However, this will not diminish the fun.

This version of Eleven also gives you the possibility of playing with several participants, one by one, betting on the successful completion of the solitaire.

CHILDREN'S
CARD GAMES

CAREFUL, FIDO!

*Fun game of seizing cards "on command" based on a good eye
and speed, guaranteeing engaging and lively rounds,
especially if there are eight participants.*

Players
Two, Four or Eight

Game Equipment
- A deck of 40 cards, from Ace to 7,
Jacks, Queens, Kings

■ Start & Object of the Game

Players decide the dealer by luck of the draw; the one who picks the highest card becomes the dealer. The dealer divides the deck between all the players, including himself, distributing to each person a pile, facedown, of 20 cards if two players, 10 cards if four players, or 5 cards if eight players.

The object of the game is to get as many cards as possible.

■ The Play

The dealer calls out "Careful, Fido!" On this command, each player has to quickly turn over the first card on top of his pile. Whichever player notices that one of his opponents has turned over a card equal in value to his own, that player has to quickly put his hand on his opponent's pile. If he does this first, he takes the card, which together with his own, is collected and put facedown in a pile next to the pile with which he is playing. If two players with equal cards touch each other's piles at the same time, it is a tie and each person keeps his own card.

The players discard in their own seized pile the single cards turned over that have not been taken.

Whoever errs in seizing the opponent's cards (for example, someone turns over a Jack and goes to take a King, confusing the cards), loses his next turn.

Having finished the round, the players prepare for the next call of "Careful, Fido!"

When all of the cards in play have been used up, each player counts the cards accumulated in his seized pile. The player with the most cards wins.

■ Strategy

The dealer, who changes from game to game, has to try to call out "Careful, Fido!" unexpectedly. A bit of small talk, or a moment of silence, creates the suspense needed to make the game lively.

I DOUBT IT

*I Doubt It is one of the most popular card games for kids (but not only!),
based on bluffing and the ability to guess when opponents
are telling the truth or not. In short, a young player of Doubt
can become a great player of Poker as an adult!*

Players
Three or more

Game Equipment
- One or two decks of 52 cards each
(use one deck for up to five players
and two decks for six or more)

▓ Start & Object of the Game

Each person picks a card; the person
with the highest card deals.

The dealer deals all the cards, one at a
time, to the players. The player to the
left of the dealer begins the game by discarding one to four of his cards facedown, one at a time, and declaring their
values.

The object of the game is to discard
all of your cards.

▓ The Play

The discarded cards are set aside facedown to form a pile that no one can view
(except whoever says "I doubt it," as we
will see).

The player discarding can either tell
the truth or lie in declaring the value of
the cards; if more than one card is discarded, all have to be of the same value
(for example, two 3s, or three 5s, or four
Jack's . . .).

The next player, during his turn, can
discard from one to four cards, provided
that he declares a value that is one point
higher than the previous player's (the
Ace is worth 1). If, for example, a player
declares four 7s, the next player has to
declare from one to four 8s, and the
next, from one to four 9s, and so on.

If the series reaches the King and the
players still have cards in their hands,
they begin again with lower value cards.

I DOUBT IT

If, after a player declares values, one of
the opponents believes that the declaration is false, that player calls out "I
doubt it!" Then, the player that just
discarded his cards facedown onto the
pile has to turn them over to show that
he was telling the truth: if he was telling
the truth, the player who mistakenly
doubted him takes the whole pile of
discarded cards and adds them to the
cards in his hand; if instead, the player
that said, "I doubt it" guessed right, the
player who bluffed has to take the whole
pile of discarded cards.

The person who gets rid of all his cards first wins.

■ Strategy

It is important to remember the cards that have already been put out and compare the declarations with the cards that one has in hand; this is the only way to unmask the liar and call his bluff.

Of course, if there are many players and two decks of cards, it is more difficult to keep count of the cards already discarded, and the game is more fun.

VARIATION OF SEQUENCES

A variation is to also declare the cards which are not equal in value, but are in sequence.

The first player can declare from one to four cards in order, for example, the 2, 3, 4, and 5 of hearts.

The next player will need to declare at least the 6 of hearts and so on.

Once one sequence is complete, you start with another.

The variation works best with two decks; however, it is easier to figure out who is bluffing.

FAMILIES

There are special decks of cards that exist for this game that have, instead of suits and values, 13 different families of animals with parents and offspring for each family: for example, lion, lioness, baby girl and baby boy cubs, and also rooster, hen, baby boy and baby girl chicks.

Players
Three or more

Game Equipment
- One deck of 52 cards

Start & Object of the Game

Each person picks a card; the one who has the highest card, counting from Ace to King, deals all the cards to the players; it does not matter if one of the players has more cards than the others.

The player to the left of the dealer begins by calling a family.

The object of the game is to reunite as many families as possible.

The Play

If playing with an ordinary deck of cards, each family is comprised of the four cards of equal value from the four different suits.

There is the family of the Aces, the family of the 2s, and so on until the family of the Kings. The first player asks another player, who is decided upon by the opponents, for a card needed to

reunite a family. If, for example, the first player already has two 3's, one of hearts and one of spades, he can ask one of the opponents for the 3 of clubs or the 3 of diamonds.

If the player who is asked for a card has that card, he must hand it over. Once the player receives the card, he can ask for another card from any of the opponents until he gets no card.

If a player asked for a card from a player who does not have it, the turn then goes to the player who was asked.

You cannot ask for cards from a family without having at least one of the cards in that family.

Each time that a player reunites a family, he lays out the four cards, face-down, in front of him.

The game finishes when all of the players have used up their cards. At this point, each player counts up his reunited families. The winner is the player who has the most families.

Strategy

In the first rounds, the questions are asked blindly. As the game proceeds, however, it won't be difficult to understand, from the requests, who has which cards in hand. The secret lies in taking advantage of this, when it is your turn.

PLAY OR PAY!

*This is a game of sequence, like Michigan, that will stimulate
even the youngest kids to recognize the Figures and values of the cards.
A touch of gambling—not with chips but with buttons, beans,
or candies—makes the game even more fun.*

Players
Three or more

Game Equipment
- One deck of 52 cards
- Tokens (or buttons, beans,
or candies)

■ Start & Object of the Game

The tokens are distributed in equal numbers to each of the players. Each person picks a card; the person with the highest card deals. The dealer deals all the cards, one by one, to the players. It does not matter if at the end of the deal, all the players do not have the same number of cards. The player to the left of the dealer goes first by putting down any one of the cards he has faceup, on the table.

The object of the game is to lay out, in sequence, all of the cards in one's hand.

■ The Play

After the first player has laid out a card, the move goes to the player on his left: if the second player has the next card in sequence, he puts it down faceup over the first one; otherwise, he has to pay a token to the pot.

In sequence means the cards from the same suit in ascending order from the Ace, which is worth 1, to the King.

A sequence can start not only with an Ace, but also with a 2, and even with cards of higher value. In that case, after the King you continue with the Ace and onward until the card that ends that sequence.

The player who finishes a sequence turns over that pile and has an extra move, in which he starts a new sequence. The first player to put down all his cards wins the game; the prize are the tokens in the pot; in addition, the winner receives tokens from the other players equal to the number of cards left in each of their hands.

■ Strategy

It is better to begin the sequence and the suit with the most consecutive cards. If, for example, a player has the 2, 3, and 4 of diamonds, he begins by putting out the 2: at this point all the opponents, in turn, have to pay a token to the pot and when it is the first player's turn again, he puts out a 3, forcing the others to pay again. Finally, he puts out the 4.

WAR

Very easy and quick, War is a game suitable for the youngest children
that is based on chance and doesn't require any special ability.
However, one game can last a long time, with unexpected reversals . . .

Players
Two

Game Equipment
- One deck of 52 cards

■ Start & Object of the Game

One of the two players deals the cards facedown, one by one, into two piles.

Both players simultaneously turn over the first card of their piles: the two cards turned over are put next to each other.

The object of the game is to win all the cards.

■ The Play

The player who puts down the higher card wins the pair of cards turned over. The two cards won are put at the bottom of the player's pile. When the player arrives at that point of the deck, the player can replay those cards.

If the players turn over two cards of the same value, War breaks out.

Should there be War, the players put three cards facedown on top of the cards just turned over, and on top of those cards, another card turned faceup. The player who has the highest card faceup wins the War and takes all ten cards, and puts them at the bottom of his pile.

If the last two faceup cards are equal in value, the War continues with the addition of three cards facedown and then another faceup by each player, until there is a winner of the War.

The player who manages to get all the cards wins the game, or alternatively, the winner is the player who has the most cards at the end of a preestablished time period of play.

■ Strategy

As already mentioned, this is a game that depends solely and exclusively on chance, but it is lively and engaging enough to amuse the youngest players and older ones who have the desire to spend some time with the children.

CONCENTRATION

A famous pastime, Concentration goes by different names,
for example, Little Piggy. It is played by children all over the world
not only with regular playing cards but also with special decks of cards
decorated with figures of animals or objects.

Players
Two or more

Game Equipment
- One or two decks of 52 cards each

■ Start & Object of the Game

One of the players shuffles the deck—or the decks if there are many players—then spreads out the cards facedown, being sure that the cards do not touch nor overlap one another *(Fig. 1)*.

The object of the game is to find as many pairs of matching cards as you can come up with.

Fig. 1 - Initial layout of the cards.

Fig. 2 - The player, during his turn, turns over one card and then another; f the cards are equal (that is, they are a pair) the player takes them.

■ The Play

The player to the left of the person who laid out the cards goes first, turning over any one card and then a second. The player is searching for a matching pair, so if the two cards are equal *(Fig. 2)*, the player takes them and puts them, facedown, in front of him in a pile.

If the player fails to find a pair, but instead finds that the two cards are different, the player turns them facedown again, putting them back exactly where and how they were. The second player then turns over one card; if by chance this card is equal to one of those previously turned over, clearly he will need to make an effort to remember where the first card of the same value is located. If he can turn over the right card, he can award himself the pair.

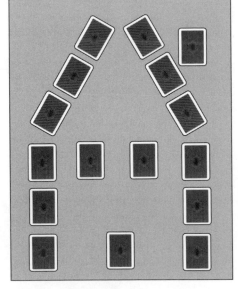

Fig. 3 - Layout of the cards placed to form a "design": helps to make the game easier.

If the player can't remember where the matching card was, or accidentally turns over the wrong one so the the newly turned over card is not equal to any of the previous cards, the player still gets another chance to find the other card to form the pair.

The player who finds two equal cards has the right to turn over a new pair of cards; if the new pair is also equal, he can turn over another pair, and so on, until two different cards are turned over. When his turn is exhausted, the play passes to the player to his left.

Obviously, the winner is the player who has more cards than the other players when all of the cards have been removed from the table.

Strategy

The strategy is inherent in the name of the game: that is, concetrating hard, to remember not only which cards were already turned over by the opponents but also, and most of all, where those cards are located.

LAYOUT OF THE CARDS

To make the game easier, the cards can be laid out in ordered lines or in geometric shapes and even figures: such as a person, a flower, a house (Fig. 3); this way, it will be easier to remember, for example, that a certain card is found in one of the petals of the daisy or along the roofline of the house . . .

MERCHANT AT THE FAIR

This is a typical family game that, like Bingo, lightens up parties
and can be played with, in addition to a normal deck of cards,
special cards that reproduce the typical products of old-time fairs:
plants, animals, various objects that were bought and sold at the market.

Players
Four or more

Game Equipment
- Two decks of 52 cards each
- Tokens (or beans, buttons, or candies)

■ Start & Object of the Game

The players decide who will play the role of auctioneer: the auctioneer does not win or lose anything but simply runs the game.

The auctioneer shuffles one of the two decks of cards, from which he randomly chooses a number of cards equal or greater than the number of players: these cards are laid out, facedown, in the center of the table: nobody can look at them until the end of the game.

The players give the auctioneer a preestablished number of tokens, which the auctioneer divides among the facedown cards *(Fig. 1)*.

The auctioneer shuffles the second deck of cards. This deck can either be distributed between the players or put up for auction.

The object of the game is to win the prizes on one's corresponding covered cards.

■ The Play

The deck can be divided equally among the players, which is possible if there are 4 or 2 players, in addition to the auctioneer.

Fig. 1 - Placement of the "prizes" on the face-down cards.

Otherwise, the deck is put up for auction. The decision to acution the deck is announced by the auctioneer who, at his discretion, shuffles the deck and then divides it into many piles, face-down, each with different numbers of cards. For each pile, the auctioneer decides upon a minimum number of tokens required to sell it: the auctioneer awards the pile to whoever accepts to pay his price or, if two or more players want the same pile, whoever offers more to buy it.

The game can also be played in both ways, distributing part of the cards and then putting the rest up for auction.

Aome card may have to be auctioned out of necessity when the number of players makes it impossible to distribute the cards equally. The auctioneer, in this case will have to offer at least some of them for auction

AUCTION OF THE DECK & BARGAINING

If the second deck is put up for auction, the auctioneer collects all of the tokens paid and puts them on the facedown cards that are on the center of the table, adding to the existing tokens.

If desired, deals can be made with the players who, once they see their cards, can sell some or ask to buy others, according to their intuition.

When the auction and bargaining is finished, the auctioneer begins to turn over, one at a time, the cards which are left in the first deck. As he turns the cards over, he announces aloud the suit and the value: whichever player has the same card in his pile has to give it to the auctioneer.

When the auctioneer finishes turning over all the cards of the first deck, it is obvious that the cards that remain in the players' hands are the same cards as the ones that are facedown with the tokens.

The auctioneer then turns over the card with the least amount of tokens: whoever has that card is awarded all of those tokens.

The auctioneer continues to turn over the cards until he awards all the tokens.

The person who at the end has the most tokens wins.

■ Strategy

The outcome of the game depends entirely on chance. Certainly acquiring the most cards means more possibilities to win the prizes, but on the other hand, it means spending a lot of tokens . . . nevertheless, the fun of the Merchant at the Fair is just that: a little like in Bingo, chance counts more than anything, but fun and suspense are guaranteed!

UNPAIRED JACK

*This game, like many others for children, can be played with special decks
of cards that show figures of different professions or with regular decks.
It is a variety of the Italian game "Peppa Tencia" dedicated to the youngest players.
Different from what happens in most of the games, in the Unpaired Jack
there is not a winner at the end but a loser...*

Players
Three or more

Game Equipment
- One deck of 40 or 52 cards

■ Start & Object of the Game

Remove one Jack from the deck. The one, from the three remaining Jacks, that ends up not being paired will be the Unpaired Jack.

A dealer is picked by the players. The dealer will deal the cards among the players; it does not matter if some of the players have more cards than the others.

Everyone looks at their own cards; if there are pairs of cards of equal value, they are discarded, facedown, in front of the player.

The object of the game is to discard all of one's cards by matching up pairs and in the meantime passing off the unpaired Jack to someone else.

■ The Play

Each player, starting from the person sitting to the left of the dealer, picks a card from the person to his left; each player holds his cards fanned out.

Once everyone picks, each person sets aside his potential pair and then the round begins again.

Whoever runs out of cards is out of the game.

The person who is left with the Unpaired Jack, once all of the other players have discarded all of their cards, loses and has to do something silly that the others decide.

■ Strategy

In order to get rid of the Unpaired Jack without having your unknowing neighbor pick cards and guess you have it, a little ability and intuition are necessary. Most of all toward the end of the hands, when the players have only 3 or 4 cards left, each round of picking will be preceded by hesitation, rethinking, urging on . . . and sighs of relief or expressions of disappointment when the cards picked do not match expectations!

STEALING BUNDLES

Perhaps the most popular game among young children, Stealing Bundles, or "Steal the Old Man's Bundles," is also the first step in Italy to become, as adults, players of Sweep (or Scopa). In fact, the rules of Stealing Bundles and the number of cards are the same. Of all the points of Sweep (or Scopa), only one counts: cards!

Players
Two or four

Game Equipment
- One deck of 52 or 40 cards

Start & Object of the Game

Each of the players picks a card; the player who picks the highest card is the dealer and deals the cards clockwise, three cards facedown for each person, the dealer included, then four cards faceup that are placed in the center of the table.

The remaining cards are set aside by the dealer for successive distribution.

The player to the left of the dealer goes first, looking at his cards and if possible, picking up a card.

Otherwise, he simply discards one of his cards, adding it to those cards already on the table.

The object of the game is to get as many cards as possible from the table and steal the other players' bundles of cards.

The Play

During each turn, a player can decide to either take a card, discard a card or steal an opponent's bundle. A player cannot refuse to play a turn.

A player can pick up a card with another of equal value (for example, a 7 of hearts with a 7 of diamonds, as in Figure 1).

Fig. 1. - *A player can pick up a card with another of equal value (for example, a 7 of hearts with a 7 of diamonds).*

Or, keeping in mind that the Ace is worth 1, a player can take two or more cards whose value adds up to the other card (for example, an Ace, a 3 and a 4 can be picked up by an 8, as in Figure 2, p. 222).

However, in this case, face cards can only be picked up by equal face cards: Jacks with Jacks, Queens with Queens, and Kings with Kings, unless a deck of 40 cards is being used in which case the

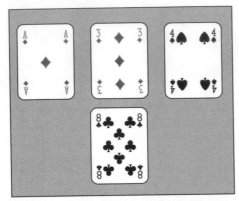

Fig. 2 - The 8 of clubs picks up 3 cards.

Jack, Queen and King are worth 8, 9, and 10, respectively.

Whoever picks up a card puts all of the collected cards faceup in a bundle in front of him.

STEALING BUNDLES

During his turn, a player can steal an opponent's bundle. This is possible when a player has a card that is equal to the top card of the opponent's bundle (Fig. 3).

When the first three cards are gone, the dealer distributes the same amount, without putting any more cards at the center of the table.

The winner is the player, who, once all the cards are used up, has the largest bundle.

■ Strategy

Even though it is a simple game, suitable for young children (as long as they know how to recognize the value of the cards), a good eye is fundamental to Stealing Bundles: often, in hjis excitement of taking one or more of the cards from the table, a player does not notice that he could have taken a conspicuous bundle from his opponent.

The reversals ahead are continuous. A player can accumulate cards for the whole game and then, by surprise, during the last hand . . . the fun of Stealing Bundles is just this!

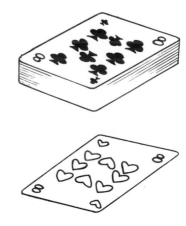

Fig. 3 - The bundle can be stolen!

ANCHORS AWAY!

*Fun and quick, "Anchors Away!" provides for an exchange of cards
between players and, like in Ramino, the formation of a game
in one's hand, in this case, a particular suit.*

Players
Four to seven

Game Equipment
- A deck of 52 cards

Start & Object of the Game

The players decide among themselves
who will be the dealer: the dealer deals
seven cards to each player, including
himself.

Each player looks at his cards, arranging them by suit.

*Fig. 1 - Players try to get 7 cards of the
same suit.*

The object of the game is to get 7
cards of the same suit *(Fig. 1)*.

The Play

The players all discard a card facedown
at the same time and then each player
passes that card to the person on his left.

As the players pick up the cards
passed to them, they reorder their hands,
deciding what to discard, and then repeat
the same action just described.

The first player who manages to get 7
cards of the same suit calls out "Anchors
Away!" and of course wins the game.

Strategy

Usually, a player starts the game by trying to get cards of wahtever particular
suit is most numerous in the hand he
was dealt.

However, in the course of the game, a
player may change his mind according to
the discarded cards he receives from his
neighbor and also according to how
much he can figure out about his neighbor's cards.

If, for example, a player is trying to
get hearts, and his neighbor discards
only spades, diamonds, and clubs, the
player can guess that his neighbor is also
collecting hearts and therefore it would
be better to change suits.

SNAP!

A noisy game, and for this reason, very fun,
Snap is undoubtedly one of the most loved by children.
It has the reward of being played with incomplete decks of cards
or with old ruined cards that adults would not use anymore.

Players
Two or more

Game Equipment
- One or two decks of 52 cards
or incomplete decks

▧ Start & Object of the Game

If there are three or more players, use
two decks of cards.

The players decide who will deal. The
dealer will deal all the cards, one at a
time, to the players, including himself,
forming facedown piles in front of each
person.

The player to the left of the dealer
goes first, turning over the top card on
his pile and putting it faceup, next to his
own pile.

The object of the game is to win all
the cards.

▧ The Play

Each player, during his turn, turns over
the top card on his pile putting it on the
faceup pile.

Whoever notices that any two faceup
piles have cards of the same value on top
calls out "Snap!" and takes both piles.

If two or more players yell "Snap!" at
the same time, the two piles in question
are put together into one pile, still faceup, which is then placed in the middle of
the table.

This new pile can also be taken by
whoever notices that the top card is
equal to the top card of another pile by
yelling "Snap!"

Whoever gets rid of all his facedown
cards, then takes the faceup pile, turns it
over and continues to play.

The person, who manages to take all
the cards, leaving his opponents without
any piles, faceup or facedown, wins.

Whoever yells "Snap!" inappropri-
ately pays, as a penalty, one card from his
facedown pile to each of the other players or is forced to put his faceup pile in
the center of the table.

Of course, the players need to decide
before starting the game which of these
two penalties to use in case of error.

▧ Strategy

A good eye and a spirited delivery of the
call "Snap!" are key ingredients to avoid
letting equal piles get by you, especially
if there are many players.

SNIP-SNAP-SNOREM

*Snip-Snap-Snorem is a fun game of sets,
enlivened by loud yells which, as always,
make it fun for youngsters.*

Players
Three or more

Game Equipment
- One deck of 52 cards

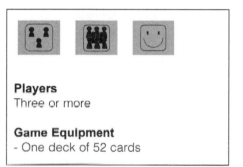

Fig. 1.

Start & Object of the Game

The players decide who the dealer will be; the dealer deals the cards clockwise, one by one, to all the players. It does not matter if one of the players has more cards than the others. The player to the left of the dealer lays down any one of his cards, faceup, on the table.

The object of the game is to get rid of all your cards before the others do.

The Play

The game is played in a clockwise motion. Let's say that the first player discards a 5. The player after him, if he has another 5, puts it next to the first yelling "Snip!" *(Fig. 1)*. If, instead, the second player does not have a 5, he passes.

Whoever has the third 5 discards it, during his turn, yelling "Snap!" Finally, whoever has the fourth 5, always during

his turn, discards it yelling "Snorem!" and has the opportunity to begin the next round.

Only one card can be discarded per turn. If a player has two cards equal to the one on the table, he can discard only one: to discard the second one, he has to wait for his next turn.

The player who discards all the cards in his hand first wins.

Strategy

If a player has two or three equal cards, it would be best to use them to begin a round, given the opportunity to do so.

The players can decide that the person who has two or three equal cards can discard them, one after the other, during the same turn: this makes the rounds go quicker.

SPIT

*Suitable for older children who know the cards well, Spit is a game
that combines Solitaire and Dare, making it one that adults will like, too.*

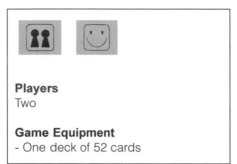

Players
Two

Game Equipment
- One deck of 52 cards

■ Start & Object of the Game

The players decide who will be the dealer. The dealer will then deal the cards one at a time to each person (for a total of 26 cards each), forming two facedown piles.

Each of the players prepares his "solitaire set-up" explained below. After this is done, one of the two players begins the game by yelling "Spit!"

The object of the game is to get rid of all of your cards first.

■ The Play

Each player prepares his solitaire set-up *(Fig. 1)* according to the following rules:
● Take the first three cards from the deck and put them facedown in a row, from left to right; the fourth card is put at the end of the row, faceup.
● Put two cards facedown and one faceup on the first of the three facedown cards.

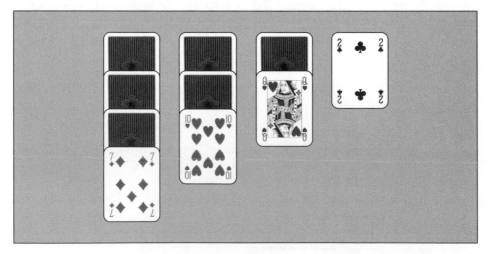

Fig. 1 - Setup of the cards in preparation for play.

- Put one card facedown and one faceup on the second of the three facedown cards.
- Last, put one card faceup on the third facedown card.

The remaining 16 cards are kept facedown in a pile.

Whoever yells "Spit!" begins the competition.

Each player takes the first card on the top of his pile and turns it over: these two cards will be the base cards.

Each player can put, on one of the base cards, one of the faceup cards from his solitaire setup that has a value greater then or less than the base card: for example, a 10 or a Queen can go on a Jack. The Ace is worth more than a King and less than a 2, therefore a King or a 2 can go on an Ace.

When a player uses a card from a solitaire pile, he turns over the next card in the pile.

SECOND PHASE OF THE GAME

When both players have played all of the possible cards from their solitaire piles, one of the two calls out "Spit" and the game moves on to the second phase of the game.

Each player takes the top card from the facedown pile, turns it over putting it in the center of the table and begins his own discard pile.

Each player starts playing again, if possible, by moving the cards from the solitaire piles to the discard pile.

When the round finishes, one of the two players calls out "Spit!" and both players turn over the top card of their facedown pile and put it on top of their discard pile. If a player uses up all the cards in his facedown pile before having played all the cards in his solitaire piles, he can take his discard pile, turn it over, and play with this pile.

The player who move all of his cards from the solitaire piles to the discard pile calls out "Stop!" and wins the hand.

■ Strategy

A good eye and speed allow the players, in the first part of the game, to play their cards before their opponents.

In the second part of the game, speed is important but players always need to keep an eye on their own solitaire piles, so that they don't let a move go by in the rush to finish the hand.

LOSE YOUR SHIRT

Like many other children's games, Lose Your Shirt
consists of trying to win all of the cards in play.
As always, when the player least expects it, his luck can change,
making Lose Your Shirt lively and fun.

Players
Two to six

Game Equipment
- One or two decks of 52 cards each

■ Start & Object of the Game

If there are more than three players, shuffle two decks together.

The players decide who will deal the cards. The dealer deals the cards clockwise, one at a time, making a face-down pile for each person, himself included.

It doesn't matter if one of the players has more cards than another.

In turn, the players turn over the top card of their respective piles, putting these cards in a central discard pile.

The object of the game is to win all of the cards.

■ The Play

Each time a player, when turning over his cards, puts an Ace or a face card on top of the pile, the player to his left is forced to pay a certain number of cards. These payment cards are also turned over, one at a time, and placed faceup on the discard pile:

- Four cards are paid for an Ace;
- Three cards are paid for a King;
- Two cards are paid for a Queen;
- One card is paid for a Jack.

If the player that is paying cards turns over an Ace or a face card, he stops paying cards: at this point, the player to his left will need to pay the cards from the last turn.

When a player is forced to pay without turning over an Ace or a face card, the player who turned over the last winning card takes the entire discard pile, turns it over, and puts it at the bottom of his pile.

The player who manages to get all the cards, or who has the most cards after a certain amount of time, wins the game.

■ Strategy

Lose Your Shirt is a game of pure chance. As such, no special ability nor a good eye nor speed is necessary. It is, however, a very fun game and most of all very easy to learn and to play.

DICE GAMES

"36"

This is a game of chance for several players, with rules similar to those of card games such as Black Jack or Seven & a Half.

Players
Two or more

Game Equipment
- A die numbered from 1 to 6
- Chips

Start & Object of the Game

Each player will roll the die once: the player who has the highest number will start the game; the others will play when their turn comes, in clockwise order.

Players agree on the bet, and must place the bet in the pot at the beginning of each hand.

After each player has anted up, the first player will roll the die and will loudly declare the obtained number.

The object of the game is to be the one who reaches a total as close as possible to 36 or even to obtain exactly 36 points.

The Play

After the first player, the second player will roll the die and declare loudly the sum of his points with the one of the previous player.

The third player will roll the die and loudly declare the sum of his roll with the preceding ones.

This goes on until one of the following possibilities is met:
● After rolling the die a player reaches 36 and thereby wins the pot;
● A player exits the game by exceeding 36. In this case the previous player wins.

The player who has enough points can declare that he is "staying" and refrain from rolling the die. The player immediately following him can accept the declaration of his opponent, who in this case would win the hand and the pot, or defy it, and roll the die. Naturally, if this player exceeds 36, the pot goes to the player who "stayed."

A player cannot stay if the previous player has just declared staying.

The game is won by the player who has collected the most chips after a preestablished number of hands or a preestablished amount of time.

Strategy

Success at the game depends on the roll of the die and the judgment of the player of whether to roll or "stay."

You can use some reasoning to decide whether to stay or not or to decide whether to accept an opponent's declaration of staying by quickly figuring your chance of exceeding 36.

ANCHOR & CROWN

This is a fast-paced real game of chance which is popular among American marines. It is, however, very biased in favor of the bank, which always wins in the long run. Try it to believe it!

Players
From two to six against the bank

Game Equipment
- A board divided in six sections, with the four suits in the corners (hearts, spades, diamonds, clubs), and, in the center, a crown and an anchor *(Fig. 1)*. The board can also be round and divided in six *(Fig. 2)*
- Three special dice, which have the same symbols as the table, with the crown at the opposite pole of the anchor, spades opposite the clubs, and hearts opposite diamonds *(Fig. 3)*

Fig. 1 - The board used for the game.

■ Start & Object of the Game

You will establish, by choice or by luck of the dice, which player will be the bank (for the round or for a preestablished number of hands).

The players place their bets on one or more symbols of their choice.

The bank rolls the dice, and, if the symbols on which the players have bet are shown, it will pay out the bets, otherwise it wins them.

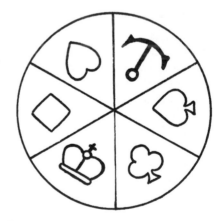

Fig. 2 - Another version of the board.

■ The Play

The bank rolls all three dice at the same time. If one dice shows one of the symbols the players have bet on, the bank pays the bet.

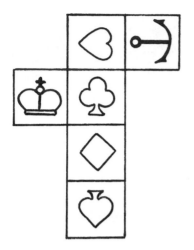

Fig. 3 - The symbols on the special dice, which are the same symbols on the table, with the crown at the opposite pole of the anchor, spades opposite the clubs, and hearts opposite diamonds.

If two dice show the symbol a player has bet on, the bank pays the player twice the bet.

If all three dice show the symbol a player has bet on, the bank pays the player three times the bet.

All the bets that do not match any of the symbols shown by the dice will be won by the bank.

◼ Strategy

Anchor & Crown is a game of pure luck, at least as far as the players are concerned. As you can imagine, in the long run the bank always wins.

In order to have a balance it is important to rotate the bank so that all players can have fun, and also not to have disproportionate wins.

CHEERIO

This is a game of combinations which can be played even with a very high number of participants. The name, Cheerio, indicates its British origins. This is a fun pastime for reunions among friends and can be made more interesting with a certain amount of risk.

Players
From two to twelve

Game Equipment
- Five dice, numbered from 1 to 6
- A dice-box
- A table in which to write down points *(Fig. 1)*

■ Start & Object of the Game

To decide who starts, the players take turns rolling a die. The player with the highest value begins.

The play moves from player to player in clockwise order.

The object of the game is to obtain the most points for each of the possible combinations that are descibed on the next page. The player who gets the highest points of all is the winner.

	Player	Player	Player	Player
1				
2				
3				
4				
5				
6				
Minor straight				
Major straight				
Full house				
Big hand				
Cheerio				

Fig. 1 - The scoring sheet on which to record points.

The Play

Players take turns rolling the five dice; if a player wishes, he can set aside some dice, and roll the remaining ones once again, trying to better his combination; either way, each time after a player rolls the dice the points for the combination he has rolled are recorded.

The combinations do not necessarily have to be obtained by the players in the order indicated by the scoring sheet: at each turn a player can choose in which field of the table to write down the obtained points.

COMBINATIONS

The combinations and the points that must be recorded are explained below:

● One: a player gets one point for each one that is shown by the dice; the minimum points is one, the maximum, five.

● Two: a player gets two points for every 2; the minimum is 2, the maximum 10;

● Three: a player gets 3 points for every 3; the minimum is 3, the maximum 15;

● Four: a player gets four points for every 4; the minimum is 4, the maximum 20;

● Five: a player gets 5 points for every 5; the minimum is 5, the maximum 25.

● Six: a player gets six points for every 6; the minimum is 6; the maximum 30.

● Minor straight: a player gets 20 points for a straight of 1, 2, 3, 4, 5;

● Major straight: a player gets 25 points for a straight from 2, 3, 4, 5, 6;

● Full house: a player gets the points corresponding to the dice that form the full house, which, as in poker, is formed by a pair and three of a kind; the minor full house is formed by three 1s and two

2s, which is worth 7 points; the major full house is formed by three 6s and two 5s, which is worth 28 points.

● Big hand: the player gets the points corresponding to the points of the six dice; the minimum is 5 (five 1s); the maximum points is 30 (five 6s);

● Cheerio: you get 50 points for five of a kind (poker);

● Cheerio is always worth 50 points, be it made up by five 1s or by five 6s.

RECORDING THE POINTS

Once a player has recorded points, he cannot in that same round get credit for that same combination. For example, the player who gets three 5s and writes down 15 in the field of 5, cannot later write down 20 in the same field if he has rolled four 5s.

The player who wants to do the second partial roll does not have to declare which combination he has in mind: only once the rolls are done can he freely decide in which field to record the points; this means that, for example, a full house of three 3s and two fives can be recorded either as a 9 in the field of 3, a 10 in the field of 5, or a 19 in the field of full house, as long as the fields are free and as long as the player has not yet recorded points in them.

A player may not refuse to record points. When towards the end of the round there have remained few empty fields (and usually those are the most difficult ones, such as cheerio), the player must record 0 points in one of the fields of the combinations that has not yet benn achieved.

The round is won by the player who, at the end of 11 hands has acquired the highest number of points abtained yb adding up the points achieved for every single combination.

■ Strategy

Cheerio depends on luck, but also on a certain strategy in recording the points.

In a roll with two 2s, two 5s and a 1, for example, it might be more convenient to record 4 in the field of two, or 1 in the field of one, rather than 10 in the field of five.

However, when you get five of a kind, even one of five 6s, it is best to write it down in the field of Cheerio, where it is worth 50 points, rather than in the field of 6, where it is worth only 30 points.

THE BIG HAND

The field of "big hand" is a way of writing down points in a roll that otherwise does not have any useful combinations.

This offers a good opportunity which should not be wasted but taken advantage of as much as possible when, for example, you get two high pairs, with a fifth dice with a high value as well.

CRAPS

*Craps is undoubtedly the most popular dice game
in the entire world. It's been exported from the United States
to every corner of the globe, and is played in gambling houses
and casinos as well as among friends.*

Players
Five or more

Game Equipment
- Two dice, numbered from 1 to 6
- Chips

▓ Start & Object of the Game

Each player must roll a die: the player who has the highest roll is the bank. The object of the game is to beat the bank by accumulating a winning score.

▓ The Play

The game always happens between only two players at a time: the bank and the player seated to his right. The other players can, if they wish, bet on one or the other, as they await their turn to join the game. The opponent of the bank makes a bet, then takes the dice and rolls them. If in the first roll the total score is 2, 3, or 12, the player loses the bet, which is taken by the bank. Then the player will pass the dice to his right, and become banker.

If the player gets a 7 or 11 in the first roll, he wins the amount of his bet from the bank. Then he has the right to make a new bet and roll the dice again.

If in the first roll the player gets any other total (4, 5, 6, 8, 9, 10), he can throw the dice again, as many times as it takes until he gets his first total again; for example, the player who got a 5 and a 3 (a total of 8) in the first roll, must roll the dice until he gets another 8 (which can be 1 + 7, 2 + 6, 3 + 5 or 4 + 4).

If, however, in this series of rolls he gets a 7, he loses the bet and passes the dice to the player at his right and becomes banker.

The winner is the player who, after having had the bank once or twice (as established at the beginning of the game), has acquired the highest number of chips.

▓ Strategy

Craps, or Seven-Eleven as some call it, is a game of pure chance that favors the bank, which is why the rotation of the banker is written into the rules of the game and is not left up to the players.

Considerable wins occur not only when one is banker or opponent but also when one is a spectator and decides to bet on one of the players.

INDIAN DICE

*Indian Dice is a classical pastime at bars that is very popular in the United States.
It is based on poker and can include placing bets,
thus making it a very fast-paced and amusing game of chance.*

Players
Two or more

Game Equipment
- Five dice numbered from 1 to 6.

■ Start & Object of the Game

Each player will roll a die: the one who gets the highest score begins the game; the other players take turns in clockwise order.

The object of the game is to obtain the highest poker combination, keeping in mind that the 1 is the joker, and the 6 has the highest value.

■ The Play

The first player rolls the dice. According to the combination he has obtained, he can choose to reroll one of the die or all five of them; this second roll can be followed by a third one, as desired.

After the first player has finished his series of rolls, his points are recorded (including the value of the unimportant die at the end of the combination). The dice is passed to the next player.

The players following the first player may not roll the dice more times than the first player has; if, for example the first player rolled twice, the players following him may make one or two rolls, but not a third.

The game is won by the player who has the highest poker combination, keeping in mind that the 1 (the joker) can take on any value.

COMBINATIONS
The poker combinations valid for this game are illustrated in Figure 1 in ascending value: pair, two pairs, three of a kind, full house (a pair and three of a kind), poker (four dice equal in value) and high poker (5 dice equal in value).

WINNING A HAND
When there are two full houses the one with the higher three of a kind wins (for example, a full house of three 5s and two 2s will win over a full house with three 4s and two 6s). If the three of a kinds are equal in value, the value of the pairs becomes the deciding factor. If the pairs are also equal, then the winnings are divided between the two players.

Similarly, when there are two pokers or two two pairs of equal value, the combination with the highest fifth dice wins. If this cannot be determined, then the hand is divided. Between two three

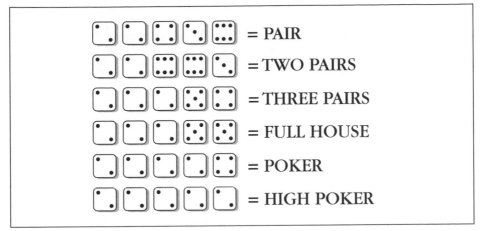

Fig. 1 - The possible combinations.

of a kinds of equal value the one with the higher sum of the fourth and fifth dice wins.

The hand is won by the player with the highest combination, who will then begin the next hand.

The game is finished after a certain number of hands or after a preestablished amount of time. The player who wins the most hands wins the game.

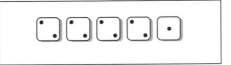

Fig. 2 - The one (1) is the joker.

THE JOKER

The one (1), being a joker, can take any value: the poker (four of a kind) in Figure 2 becomes high poker (five of a kind); however, if another player during the same hand gets high poker without a joker (clean high poker), he wins.

Attention! A full made up of 3 values and two jokers is actually five of a kind, or high poker!

▮ Strategy

The outcome of a roll of the dice is never predictable.

Still, you need to learn to weigh your options in deciding to make several rolls, especially when you are the player who begins the hand, carefully evaluating the potential obtaining combinations.

Before starting the game, players should agree to place bets in the pot at the beginning of each hand.

With every roll, a player can bet and raise. The other players can accept the bet or not, just like in Three-Seven (Teresina) with every new card.

DICE POKER

*Captivating and intriguing like poker, fast-paced and fun like a game of dice,
this version of Dice Poker combines the best qualities of America's
two favorite pastimes and it is popular all around the world.*

Players
Two or more

Game Equipment
- Five special dice, which have the
following values, in decreasing order:
Ace, King, Queen, Jack, 10 and 9
- Chips

▓ Start & Object of the Game

The players take turns rolling one die:
the player who gets the highest value,
from the Ace to the 9, goes first; the others follow in clockwise order.

Each player puts an agreed upon bet
of chips in the pot.

The object of the game is to accomplish the highest poker combination.

▓ The Play

After rolling the dice, players can choose
to make a second roll using from one to
four dice.

After the second roll, the player
records the combination obtained, and
passes the dice to the next player.

The combinations in decreasing
order, are: high poker (five equal dice),
poker (four equal dice), high flush (from
the Ace to the 10), low flush (from the
King to the 9), full house (three of a kind
and a pair), two pair, and a pair.

The player who wins a hand takes the
bet and starts the next hand.

The game is won by the player who
has won the most chips after a preestablished number of hands or a preestablished amount of time.

▓ Strategy

Luck and some amount of reasoning in
making the potential second roll are the
ingredients in this fun dice version of
poker.

Players can decide for the entire
length of the game, or only for a few
hands, to bet and raise at every roll,
thereby considerably increasing the
amount of chips in the pot.

You can also decide to play with the
Aces functioning as jokers, taking into
account that a clean combination always
wins over a "dirty" combination containing one or more jokers.

EVEREST

This original pastime recalls, in the mechanism of the game, the folk game Close the Box. The name probably comes from the score chart that must be climbed up and then climbed down.

Players
Two or more

Game Equipment
- Three dice numbered from 1 to 6.
- A chart for each player in which to record the points, as shown in Figure 1.

			12						1		
			11						2		
			10						3		
			9						4		
			8						5		
			7						6		
			6						7		
			5						8		
			4						9		
			3						10		
			2						11		
			1						12		

Fig. 1 - Chart in which to record points.

▩ Start & Object of the Game

Each player rolls a die in order to decide who goes first.

The object of the game is to cancel out all the points in one's own chart.

▩ The Play

For each roll of the dice, you can cancel in any of these ways:
● The three points corresponding to each of the single dice.
● The points corresponding to the sum of two of the dice and the value of the third one separately.
● The points corresponding to the sum of all three dice.

If, for example, you get a 1, 2, 3, you can cancel: the 1, the 2, the 3, or the 2 and the 4 (1+3), or the 1 and the 5 (2+3), or only the 6 (1+2+3).

Each value must be cancelled twice, once in the column on the right, and once in the column on the left.

If in a roll you obtain a pair, you can cancel that number in both columns.

The winner is the first one to cancel all the numbers in his table.

▩ Strategy

You must pay attention to the numbers rolled, not to miss canceling a number.

FIFTY

*Fifty is a very simple but fun game that is well suited for children.
In this game you can experience unexpected changes of leadership,
as it often happens when you trust chance.*

Players
Two or more

Game Equipment
- Two dice numbered from 1 to 6

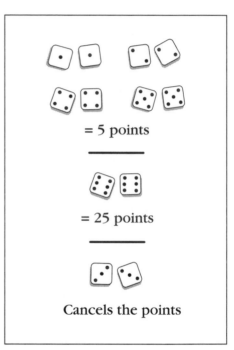

Fig. 1 - In order to make points you must roll a double.

■ Start & Object of the Game

Players take turns rolling a die: the one who gets the highest points goes first; the others take turns after him.

The object of the game is to be the first to get 50 points.

■ The Play

Each player rolls the dice in turn and records his points (if any) from the roll. Then he passes the dice on to the next player, to his left. In order to obtain points one must get doubles *(Fig. 1)*, double 1s, double 2s, double 4s and double 5s count as 5 points; double 6s count as 25 points; double 3s cancel all points obtained to that point and that player must start over.

The first player to equal or exceed 50 points wins.

■ Strategy

Winning Fifty depends exclusively on the luck of the roll of the dice.

In order to make this game more exciting you can establish a bet in advance, which can be increased with a raise suggested by the player who is the first to reach or exceed 25 points.

HOOLIGAN

*Similar to Cheerio, Hooligan is of clear British descent,
and can be played as a game of chance, although this is not
the main reason why it is fun and exciting.*

Players
Two or more

Game Equipment
- Five dice numbered from 1 to 6
- A dice-box
- A chart similar to the one shown
in Figure 1, in which to record points.

Start & Object of the Game

Each player rolls a die. Whoever gets the
highest score goes first; the other players
follow in clockwise order.

The object of the game is to accomplish, in seven hands, all the number-points required by the scoring sheet.

The Play

Each player has, with every hand, the
right to three rolls of the dice in order to

Numbers-points	Player		Player		Player		Player	
1								
2								
3								
4								
5								
6								
H								

Fig. 1 - Scoring sheet on which to record points.

accomplish the numbers on the dice, the points. After the first roll, the player must declare which numbers–points, among those not yet attained, he intends to accomplish. Based on this declaration, he will set aside the used dice and roll the remaining ones, doing the same for the third and last roll.

At the end of the three rolls, the valid points are summed up, namely the dice which have the declared value; if, for example, the player was aiming for a 3, and at the end of the three rolls he has totaled four threes, 12 will be marked in the appropriate field.

After the first roll a player can avoid making a declaration if he decides to take back all the five dice.

In this case at the second roll the declaration is mandatory, and the player has only the third and last roll to make as many points as possible.

DECLARING HOOLIGAN

Hooligan is defined as when the dice form a stragiht from 1 to 5 or from 2 to 6, each of which is worth 20 points. The player who has not yet declared Hooligan before the seventh hand is required to play it in this last hand.

The fields that have not been accomplished by the end of the seventh hand will be marked 0.

Each field can be declared only once during the round. Once a player has declared a field he cannot change his mind and, in the following hands, he cannot play that number again.

EXTRA POINTS

The player who rolls five dice the same on either the first or second roll concludes the hand (with remaining roll or rolls), and continues to set aside the used dice; if, for example, a player has totaled five 6s in the first roll, he takes back all of the dice, he chooses to set aside two 6s to be counted again, rolls three dice and makes another 6, his final total is eight 6s, for a score of 48 points, which is recorded on the scoring sheet.

The round is won by the person who, at the end of seven hands, has scored the highest number of points.

■ Strategy

Recognizing a potential Hooligan and playing for the one which is most likely is the best way of making sure that the "H" field is not left empty at the seventh and last hand, thereby losing 20 possible points. Of course, rolling the dice is always based on luck, and finishing a hand having filled in all of the fields is not easy at all.

KLONDIKE

*Very popular in American casinos, Klondike uses a table,
and instead of the traditional dice-box, prefers a long runway on which
to roll the dice. An unlimited number of participants can play against the bank.
The success of the game comes from the fact that it does not allow objections:
a player rolls and immediately knows if he's won or lost, without the possibility
of making another draw, not even a partial one.*

Players
Two or more, against the bank

Game Equipment
- Two sets of five dice, numbered
from 1 to 6
- A table with spaces marked "win,"
"lose," "beat 2 Aces," and "Klondike"
(Fig. 1)
- A long runway on which
to roll the dice
- Chips

■ Start & Object of the Game

The players choose whether to bet on
"Win," "Lose," or "Beat 2 Aces."

The bank rolls its 5 dice, which
remain in the Klondike.

The object of the game is to beat the
bank with only one roll.

■ The Play

The player at the right of the bank is the
one who starts, rolling the second series
of five dice.

The combinations are the ones of
poker, in increasing order, pair, two pair,
three of a kind, full house (three of a

Fig. 1 - The special game board.

kind and a pair), poker (four equal values), and high poker (five equal values). The 1 is the highest value (like the Ace in poker), and afterward follow in decreasing order, the 6, 5, 4, 3, 2.

The dice that are not part of a combination (in a pair, two pair, three of a kind, or poker) do not count: a poker of 4 with a 5 has the same value as a poker of 4 with a 1. However, between two full houses with the same three of a kinds, the winner is the one with the highest pair.

WIN. LOSE, BEAT 2 ACES

The player who bets on "Win" must make a higher combination than that of the bank to win.

The player who bets on "Lose" must make a weaker combination than that of the bank to win.

The player who bets on "Beat 2 Aces" must get at least two pair (or combinations of superior value), regardless of what the bank has gotten to win.

SETTLING ACCOUNTS

If the player has the same combination as the bank, the bank wins.

With each roll of the dice, accounts must be settled immediately: if the player wins, the bank pays the bet; if the bank wins, the player loses the bet; the dice are passed to the player to the right of the previous player.

The bank's initial dice combination remains in the Klondike until all of the players seated at the table have rolled the dice; only at the end of the round can the banker take back his dice, and begin a new hand.

COUNTER KLONDIKE

In "Counter Klondike," the "friendly" version (not the one played in casinos), a table is not used, and players need not bet on "Win," "Lose," or "Beat 2 Aces." but play simply against the bank, using the same rules and combinations as in the traditional game.

■ Strategy

Klondike is based exclusively on luck, and, like all casino games, is biased in favor of the bank. This is why, when playing among friends, one must rotate the bank so that everybody has fun.

THE CLOCK

*Extremely easy but still fun, this game owes its name to the table
on which points are recorded, which is designed exactly like the face of a clock.
This is a game based on luck. You can introduce chance
by rewarding the winning player with a bet.*

Players
Two or three

Game Equipment
- Two dice, numbered from 1 to 6
- A table on which to record points,
with a clock face for each player
- 12 chips for each player

▨ Start & Object of the Game

Each player rolls a die in order to see
who goes first; the others follow in
clockwise order.

The object of the game is to cancel
out all the hours in one's own face.

The Play

Each player, at his turn, rolls both dice:
according to the points obtained, he can
cover an hour on the face using a chip.
The hours must be covered in order
from 1 to 12.

For the first six hours, the player can
use either the points of one die or of
both dice. If, for example he must cover
1 o'clock and he gets a 1 and a 4, he will
ignore the 4; if, on the other hand, he
must cover 3 o'clock and gets a 1 and a
2, the sum will permit him to cover the
appropriate hour.

Naturally, from the seven on up to the
twelve the sum of the points of both dice
must be used.

If the player gets two consecutive
numbers, for example a 4 and a 5, corresponding to hours that have not been
covered yet, the player can cover both
values in the same hand.

The winner is the one who covers his
entire face first.

▨ Strategy

Since the hours must be covered in
order, the game depends on luck.

However, if one introduces the version in which hours must not be cancelled out in a particular order, the game
can use a strategy similar to that of
Everest, calculating which hours are the
best to cover based on the obtained
points. In this case the length of the
game will be shorter, but the game is
more interesting.

THE PIG

This is a game which children will enjoy very much.
It can feature a small bet, for example, chocolate chips or candy,
or, if played among adults, a preestablished number of chips,
bringing some chance to a pastime that is already a lot of fun.

Players
Three or more

Game Equipment
- Two dice numbered from 1 to 6
- A pig-shaped chart on which to record points, with the parts of the body marked for each player *(Fig. 1)*

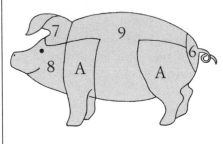

Fig. 1 - The amusing scorecard.

Start & Object of the Game

Each player rolls a die; the player who rolls highest goes first, the others follow in clockwise order.

The object of the game is to cover one's own pig before the opponents do.

The Play

With each roll one has the possibility of adding a part to one's pig, according to the points obtained by adding the two dice, if the points equal 6, 7, 8, or 9.

The legs, marked by the letter A, can be covered by rolling a double 1 or a double 6.

When you have an unusable roll (lower than 6, higher than 9, or corresponding to a part already filled out), the dice are passed to the next player.

The winner is the one who is the first to cover his pig.

Strategy

The success of the game depends exclusively on the points that are obtained when rolling the dice.

A bit of chance, which is always a plus, can be added by establishing a bet, which will be declared and put down before starting the game.

To play for a longer time, you can decide that the parts of the pig should be covered in a certain order. For example, the players can agree to cover first the 6, then the 7, then the 8, then the 9, and at last the two As, one of which (the back one) may only be covered by a double 1, and the other with a double 6.

SCARAB (or BEETLES)

Scarab, or Beetles, is a British folk game
for adults as well as children, and owes its name to the fact that,
with each roll of the dice, each player proceeds to draw
one of these undesirable creatures.

Players
From two to six

Game Equipment
- A special die which, on its six sides will have the following letters: B, H, L, E, F, T *(Fig. 1)*; or alternatively, a normal dice numbered from 1 to 6.
- A sheet to write down points, and a pencil for each player.

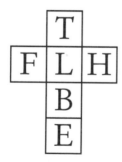

Fig. 1 - The sides of the special die.

Start & Object of the Game

Each player rolls the die. The player who gets the B (or 1 with a normal dice) starts the game; the other players follow, in clockwise order. The object of the game is to complete on one's own sheet the drawing of a beetle *(Fig. 2)* before the opponents do.

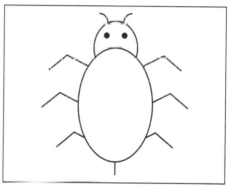

Fig. 2 - The object of the game is to complete on one's own sheet the drawing of a beetle before the opponents do.

The Play

The meaning of the letters and their corresponding numbers on an ordinary die are the following:

● B = body; with an ordinary die this would be 1.
● H = head; 2;
● L = legs; 3;
● E = eyes; 4;
● F = feelers; 5;
● T = tail; 6.

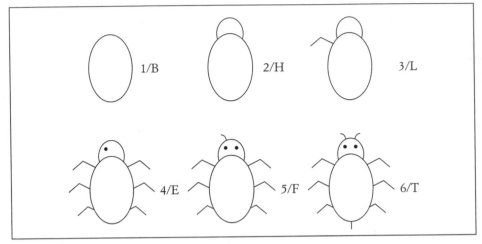

Fig. 3 - The complete order of the drawings.

The players take turns rolling the die and draw the body parts in the order shown above, starting with the body (B or 1) and finishing with the tail (T or 6).

For each roll of the die, the player will draw on the sheet the appropriate part, keeping in mind that the 6 legs can only be drawn one at a time, with six separate rolls that result in an L or a 3; the same is the case of the eyes, which will be drawn one at a time, for each of them an E being required, or a 4; the feelers will also be drawn one at a time, and will require two rolls of F or 5. The complete sequence of the drawings is illustrated in Figure 3.

The winner is the player who first finishes drawing his beetle, complete with tail and each of the required parts.

■ Strategy

There is no strategy, just lots of fun. One only needs to have some good luck in rolling the die.

The hardest part are the legs, because it is difficult to get six rolls of L, or 3, one after the other.

In order to make the game faster, players can decide that for each L or 3 all of the legs on one side of the beetle can be drawn.

SEVEN

Seven takes from Roulette the terms Manque and Passe:
as in the famous casino game you must bet on numbers against the bank.
However, in the long run, the bank always wins.

Players
Five or more

Game Equipment
- Two dice numbered from 1 to 6
- A rectangular playing board divided in twelve numeral sectors, illustrated in Figure 1
- Chips

1	2	3	4	5	6
12	11	10	9	8	7

Fig. 1 - The game board.

■ Start & Object of the Game

Each player rolls a die: the player who gets the highest points is the banker for a certain number of hands which must be established before starting. After that he will pass the bank to the player on his right, and so on, until all the players will have had the bank for a certain number of hands.

The players, except for the bank, make a bet along the top row, "Manque," or along the bottom row, "Passe."

The object of the game is to beat the bank, by guessing how much the bank will total with the roll of the dice.

■ The Play

Once the bets have been made, the bank will roll the dice. If the bank, adding the value of the two dice, obtains a number from 2 to 6, all the players who have betted on "Manque" will receive what they bet, while those who bet on "Passe" will lose their bets.

On the other hand, if the banks total falls between 8 and 12, it will pay the players who have bet on Passe, and take the bets of those who have bet on Manque. If, however, the bank gets 7, it wins all bets.

The player who bets on 1 always loses the bet, unless the bank totals 7, in which case that player wins what he bet.

■ Strategy

A good deal of luck is the only weapon that is successful in this game of pure chance which always favors the bank: this is why it is highly recommended to rotate the bank among the players.

PEN & PAPER
GAMES

ACROSTICS

*Acrostics is a word game made popular by Americans
in which words are created
from the initials of other words.*

Players
Two or more

Game Equipment
- A sheet of paper and a pen
for each player

■ Start & Object of the Game

Taking turns, the players choose a word.
Each player writes his word vertically on
the sheet of paper *(Fig. 1)*.

*Fig. 1 – First step in the game: each
player writes a word vertically
on a sheet of paper.*

Beginning from the left of the base
word, each player writes words that end
in the initials of the base word. Then, to
the right of the base word, each player
writes words that begin with each of the
starting initials.

■ The Play

In the example in Figure 2, the base
word is PEAR; the words to the left are
toP, figurE, ideA, jaR; those to the right
are Post, Even, Air, Rain.

*Fig. 2 - Example of the second step
of the game.*

The player who finishes the acrostic
in the least amount of time wins.

In a more advanced version of the
game, the players create not only two

different words for each letter but those two different words must form a third word when combined. In the example in Figure 3, the words to the right of the base word reP, bE, seA, paR, when added to the words on the left of the base word Peal, Ear, At, Rent, create four new words, rePeal, bEar, seAt, paRent.

Fig. 3 - Another version of the game.

The third and more difficult version of the game requires writing words to the right of the base word and forming a phrase related to the meaning of the base words. For example: AIR—All Inhale Regularly.

■ Strategy

Provided the players are in agreement to its use, a good dictionary helps considerably, especially when playing the second version of the game. Also with the players' consnet before they start, foreign words that are commonly used can be made permissible.

A good familiarity with the English language, or whatever language the players choose to play in, and a creative mind are a player's best assets in having fun with this stimulating pastime.

Unless you are already experienced with word games, you should begin this game using a base word of only four, or at most five letters.

ANAGRAMS

*One of the most famous word games and among the favorites
of every puzzle lover, Anagrams stimulate the imagination
of both the player who solves the puzzle and the person who prepares it.*

Players
Two or more

Game Equipment
- A sheet of paper and a pen
for each player

Start & Object of the Game

Taking turns, one player prepares a list
of words related to a common theme.
For example, if the theme is marine animals, the player writes polyp, dolphin,
dogfish, whale, and walrus.

Then, the player writes the anagrams
on sheets of paper equal to the number
of players, scrambling the letters of each
word and rewriting them randomly, for
example yolpp, hldoipn, sgfohdi, lweah,
and asluwr.

The purpose of the game is to solve
the anagrams by figuring out and writing
the original words.

The Play

The words do not have to be familiar to
all the players, but they must be plausi-
ble and easily pronounced.

Receiving the list, each player solves
the anagrams. Whoever solves all of the
anagrams first wins.

The players can agree to set a time
limt for solving the anagrams, which is
especially appropriate when the list is
very long. When the time limit has been
reached, whoever has solved the most
anagrams wins.

Strategy

A player's first glance at an angaram is
often the critical moment in figuring out
the original word. However, if the player
who prepares the anagrams scrambles
the letters of each word well (for example breaking up the syllables of the word
in order to make it more difficult, like
the syllables "wal" and "rus" of walrus),
the other players may have to try forming over and over all of the possible
combination of syllables.

MULITPLE SOLUTIONS

It is always acceptable for a player to
solve the anagram by writing a word that
is different from the initial word, as long
as it is a real word and uses all of the letters provided in the anagram. For example, if the original word is "seal" and the
anagram is "esla," a player can solve the
anagram writing "sale," and his solution
must be counted as correct.

ATTACK!

*Attack! creates on paper a simplified version
of the most popular war games, with virtual battles
that will put the participants' strategic abilities to the test.*

Players
Two or more, divided into two teams
Game Equipment
- A sheet of paper
- Three pens of different colors:
black, red, and blue

■ Start & Object of the Game

The players decide by luck of the draw
who goes first. Using the black pen, the
first player traces the borders of a hypothetical country on the sheet of paper
and marks it with the letter A *(Fig. 1)*;
and then passes the pen to an opponent.

Fig. 1 – First step of the game: the
first player traces the borders of
a hypothetical country on the sheet
of paper using the black pen and
marks it with the letter A; then passes
the pen to an opponent.

On his turn, the opponent traces
another country and designates it with
the letter B *(Fig. 2)*.

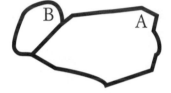

Fig. 2 – The opponent traces the borders of another country, B.

Taking turns, the players continue
until the letter T (or 20 countries).

The first player then assigns a certain
number of armies to each country, writing the number with the blue pen. The
opponent does the same with the red
pen. The two players take turns assigning the armies until all of the countries
are occupied *(Fig. 3)*.

The purpose of the game is to have
the most countries which cannot be
attacked by the opponent.

■ The Play

Each player can place up to 100 armies,
though a player can opt to use less than
100. It is also not necessary that armies
be stationed in all of the designated territories; the territories free from occupa-

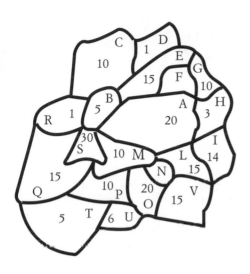

Fig. 3 – The two players take turns assigning armies until all of the countries are occupied.

tion are "neutral," but regardless of their neutral status, they will be important from a strategic point of view, acting as cushions and containing, in some cases, an enemy advance. Once a certain number of armies are assigned to a country, that number cannot be changed.

GETTING READY TO ATTACK

Once the armies are in place, the first player begins the game. Players can attack the only countries that border one or more of their own. The attack is successful if the number of armies in the country or countries that attacks is greater than the number of armies in the country attacked. When a country is invaded, its armies are captured and made prisoners and they can no longer reenter the game.

A territory invaded by the enemy cannot be reconquered.

END OF THE GAME

Taking turns, the players carry out their moves until neither of the two sides is in a position to attack the other.

At this point, the players count the territories in their possession (that is, those with armies that are still active, not prisoners). The player who has the most unoccupied countries wins.

Strategy

The configuration of the game and the positioning of the armies change with every new round of the game. Thus, the players' strategies must adapt to the different situations. It is worth noting that a country which borders many others is difficult to defend. On the other hand, a country surrounded by allies or neutral countries can consider itself safe because its allies or the neutral countries surrounding it cannot host enemy armies, even if invaded. Those countries will simply be occupied by an army and will remain in the possession of the opponent until the end of the game. This fact demonstrates the importance of the progression of an attack and, above all, the preliminary positioning of the armies.

BATTLESHIP

A very popular strategic game with relatively simple rules.
However, it is an enthralling pastime in which the players must rely
on their intelligence in order to effectively arrange a fleet and,
at the same time, predict the enemy position.

Players
Two

Game Equipment
- A sheet of paper and a pen
for each player.

■ Start & Object of the Game

Before they can start the game the players prepare their sheets of paper by drawing two squares each, side by side, with ten vertical rows marked by the numbers 1 to 10, and ten horizontal rows marked by the letters A through J *(Fig. 1)*. The players then position a barrier of some sort between themselves that will allow them to hide their sheets of paper from each other's sight.

Each player starts with his own naval fleet composed of a battleship of four squares in length, two cruisers of three squares in length, three destroyers of two squares in length, and four submarines of one square in length *(Fig. 2)*.

The players set up their battle positions by filling in the squares in the left diagram indicating each ship *(Fig. 3)*. The purpose of the game is to locate, hit, and sink your opponent's fleet.

Fig. 1 – Each player draws two diagrams in order to play the game.

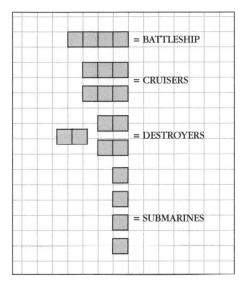

Fig. 2 – Each player has a fleet composed of a battleship of four squares in length, two cruisers of three squares in length, three destroyers of two squares in length, and four submarines of one square in length.

■ The Play

The ships can be placed horizontally or vertically, but they cannot touch each other and there must be at least one square which separates the ships.

The players decide by luck of the draw who will begin the game. The first player attacks a square on the diagram of the opponent, stating aloud the corresponding letter and number, for example, A4.

The opponent must respond by saying "hit" if a ship (or part of a ship) is in that square, and "miss" if the square is empty.

HITTING & BEING HIT

After launching an attack on the opponent, the player marks the move in the corresponding space in the right diagram to keep track of the attack; every time a ship is hit, the corresponding space is marked with an X.

Each time players successfully hit an enemy ship they get another turn, and they continue their turn until they miss by attacking an empty space. When a player has missed in his attack, the turn shifts to the opponent who launches a counterattack.

When players receive a fatal hit to a ship (either the single square of a submarine is hit, or the final square of a ship), they must say "hit and sunk," and the ship is out of the game.

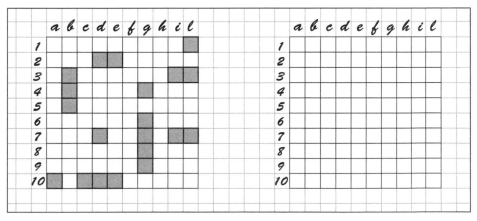

Fig. 3 – Each player arranges a fleet on the diagram to the left.

The player who sinks all the opponent's ships first wins.

■ Strategy

Some believe it is better to arrange the ships on the perimeter of the diagram because the common tendency is, at least in the beginning, to attack the middle of the diagram rather than the borders. That method, however, is a psychological game which, once detected, can lead to a rapid defeat. Instead, it is better to change strategy from one game to the next, especially if you always play with the same opponent who, after a while, will guess your mode of reasoning and predict your moves.

CRYSTALS

This game stimulates a player's imagination and creativity.
Crystals can be played with school-aged children who are learning
the fundamentals of geometry.

Players
Two or more

Game Equipment
- A sheet of graph paper or paper
divided into squares
- Different colored pencils
for each player

■ Start & Object of the Game

First, one player sets up the game on the sheet of paper: a large square which from its center will have as many smaller squares as there are players (or, perhaps, 20 squares for two players, 30 for three, and so on). With their pencils, the players take turns coloring in the squares trying to form symmetric crystals. The purpose of the game is to design the most extensive "crystals."

■ The Play

To count, a "crystal" must be symmetric on four axes simultaneously: horizontal, vertical, and two diagonal *(Fig. 1)*. A crystal must be formed of squares that touch on at least one side. Unions creat-

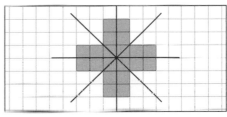

Fig. 1

ed by the corner of one square touching the corner of another are not allowed.

Once there is no more space to complete other squares, the game is ended. At this point, the players decide which crystals are valid and they count how many each player has from the amount of squares formed. Whoever has the highest number of squares inside their crystals is the winner.

■ Strategy

At the start it is wise to distribute small squares inside the different bigger squares. Those smaller squares will become the seed for the successive expansion of other crystals.

An irregular crystal, while not counting, may be a good strategic move, since it can limit the expansion of an opponent's crystal. Therefore, sometimes it is worth the effort to create an irregular crystal to stop an opponent advancing rapidly.

CATEGORIES

Name games are a pastime for everyone. Thanks to the diversity of categories, this game can be adapted, for example, to a group of film buffs who play with Titles, Actors, Actresses, and Directors, or to a group of animal lovers who identify Fish, Reptiles, Birds, and Mammals.

Players
Two or more

Game Equipment
- A sheet of paper and a pen for each player

■ Start & Object of the Game

The players choose four or more categories, for example, proper names, cities, fruits, or animals. Each player prepares a diagram with the names of the categories written on the top of the page, a column in which to write the letters chosen at each turn to the left, and finally, a column in which to record the

letter	proper names	city	fruit	animals	Points

Fig. 1 - Each player prepares a diagram with the names of the categories written on the top of the page, a column in which to write the letters chosen at each turn to the left, and finally, a column in which to record the player's score in each round to the right.

letter	proper names	city	fruits	animals	Points
D	Daniel	Detroit	Dates	Dog	8

Fig. 2 – After designating a letter, each player fills the corresponding spaces of the different categories. If, for example, the letter chosen is D, a hypothetical player could write Daniel, Detroit, Date, and Dog.

player's score in each round to the right, as is indicated in Figure 1.

Taking turns, players choose a letter or with their eyes closed they point to a letter on a sheet of paper that contains all of the letters of the alphabet—leaving out difficult letters such as Q or X, especially if you are playing with children. In the course of the game, the same letter may be used twice. The purpose of the game is to fill the categories with words beginning with the designated letter.

■ The Play

After deciding the letter, each player fills the corresponding spaces in the different categories. If, for example, the designated letter is D, a hypothetical player could write Daniel, Detroit, Dates and Dog (*Fig. 2*).

The players can set a time limit to complete the categories (for example, twenty seconds); or, the first person who finishes counts to ten after which time all the other players must stop writing.

The next step is to count the points: two points for each written word, only one point if the word was written by two or more players, and zero for each category left blank.

■ Strategy

Quickness and mental flexibility are the indispensable qualities necessary for playing Categories.

A dictionary and a small, condensed encyclopedia will help in case there are doubts about the validity of a word. Or, the players can choose the most impartial person to act as judge.

AND IT HAPPENED THAT . . .

This is a great pastime and fun for everyone. The advantage of this game is that there are no winners, only guaranteed laughs.

Players
Three or more

Game Equipment
- A sheet of paper and a pen for each participant

■ Start & Object of the Game

On their own sheets of paper, the players write the beginning of a story. Then, folding the edge of the paper in order to hide what they have written, each of the the players passes the sheets of paper to the left. The purpose of the game is to have fun completing as many stories as there are players and in the end reading all of the stories aloud.

■ The Play

The "plot" around which to sketch a story is the following:
● First turn: Her (everyone writes the name of a famous woman, historical or fictional, or of a woman known by all the players);

● Second turn: Him (do the same as the first turn, but write the name of a famous man);
● Third turn: Where (write a place);
● Fourth turn: He says to her . . . (write a sentence that the man says to the woman);
● Fifth turn: She says to him . . . (write a sentence that the woman says to the man);
● Sixth turn: And it happened that . . . (draw the story's conclusions);
● Seventh (and last) turn: and the people said . . . (report the public's comments on the events of the story).

Naturally, from turn to turn the players will continue their own stories, writing their remarks on a sheet of paper, then folding the edge and passing them to the left. At the end of the seventh turn, the players open the sheets of paper and they read the improbable and entertaining stories.

■ Strategy

A little humor will make funny stories absolutely irresistible, especially if the players choose people, places, and dialogues that seem funny and even outside of the context of the game are entertaining enough to make everyone laugh.

TIC-TAC-TOE

This classic challenge, known as Tic–Tac–Toe, is one of the oldest, best-known and most-played games in the world, and its simple rules make it appropriate even for the very young.

Players
Two

Game Equipment
- A sheet of paper
- A pen for each player

▧ Start & Object of the Game

One player draws a diagram of four lines which cross each other, two vertical and two horizontal, as in Figure 1.

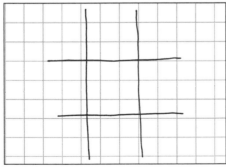

Fig. 1 – The basic diagram.

The two players decide who will go first, and the first player draws an X in

one of the nine spaces on the diagram, as seen in Figure 2.

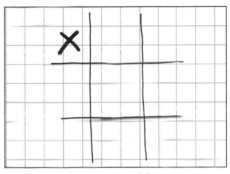

Fig 2. – The players decide who will go first, and the first player draws an X in any one of the nine spaces.

The object of the game is to create a complete line in the diagram, that is, to put three symbols in a horizontal, vertical, or diagonal row (the first player tries to place three X's in a row, and the second player tries to place three circles in a row).

▧ The Play

The second player draws a circle in any of the remaining empty spaces (*Fig. 3, on page 268*). The two players then take turns filling in the remaining spaces trying either to create a complete row or to block their opponent from creating one.

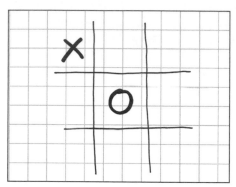

Fig. 3 – The second player traces
a circle *in one of the remaining spaces
of the diagram.*

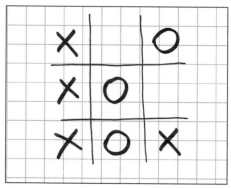

Fig. 4 – *Whoever creates three in a row
first wins the game.*

Whoever creates a complete row first
wins the game *(Fig. 4).* If neither of the
two players is able to complete a row
and all of the spaces are filled, the game
is a draw.

■ Strategy

As you play, you will discover that whoever begins has the advantage. For this
reason, it is necessary for the two players
to take turns beginning the game.

Whoever creates a double possibility
of making a complete row, as shown in
Figure 5, will automatically win the
game. In fact, in our example, the first
player now has two X's in two opposite
corners of the diagram and another in
one of the remaining corners. The second player has aa circle in the center and
in the other corner. On his next turn, the
second player places at the bottom middle between the two X's in opposite corners on the diagram, but the first player
will still able to complete a row by drawing a circle and creating a row vertically.

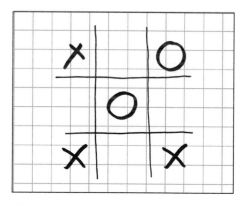

Fig. 5 – *Whichever player creates a
double possibility of making a complete
row will automatically win the game.*

SQUARES

*This is a small, but fun strategy game which is very simple,
but at the same time exciting. The game can be made longer
depending the size of the diagram the players agree to at the start.*

Players
Two

Game Equipment
- A sheet of paper
- Two different-colored pens,
one per player

▉ Start & Object of the Game

The players draw a certain number of
points on the sheet of paper which correspond to the corners of the squares,
for example, six rows of five points each.

The object of the game is to close the
most number of squares as possible.

▉ The Play

One player starts by connecting two
adjacent points which are linked either
horizontally or vertically, but not diagonally. The second player does the same.

The game proceeds with the players
connecting two adjacent points trying to
complete the squares.

When a player closes a square, he or
she signs it with his or her initials (*Fig. 1*)
and can then takes another turn and
draw another line.

Fig. 1 – *Whoever closes a square signs
it with his or her initials.*

When the diagram is complete, the
players count their squares. Whoever
has the most complete squares wins.

▉ Strategy

Two strategies are used; each tries to
complete as many squares as possible
and, at the same time, tries to block the
opponent from completing squares.
When playing with a large diagram, it is
better to concentrate on completing
squares rather than on blocking your
opponent, but players must be attentive
not to overlook closing a square that
they may missed because it was part of
an effort to block the opponent.

TELEGRAMS

*This is a classic word game, ideal for creative people
who have a vast knowledge of the English language
or, in a simplified version, ideal also for children
who are developing their creativity and imagination.*

Players
Two or more

Game Equipment
- A sheet of paper and a pen
for each player

■ Start & Object of the Game

On their separate sheets of paper, the
players write down words with a total of
12, 13, 14, or more letters (but all must
have the same number of letters). They
then fold the sheets of paper in order to
cover the words and they mix up the
sheets of paper and redistribute them to
all of the players.

The object of the game is to compose
a complete sentence from words that
begin with the single letters of the base
words in the order they are written.

■ The Play

The telegram must be a complete sentence. In the sentence, you can freely
insert punctuation (or, for a greater
"telegram effect," you can substitute the
punctuation with the classic "stop").

Inside the telegram, the players can
insert proper names of localities, etc.
The last letter of the base word can be
used as a signature.

If, for example, the base word is
OVERBEARINGLY, a valid sentence
would be Only Very Eager Rabbits
Breed Stop Every Animal Rears Infants
Stop Nature Gives Life—Young.

Whoever completes a telegram first
wins if, according to the judgment of the
other players, he or she has written a
sentence that makes sense.

If they would like, the players can
write on the pieces of paper fifteen or
more letters instead of a word. It is
important that the telegram be composed in the same order as the letters. If,
for example, the letters are AFNWB-
HGLPFDCHSB, the sentence can be:
Arrived Fourth November With Brian
Stop Hotel Glorious Luxurious Pool
Food Delicious Stop Call Home Soon—
Barbara.

■ Strategy

This game requires a healthy dose of creativity. As always, in this type of word
game it does not hurt to have a dictionary at hand.

If you want to play with young children, use easy and short words.

OLD FAVORITES

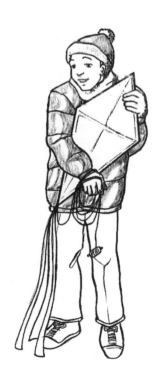

ANIMAL, VEGETABLE, MINERAL

This is a game several people can play together. It stimulates the imagination, and players can compete individually or in teams. The level of fun will escalate with players who can think up creative and challenging subjects for the group to guess.

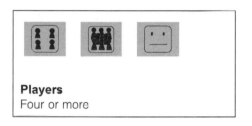

Players
Four or more

▤ Start & Object of the Game

One player must be the judge; another player will be the arbiter who thinks up a subject for the others to guess.

The remaining players (divided into teams) must try to guess the subject the arbiter chooses.

▤ The Play

The arbiter secretly tells the judge the subject, and he then tells the remaining players which of the three categories it falls into: animal, vegetable, or mineral.

All living beings are animals, and so are all the objects obtained from a living being. Thus, the category of animal includes, for example, both a cow as well as shoes that are made of leather.

All plants, flowers, fruits, and roots are vegetables, and so are the things made from them, such as a table of wood.

All inorganic substances are minerals, and so are the things that come from them such as a stone or a mirror.

After the nature of the subject to be guessed is stated, the participants, or the teams, take turns asking the arbiter 20 questions, to which the arbiter can respond only by saying "yes" or "no."

Every player, or team, has three tries to guess the answer.

The judge keeps count of the questions and clarifies whether the questions as well as the responses given by the arbiter are correct. If there are disputes, the judge and the arbiter may consult each other during the game. In the end, the judge makes the final decision.

The first player, or team, who guesses the subject correctly at any point wins.

▤ Strategy

The mode of asking the questions is important. It is better to ask more general questions in the beginning in order to narrow down the field. As the game continues, it is a good idea to ask more specific questions which focus in on the answer.

Everyone also needs to pay attention to the questions asked by the opponents. Even if they do not follow your same logic, they can provide you with useful hints in figuring out the subject. Also, before trying to guess the answer, think about it carefully. Three tries can be used up quickly!

KITES

People fly kites all over the world, but especially in the Far East where they are often used to evoke historical events and ancient legends, or as parts of a ritual, or in actual competitions or even in battles, during which the tail of the kite is constructed with materials that make it strong and sharp. In these types of battles, the participants try to intercept the tails of the opponents' kites and to cut them down, in order to destroy the opponents' kites.

Players
One or more

Game Equipment
- One kite for each player

■ Start & Object of the Game

In order to fly a kite alone, you need to hold it with one hand, giving it a nudge so it will rise into the air, and then moving back into the wind while letting more and more of the string out.

Having someone release the kite will allow you to launch it more easily, and little by little the wind will lift it. The string will continue to unwind slowly from the reel and the kite will be flying.

■ The Play

Naturally, in order to fly a kite, the presence of wind is necessary; a breeze, even if it is modest, is more than sufficient for kites, which are very light objects.

More complex and heavy kites will need a more sustained wind and definitely need the help of a second person during the launch, while you gradually unwind the kite's string from the reel.

MAKING A KITE FLY WELL

It is best if the string is always a little tense, and at the first instance of a loss of control, you immediately have to reel in enough string in order to stabilize the kite's flying position.

Furthermore, you always have to be ready for a sudden stop of wind. When this happens, reel in enough string quickly until you find another current of wind that will hold the kite in the air.

There is also the risk of tangling the string of your kite with the string of another person's kite. When this happens, both kites usually fall instantly!

Each time before flying your kite, make sure it is not damaged (the supporting structure of the kite, the canvas, or the paper) and make sure the string is securely attached to the kite.

When flying kites with other people, each with his own kite, it is exciting to compete to see who can fly their kite at the highest altitude.

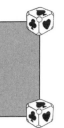

JACKS

Originally, the game Jacks was played with the small bones in a sheep's ankle, which since antiquity were used both to predict the future, and for pure entertainment. The ritual component of Jacks has long been lost, but the game of Jacks, or the Game of the Five Stones, is still enjoyed all over the world as a pastime which tests a player's ability, and allows participants to place bets on the outcome.

Players
From one to four

Game Equipment
- Actual Jacks, or five small stones all of the same size, or small plastic cubes *(Fig. 1)*
- A small ball (for variations)

Fig. 1 – The Jacks.

■ Start & Object of the Game

If you play with other people, all of the participants decide by luck of the draw who goes first. The remaining players then take turns.

The object of the game is to toss and catch the small Jacks according to the preestablished rules and plans.

■ The Play

One way to start the game is for each player to carry out an initial toss, called flipping. Gather the Jacks in the palm of your hand, tossing them in the air and catch them on the back of your hand; then, continue by tossing the ones you caught in the air again but catch them in the palm of your hand *(Fig. 2)*.

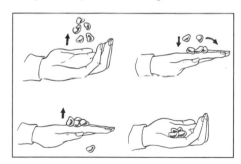

Fig. 2 – In order to begin the game, you need to carry out the initial toss.

If a player does not catch any of the five Jacks, he passes his turn.

"ONESIES"
On the other hand, if a player catches at least one Jack, he may continue with the game known as "Onesies." The player leaves the fallen Jacks where they are, and keeps only one, the "father," in his

hand. The player tosses the "father" in the air and quickly grabs one of the Jacks from the ground before catching the "father" in the palm of the hand again. If the player does it without letting the father Jack fall, he then places the Jack grabbed from the ground to the side and continues tossing until he has collected all of the Jacks. Once finished gathering the Jacks, the next player takes a turn. Instead of the father jack, a small ball can be tossed in the air and let to bounce and then caught, while before it is caught a jack is scooped up.

"TWOSIES" & OTHER VARIATIONS

"Twosies" begins with 4 Jacks on the ground and one in hand. The player tosses as in "Onesies," but in this game each time the player tosses the father Jack in the air, he must grab two Jacks before catching the father. The player then puts those two Jacks to the side and tosses the father Jack again in order to grab the last two Jacks. This can be played tossing a small ball in the same way as for onesies.

You can play "Threesies" in a similar way (while tossing the father Jack in the air, grab three and then only one Jack. In "Foursies" all four jacks on the ground are picked up at once *(Fig. 3)*.

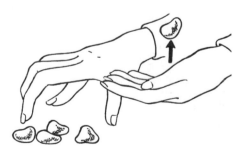

Fig. 3 - In Foursies four jacks are picked up at once.

The number of Jacks on the surface to be picked up can be increased to ten, and the same game played from Onsies to Tensies and back again.

In another variation of "Onsies" the players put four Jacks on the ground, and then one player tosses the father Jack in the air and grabs one Jack from the ground before catching the father Jack. Then, keeping the collected Jack in hand, the player tosses both that Jack and the father Jack in the air and grabs a third Jack from the ground before catching the other two. The player continues tossing and catching the Jacks in this manner until he tosses four Jacks in the air and grabs the fifth. The player then concludes his turn with the initial toss of all the Jacks (palm-backhand-palm).

MAKING MISTAKES & WINNING

Each time you make a mistake, the turn automatically passes to another player. On your next turn, you begin exactly where you left off on your last turn. Whoever completes the entire sequence first wins the game.

◼ Strategy

Lots of practice with Jacks is absolutely necessary in order to succeed at this game. It is a very entertaining pastime which may also help enhance the players' imagination by creating personalized versions of the game and challenging their friends.

FANCIES

Fancies are specialty jacks rounds, in which the players decide how many and what kinds of tricky ways (fancies) of picking up the Jacks will be included. A certain pattern of activity would make up a single, personalized fancy.

MARBLES

*This is a popular game all over the world and throughout time,
from Ancient Egypt to the United States of America, the game of marbles—
of whatever type and size—is a favorite pastime of millions of children and adults!*

Players
Two or more

Game Equipment
- Marbles

Start & Object of the Game

Many versions of marbles exist and we will describe some of them below. First, we will explain the best technique for shooting a marble.

Put your hand on the ground with the index finger touching the surface. Then, press the tip of the thumb against the middle finger behind the marble.

In the games that require shooting the marbles from the point at which they are found, the hand is then positioned in the same way next to the marble.

Before shooting the marble, the player aims and then springs the middle finger off the thumb and flicks the marble in the desired direction.

Nearly all of the games require shooting the marbles in a set direction or directly at the other players' marbles, which, if hit, are collected. The play is either "for fair," accumulating points and returning marbles to the owner, or

"for keeps," winning the marbles according to the rules agreed on at the outset of the game.

Whoever has the most points or the most marbles or captures all the marbles wins the game.

The Play

The most common version of marbles is called "Boss Out" and is played with two or more players. The first player shoots one of his marbles, and the second player does the same aiming at the opponent's marble; if the second player hits the opponent's marble, he captures it and keeps it. At the next turn, the first player must use a new marble. After shooting that marble, the second player tries to hit it and capture it on his turn. If the marble the player shot does not hit the other marble, then, if the two marbles are close enough, he can attempt to "span" them. He places his index finger on his opponent's marble and his thumb on his own marble, and then draws his hand up while bringing his fingers together. If the two marbles hit, he collects both marbles. If he misses, the first player may shoot at either marble on the ground. Whoever captures all of the opponent's marbles or the most marbles after a preestablished number of turns wins the game.

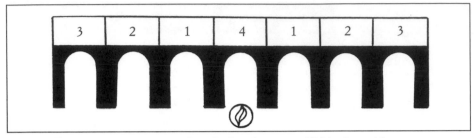

Fig. 1 – The necessary structure for playing the game "Bridgeboard."

BRIDGEBOARD

To play "Bridgeboard," players need to make a small wood board or cardboard with cutouts *(Fig. 1)*. Each arch corresponds to a certain number of points (3 for the farthest arches, then 2, then 1, and finally 4 for the center). Players can make bridges with more or different-sized arches. The greatest number of points is assigned to the smallest arch. The players take turns shooting their marbles and they aim for an arch (without hitting the borders!). The players keep score as the game proceeds. After the players finish a certain number of preestablished turns, whoever has accumulated the most points wins.

RINGER

In the game "Ringer," the players draw two concentric circles on the ground, one of about 12 inches in diameter, and the other of about six to ten feet. Each player puts several marbles inside the small circle (the players can decide on the number of marbles). Taking turns, each player shoots a marble from the boundary of the big circle. If a marble hits another marble or pushes another marble outside the boundary of the small circle, the player captures that marble and gets another turn to flick his marble from whatever point it may be

within the boundaries of the game. If a player does not hit another marble, he leaves the marble where it is (each player begins his next turn from the place he last hit the marble) and the next player takes a turn. If there are marbles in the large circle, and they are hit or pushed out of the boundaries of the game (not inside the small circle, however), they are also captured. The game ends once there are no more marbles left inside the two circles. The players collect their initial marbles and then they count the number of marbles they captured from each player. Whoever captures the most marbles wins the game, and the winner also collects all the marbles that remain outside of the circles.

■ Strategy

The strategy is all in the shooting. In order to perfect shooting the marble, you must practice. There are no precise rules for how a player must shoot a marble. The method described here is considered most effective, but everyone is free to "invent" his own style. The number of marbles per player varies because everyone will have their own marbles and will play with those. Also, the number of marbles increases or decreases with every game based on who wins.

BOCCE BALL

The game of Bocce Ball is very popular in France and Italy.
North of the Alps, Bocce Ball is called Petanque and has ancient origins.
This pastime may even date back to Greece in the third century B.C.
and to Ancient Rome. In French villages today, you can still find dedicated teams
of Bocce Ball players who challenge each other everywhere, in the garden,
in the town square, on the street, or even on official Bocce Ball fields
which are usually surrounded by other players as well as curious spectators.

Players
Two or more (up to six, or eight) divided into two teams

Game Equipment
- Three or four bocce balls per team, usually made of iron (or of wood, or hard rubber), 3¼ inches (8 cm) in diameter
- One small bocce ball, 1½ inches (4 cm) in diameter, which is the target

■ Start & Object of the Game

The players can establish a field of any dimension or follow the French version, "Pentaque," for a regulation field 13 meters long by 3 meters wide (approx. 43 feet by 10 feet).

The players decide by a coin toss which team will begin the game. One player from the team that won the toss throws the small ball from one end of the field. The throw should be between about 15 and 30 feet (5 and 10 meters)— neither shorter nor longer.

Taking turns, the players of the two teams throw their own balls trying to get them closest to the small target ball.

■ The Play

If the initial throw of the small ball is not valid, the turn passes to the opposing team to rethrow the target ball.

Once the small target ball is in position, a player begins by throwing one of the larger balls in the direction of the smaller one. The player may roll the ball on the field or may throw it. After one player takes a turn, the opposing team designates a player to throw.

MAKING THE BEST THROW
A player throws a ball with the aim of placing it closer to the small target ball than the opponent. If the player does not succeed, he throws another one, until he has a ball in a better position than the opponent or the opposing team (and then the turn changes) or until a player or team has no more balls.

In the case that the turn passes to the other team because a player placed a ball closer to the smaller ball, the next player then tries to make an even better throw.

In the case that a team is forced to pass the because the player threw all of the balls, the opponent will then throw all of his balls, trying to throw them closer to the small target ball.

WINNING THE ROUND

Whoever threw the ball which landed closest to the small target ball than all the others wins the round and counts one point for every ball of his that is closer to the target ball than his opponents.

For example, a player who has a total of two points, one point for the first ball (the ball closest to the small target ball) and one point for the fourth ball (because the second and third ball were surpassed by the opponent's balls) wins the hand.

Whoever reaches 13 or 15 points first wins the game.

HITTING ANOTHER BALL

If one ball hits another ball (a player's own ball or an opponent's ball) or the small target ball, and moves it, nothing changes except the situation on the field. Indeed, the first rule of the game is that the point is always determined depending on where the small target ball winds up, even if that ball is hit and moved several times throughout the game.

THE ITALIAN VERSION

In the Italian version of Bocce Ball, there is a small peg in the center of the field—the field is 18 meters long and 2.5 meters wide (approx. 60 feet by 8 feet) At the beginning of the game, someone must throw the small ball from one end of the field to at least within 1.5 meters (5 feet) of the peg and more than 30 cm (1 foot) from one of the two sides. Taking turns, the players then proceed to throw the balls with the same rules as Petanque, except that if a ball that is rolled hits another ball or the small target ball it is disqualified, but this rule does not apply to a ball that is thrown (this is done to hit or move an opponent's ball or the small target ball on purpose). If the ball, however, fails to hit any target it is disqualified. Once all the balls are thrown, the players check to see who won the round and they count the points in the same way as in the French version. After each round, the teams change sides on the field.

Whoever reaches 15 or 18 points first wins the game.

■ Strategy

A player can also gain a point by moving the ball of an opponent or by moving the target ball, such as when an opponent's ball is so close to the target ball (a few centimeters) that it would be nearly impossible to make a better throw. The player may decide to try to hit the opponent's ball (or the target ball), in a way that changes the situation on the field. The best throw when making this move is to throw the ball in the air. After a long throw, your ball will land on that of your opponent and move it.

In order to identify your team's balls, some players put a symbol or name on them. Alternately, you can designate a judge who keeps track of the various balls and to whom they belong, or you can choose different colored balls.

At the end of a round, disagreements usually arise concerning the distance of the balls from the target ball. To avoid these disagreements, it is best to keep a tape measure or a measuring stick close by in order to measure the distances in an exact and irrefutable manner.

BUBBLES

Children and even babies love bubbles
almost as much as adults do.

Players
One or more

Game Equipment
- A bottle of prepared bubbles
(or soap water)
- A straw or a plastic bubble blower

■ Start & Object of the game

Dip the straw or the bubble blower in the bubble solution, then blow slowly and continually in order to create a big bubble which, with one decisive blow, will break away from the straw or bubble blower and float off.

■ The Play

With two or more people, you can compete with each other to make the biggest bubble, or to make the bubble that floats the highest or the farthest before popping.

Designate boundaries for the game about 10 feet by 10 feet, and draw a line on the ground that divides the players into two teams.

Each player, or team, stands in one half of the playing field. Players decide by luck of the draw who goes first. One player or one team then blows the biggest possible soap bubble with the straw.

As soon as the bubble breaks away from the straw, you must blow it (always using the straw) onto the opponents side of the field. When a bubble crosses the line to the opponent's side, your team gains a point.

On the other hand, if a bubble pops before crossing the line, the other team takes a turn. Whichever player or team reaches the preestablished number of points or accumulates the most points within a designated amount of time wins the game.

■ Strategy

One slow and measured blow usually creates one single bubble that will also be quite large. A fast blow, on the other hand, will produce a stream of different-sized bubbles. If you want to make a homemade bubble solution mix a cup of water and 4 tablespoons of liquid soap or glycerin.

Bring to a light boil and remove from the stove. Let the solution cool completely before using the "magic" mix!

If you do not want to use a straw, you can prepare a bubble blower (usually you find these bubble blowers inside the bubble solutions sold in stores) by folding a thin piece of wire into a hoop.

TREASURE HUNT

This is an entertaining game to play in teams outdoors,
or inside the house on a rainy day. With an able and imaginative organizer,
this game guarantees several hours of fun for everyone.

Players
Four or more, divided into at least
two teams, with one organizer

Game Equipment
- Small pieces of paper for writing
down instructions
- A treasure

▮ Start & Object of the game

The organizer creates the small pieces of
paper on which he writes instructions or
clues for finding the treasure. The organizer then hides the pieces of paper and
the treasure. Once teams are formed, the
organizer hands out a piece of paper
with the first hint to the whereabouts of
the other pieces of paper that are neede
to find the treasure.

The object of the game is to find all
the pieces of paper and win the treasure.

▮ The Play

The hints should be written in a such
way that everyone is able to figure out
the hiding place of the next piece of
paper and eventually the treasure.

The first hint should be written on as
many pieces of paper as there are teams.
The subsequent hints should be written
on one piece of paper only. The team
that finds the piece of paper should read
it and then hide it again exactly where
they found it, so that the other team or
teams can find it. The hints can be written as riddles as long as they direct the
players in the direction of the next piece
of paper. Whichever team finds the treasure first wins the game.

▮ Strategy

In another version of the game, players
can substitute the pieces of paper with
objects they must find. In that case, an
entire list of objects should be given to
the teams at the outset of the hunt (one
list per team) or the organizer must give
hints about the next objects right after
the preceding object has been found.
Whichever team gathers all of the
objects first and brings them to the organizer wins the game.

A good treasure hunt depends in
large part on the ability of the organizer
who will have to hide the hints, compose
challenging riddles, think of hard-to-
find objects for the players to search for,
and hide an inviting treasure, such as a
painted treasure box full of candy and
chocolate or a box full of gifts.

DARTS

There is not a pub in England without a dart board up on the wall. This British national pastime recalls the glorious tradition of medieval archery, when players used a section of a trunk as the center target and arrows used in battle for man-to-man warfare for darts.

Players
Two or more, divided into teams

Game Equipment
- A series of three darts for each player or team, about 6 inches long with a heavy point made of metal, a handle made of coarse metal (usually brass) or of wood, and a tail with feathers of plastic, paper or of actual feathers *(Fig. 1)*.
- A dart board made of cork, bristle or elm wood, 18 inches in diameter, divided into 20 numbered segments; with one outer circle for double points, and another for triple points; a center called a "bull's-eye" also with an outer circle; the adjacent sections are distinguished by color *(Fig. 2, p. 284)*
- A chalk board for keeping track of points

Fig. 1 - Typical darts.

Start & Object of the game

Each player, or a member of each team, throws a dart. Whoever throws the dart closest to the center of the board begins the game.

When people play in teams, the players establish the order each member will throw for each team.

The object of the game is to decrease to zero the initial score beginning at either 301, 501, and 1001 points.

The Play

The target must be hung vertically so that its center is 5 feet 6 inches (1.7 meters) from the ground, and the players throw 8 feet (2.5 meters) from the target.

On every turn, each player throws all three darts one at a time. The score is calculated by the number of the section where the dart lands. That score is multiplied by two if the dart lands in the outer circle and by three if it lands in the inner circle. The "bull's eye" is worth 50 points, and its outer circle 25 points.

SUBTRACTING POINTS
At the end of a turn, the player subtracts the sum of the points on the dart board

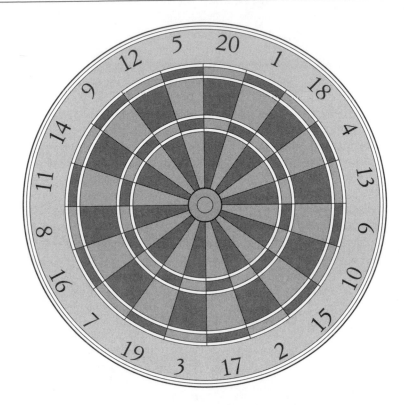

Fig. 2 – The organization of the different sections and relative points on a dart board.

from the total and writes down the remaining points on the chalk board. If, for example, the game begins at 301 points and the first player hits a double 5, a 13, and a 7, the player will subtract 30 points from 301 and will write 271 on the chalk board.

In order to begin subtracting points, it is necessary to hit a double in the beginning of the game. Its value and that of all the points obtained afterwards are subtracted from the total.

The player, or the team, who subtracts the total number of initial points first wins the game. The subtraction process must be accomplished with an exact score.

If at the end of three throws (that qualify as a total, not subtracted individually, but altogether), a player obtains a score too high to be subtracted, the entire turn is disqualified.

■ Strategy

Everyone must create his own way of throwing the darts. In general, the dart is gripped with the thumb, index, and middle fingers. You take aim, practice the motion and finally throw it according to your own style. Of course, you must remain the required distance from the dart board and throw with your feet together.

KIM'S GAME

A fun and instructive game, especially for very young children
(but depending on the difficulty it is appropriate really for everyone).
Kim's Game stimulates observational and memory skills of the participants.

Players
Two or more, divided into teams,
with one organizer

Game Equipment
- A tray
- Ten or more small and different
objects that can be placed on the
tray
- A cloth napkin large enough to
cover the tray
- A piece of paper and a pen
for each player or team

▧ Start & Object of the game

The organizer prepares the tray with
objects which are unknown to the participants and he then covers the tray
with the cloth napkin.

Each participant, or team, is given a
piece of paper and a pen.

The organizer uncovers the tray in
front of the participants, showing them
the objects (Fig. 1) for only a brief
moment, 30 seconds to two to three
minutes—dpending on the number of
objects, on the ability and age of the participants, and on the number of members on each team. Finally, the organizer
covers the tray again.

The object of the game is to list as
many objects as you can remember.

Fig 1 - Example of objects to put on a tray.

■ The Play

During the observation of the objects, taking notes is prohibited. Participants can use the pen and paper only once the tray is covered again.

The organizer establishes a time limit (for example one turn of an hourglass) after which the participants must give the pieces of paper with their lists written on them to the organizer.

The player or team who listed everything or the most objects wins the game.

■ Strategy

Everyone has his own method for remembering objects. Whoever is blessed with a photographic memory, for example, will use the time to view the objects to make a mental picture of the contents on the tray.

Or, you can try to construct a sentence that contains the names of the objects in order to remember.

For example, the tray in Figure 1 contains a pen, a glass, a necklace, a teddy bear, and a magazine.

You can construct this sentence: "With the pen, I designed a teddy bear wearing a necklace who drank from a glass on the magazine."

Naturally, this system only works with a few objects, or if you have a lot of time to observe the objects, otherwise you will need a good imagination and a bit of creativity to come up with a quick way to remember the objects.

THE RING GAME

This game, also called Quoits, is popular throughout the world and has rural English origins. It is true that in place of rings, villagers in 1400 used horseshoes, a version that has become popular in the United States.

Players
Two or more, divided into teams

Game Equipment
- Two strong bases into which are driven two pegs *(Fig. 1)*
- Two rings, one per team

Fig. 1 – The bases with the peg.

■ Start & Object of the game

The players situate the bases with the pegs 50 feet from each other.

The players decide by luck of the draw which player or team goes first. When playing in teams, the teams decide the order in which each player will toss the ring.

The object of the game is to arrive at the established number of points first, for example, 11 or 20 points.

■ The Play

The players take turns throwing. Each player, or member of a team, positions himself directly in front of the team's base (the player's heels must touch the base) and he throws the ring toward the opponent's base. Whoever rings the peg, scores a point and can take another turn.

If the ring does not fall around the peg, the turn passes to the other player or team.

Whoever arrives at the established number of points first, wins the game.

■ Strategy

It is best to throw the ring while holding it horizontally and parallel to the ground. The more your hand moves in a straight line and the less it curves, the more the throw will be precise. Also, as in all games that require throwing, everyone will eventually create his own throwing technique.

Another version of the game has a different kind of base with pegs of different heights which are worth a different number of points (inversely proportional to the height of the peg).

HOPSCOTCH

Originating in ancient Rome, this is undoubtedly a popular game among children who draw Hopscotch courses on pavements all around the world.

Players
Two or more

Game Equipment
- A piece of chalk to draw the Hopscotch course
- A pebble for each player (approximately the same size for each)

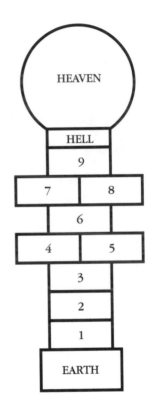

Fig. 1 Pattern of the game to draw with the chalk.

■ Start & Object of the Game

Draw the pattern as shown in Figure 1 with the chalk on the ground.

Players decide by luck of the draw who goes first.

The purpose of the game is to get through the whole pattern with your pebble, jumping from square to square.

■ The Play

The first player starts from Earth and throws the pebble into square 1; hops on one foot from Earth to square 1; bends (always standing on one foot) and picks up the pebble. Then the player returns to Earth, where she can stand on both feet. Here the player gets ready to throw the pebble again, this time into square 2, to which the player must jump on one foot, and so on until square 9.

Whoever arrives at square 9 throws the pebble into Heaven, where, after arriving by jumping on one foot, the player can stop to rest on both feet before starting the return, which is to say from Heaven to square 9, then to square 8, and so on until she reaches Earth.

Whoever throws the pebble in the wrong square, on the line, or outside of the pattern and/or who supports herself with both feet while jumping or picking up the pebble, looses her turn and the turn passes to the next player. When it is her turn again, the player will start from where she left off.

Whoever throws the pebble into the Hell square looses her turn, and when it is her turn again, must start all over from Earth, instead of the point where she previously was interrupted.

THROWING THE PEBBLE

Whoever completes the whole route from Earth to Heaven and back stands on the Earth square facing in the opposite direction of the pattern and throws the pebble over her shoulder. If the pebble lands in a square, this square will be marked with her name. In the subsequent rounds of the game when the player arrives in the square with her name, she may rest there with both feet; meanwhile, all the other players must skip the square with her name. Pay attention though: if the pebble lands on a square, which has already been marked by the name of another player, or on Hell, the toss is no good and cannot be repeated.

SUBSEQUENT SEQUENCES OF STEPS

Once one sequence is completed, the following rounds become more and more difficult.

Once the player picks up the pebble from square 1, she must throw it on Earth in order to come back. The same for square 2, etc. until square 9. Then, the players do the same only this time throwing the pebble to Heaven.

Upon finishing this round, the player throws the pebble over her shoulder and she marks this square with her name, if this square has not been marked before by the names of other players.

Then, the players must go through the whole pattern in both directions, by pushing the pebble (i.e., not throwing it) with the tip of the foot each jumps with; then, by keeping the pebble in balance on the back of the hand and then on the head, stopping whenever the pebble falls.

At the end of every round, the player tries to conquer a square by marking it.

The first player who either accomplishes all the sequences agreed upon at the beginning of the game, or throws the pebble over her shoulder conquering Heaven wins.

■ Strategy

The true and only secrets of succeeding in this game, of which only one among more than a thousand variations has been shown here, are a good aim to reach each square with one's own pebble and a sense of balance to jump easily from one square to the next.

Before starting the game, the most important thing is that all the players agree upon the rules by which they will play and the sequences they will follow.

MIKADO

This popular pastime, also known as Shanghai, clearly has a Chinese origin;
nowadays, it has spread all over the world.

Players
Two or more

Game Equipment
- A bundle of sticks with different colors. There should be 40 sticks, of which 20 are yellow, 10 are red, 5 are blue, 3 are green, and 2 are white-red striped

■ Start & Object of the Game

A player gathers the bundle of sticks in his hands, and then opens his hands, letting the sticks fall so that they form a casually scattered heap. The play moves in clockwise order from the player who dropped the sticks.

The player who dropped the bundle starts first, picking up the sticks from the heap.

The object of the game is to pick up the sticks with the highest score.

■ The Play

Each stick is worth a number of points: the yellow sticks are worth 3 points, the red sticks 5 points, the blue sticks 10 points, the green sticks 15 points and the white-red sticks 20 points *(Fig. 1)*.

Once a stick has been touched, it must be picked up: a player may not change his mind. Even when a stick (besides the one the player tries to pick up) has been slightly touched, the turn passes on to the next player. A stick that has been touched and has changed position must be left as is. Whoever picks up one of the two white-red sticks can use it to pick up the remaining sticks. When there are no more sticks left, each player calculates his score. The player with the highest score wins.

■ Strategy

Patience, carefulness, and a steady hand are really fundamental for this game. At each move one needs to observe carefully the position of the sticks in order to mark out the easiest to pick up.

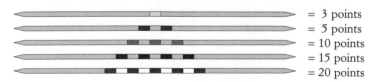

= 3 points
= 5 points
= 10 points
= 15 points
= 20 points

Fig 1- The sticks for the game.

ODDS & EVENS

Known all over the world from Italy to China
(homelands of the two most widespread versions), Odds and Evens
probably owes its fortune to the fact that it does not require any equipment,
hence, this game can actually be played anywhere and at any time.
Moreover, it gives the possibility to bet (for the players
and for the spectators) on the outcome.

Players
Two

Game Equipment
- Nothing but hands!

■ Start & Object of the Game

One of the two players counts: "One, two, three," then both players show two or three fingers and at the same time they both say if the total is even or odd. Whoever guesses the correct answer gets

2 points. If neither player guesses the outcome because, for example, both say "odd," and it comes out even, the turn is void. If both guess correctly, they each get one point.

■ The Play

The players alternate starting the turn with the typical technique of counting out. The player with the highest total after 10 or 15 hands wins.

A VARIANT OF "ODDS & EVENS"

A variant of this game is for the players to take turns saying either "even" or "odd" before revealing fingers. In this case, there is no tie because if one says "even," the other automatically gets

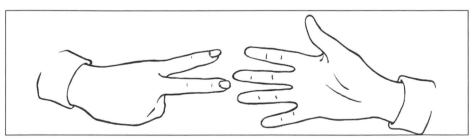

Fig. 1 - In a classical variation (see page 292) one of the two players counts: "One, two, three," then both players show a certain number of fingers and at the same time each says a number to try to guess the total.

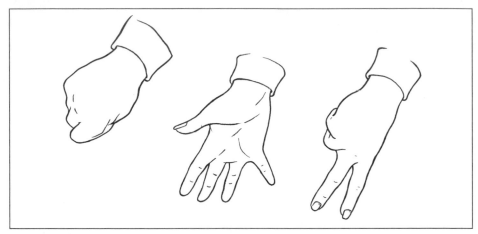

Fig 2 - The different "Figures" of Rock, Paper, Scissors.

"odd." Whoever wins gets one point. If the player who is taking the turn is wrong, the point goes to the opponent.

A CLASSICAL VARIATION

In a classical version of Odds and Evens one of the two players counts: "One, two, three," then both players show a certain number of fingers and at the same time they both say a number *(Fig. 1, on page 291).*

The object of the game is to guess the total of the fingers "played" (one 's own and those of the opponent).

The players alternate starting the turn with the typical technique of counting out.

The player may show from one to five fingers or a closed fist, which stands for zero. If a player says "Ten!" he plays 5 fingers and counts on the chance the opponent will do the same. Whoever guesses the total of the fingers that have been shown wins the turn, and gets 2 points. If neither player guesses the exact total, the turn is void.

If both the players guess the total outcome, they each earn 1 point. The play-er who has the highest total after 10 or 15 hands wins.

■ Rock Paper Scissors

The game Rock Paper Scissors is of Chinese origin and is more appropriate for younger players since it is not based on counting fingers, but on Figures that are made with the hand after the usual counting "one, two, three" (to be done in turns).

The closed fist stands for a stone, the opened hand for paper, and the index and middle fingers forming a V (with the other fingers closed in a fist) indicate the figure of scissors *(Fig. 2).*

Rock wins over scissors because scissors cannot cut stone; scissors win over paper because the scissors can cut paper; paper wins over stone because paper wraps the stone.

If both players show the same Figure, the turn is void.

The player who wins the turn gets one point.

The player who gets the highest score after 10 or 15 hands wins.

TIDDLYWINKS

Tiddlywinks is a familiar game for children which actually requires some skill, making the game fun even for grown-ups. In any case, it is a favorite with those who have a good aim and the instinct to guess at the trajectory of the winks that when flicked can also take unexpected directions.

Players
Two or more

Game Equipment
- A set of 4 winks (small disks made of bone or plastic of one-half to one inch diameter) per player;
- One shooter for each player (Fig. 1)
- A cup

Fig. 1 – The shooter and a set of 4 winks.

Start & Object of the Game

The play area must be established. A part of the floor or the surface of a round table works well.

Place the cup in the center of the play area that has been agreed upon.

Each player shoots a wink from the edge of the play area: the player who gets closest to the cup starts to play, the other players follow in clockwise order.

The object of the game is to shoot all your winks into the cup.

The Play

The players begin at the border of the table or play area. From there they can shoot any of their winks, unless they are blocked. To shoot a wink, one must press firmly upon the edge using the biggest wink *(Fig. 2):* this will make the wink fly.

Every time a player manages to get a wink in the cup, he continues his turn. However, if the wink does not land in

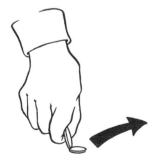

Fig. 2 - To shoot a wink, one must press firmly upon the border using the biggest wink: this will make the wink fly.

the cup, the player leaves it where it is (from there, he can start again if he wants, in the next turn) and passes the turn.

BLOCKED WINK

A wink is temporarily out of play if it is blocked or only partly blocked by an opponent's wink *(Fig. 3)*. The owner can again play with his blocked wink only after the opponent's wink, which covers it, has freed it (by shooting the wink on top). Or, the owner can free it by himself by hitting the opponent's wink with one of his own winks.

Fig. 3 - A wink is temporarily out of play when it is blocked or only partly blocked by an opponent's wink.

A wink that is unstable, vertical, or leaning against the outside of the cup *(Fig. 4)* is also blocked. It can be freed by another wink belonging to the same side or to the opponent that hits it and

Fig. 4 - A wink that is unstable, vertical or leaning against the outside of the cup is also blocked.

causes it to fall flat on the surface of the play area.

When playing on a table, a wink that falls off the table is picked up and placed on the edge of the area from which it fell.

The first player who gets all his winks in the cup or, alternatively, who after a preestablished number of turns has the most winks in the cup wins.

■ Strategy

The strategy is in the successful shooting of the winks. The shooter must touch a very small part of the wink's edge so that the leap is precise. Moreover, it is necessary to skillfully balance the amount of pressure exercised on the shooter in order to avoid very long leaps.

JUMP-ROPE

*Children all over the world have jumped rope, alone or in groups,
since the beginning of time. This is a jumping game
that, besides being an enjoyable pastime, is also aerobic exercise
included in the training of athletes, especially boxers.*

Players
One, two or more

Game Equipment
- A rope with two handles
at its ends, usually made of wood
or plastic *(Fig. 1)*

Fig. 1 - A typical jump rope.

■ Start & Object of the Game

Playing alone, one holds the rope at
both ends, one in each hand, keeping it
behind the legs. Then, one moves the
arms so that an arc is formed with the
rope. When the rope reaches the feet in
front of oneself, it must be jumped with
both feet together or one foot at a time.

When there are two players, one hand
of the rope is attached to a pole, and the
other is held by one of the two players.
The player then begins turning the rope,
which forms an arc in which the play-
mate jumps.

When there are more players, two
players turn the rope and the third
jumps. The other participants take turns
jumping after her.

The object of the game is to accomplish certain figures.

■ The Play

This game is generally played in large
groups in which two players turn the
rope and the others enter the arch and
leave it, doing the established figures.

If one jumps alone or with a group,
songs or nursery rhymes can be sung to
help keep the pace. One can also change
the jumps (from both feet to one foot at
a time) and the direction (from back to
front and vice versa).

THE GAME OF BOSS
In this game a boss must be nominated,
who enters first, singing the chorus of a
song or of a nursery rhyme, and at the

same time, she has to complete a certain number of jumps. Then, she leaves and lets the second player enter, who must complete the same number of jumps and sing the same chorus, and so on.

Alternatively, the boss chooses a song or a nursery rhyme that everybody knows and starts with it, completing a certain number of jumps: the others must do the same number jumps and at the same time continue the song verse by verse. Whoever makes a mistake in singing or jumping replaces one of the players turning the rope.

THE GAME OF JUMPS

In the game of Jumps, two participants turn the rope and the others take turns entering the rope, jump once, and leave. On the next turn, they enter, jump twice and leave, and so on.

Whoever makes a mistake substitutes one of the players holding the rope.

THE BOAT

The rope is not turned but only swung, at the beginning close to the ground, by two participants, while the others jump it by turn, one or two times, without touching it with their feet. After the first turn, the rope is swung higher off the ground and so on. Whoever grazes against or stumbles over the rope in their jump is eliminated from the game. The last player who remains in the game after not touching the rope wins.

■ Strategy

Being in good shape is a fundamental requirement to jump rope. It is important that whoever turns the rope keeps a constant rhythm. While the others jump, everybody has the time to observe this rhythm and get used to it, managing to enter the game at the right moment, avoiding stumbling.

TOPS

*Since ancient Rome, Tops have been a favorite game of children
and at the same time are an instrument for both pagan
and Judeo-Christian rituals almost everywhere in the world.*

Players
One, two or more

Game Equipment
- A top with a handle *(Fig. 1)* or shaped as a "peg top" provided with a thin cord to put it in motion

Fig. 1- A top with a handle.

■ Start & Object of the Game

Place the top on the ground on its tip, keeping it perpendicular to the surface upon which it stands.

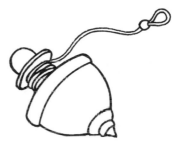

Fig.2- A top known as "peg top" provided with a thin cord to put it in motion.

Grasp the top by the handle, set it in motion with a clean spin, and quickly release it.

The top with the thin cord must be held with one hand while the other pulls the cord in a quick, fluid motion.

The goal of the game is to set the top spinning so that it keeps spinning on its tip as long as possible.

■ The Play

The tops may be spun for fun alone, trying to keep them in motion as long as possible.

THE WAR OF THE TOPS
Wars can be fought, playing together with other playmates. Whoever is able to intercept and push over the opponent's

top, and prevent his own top's stopping spinning, wins. If, however, both tops stop spinning in the collision, the war is only a draw.

HITTING BULL'S-EYE

A circle with concentric rings numbered 1 to 10 (from the outside to the center) is drawn on the ground with a piece of chalk.

The players take turns setting their tops in motion, directing them toward the center of the drawing.

When the top stops spinning, each player marks the points in the circle which correspond to where the top stopped.

The first who earns an established number of points wins.

■ Strategy

In tops, one needs to become good at spinning successfully and to gauge the strength applied with the hand in order to keep the top spinning steadily for as long as possible.

IMPORTANCE OF SPEED

It must be noted that the faster a top spins, the less it moves forward, the technique that results in winning the bull's-eye game mentioned above.

As well a fast-spinning top is very difficult to push over; therefore, this technique works well in the game of war, since in order to win the game the top must continue to spin after pushing over the opponent's top.

PUZZLES

BILBOQUET

A pastime requiring a good deal of skill, Bilboquet was played in the French court
of the past, as well as among Eskimos and Native Americans, who today
remain the real wizards of this game that is endowed with ritual meanings,
which, as it often happens, come from these peoples.

Players
One

Game Equipment
- A bilboquet made with a handle
that ends in a tip and a pierced ball,
which is attached to the handle by a
thin rope *(Fig. 1)*

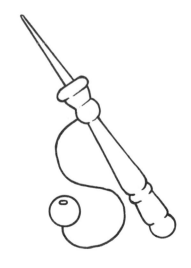

Fig. 1- A classic bilboquet.

Start & Object of the Game

Grasp the Bilboquet and with a quick
hand motion, cast up the ball, trying to
thread it directly on the tip.

The Play

The Bilboquet used by the Eskimos has,
instead of the ball, fragments of bones
that may have more holes. According to
their dimensions, it is more or less difficult to thread them.

Similarly, there may be more balls
(two or three). The skill does not rest
only in threading them all, but also in
not accidentally unthreading the first
ball when you are attempting to thread
the second.

Finally, there is a variation, where at
the top of the handle a cup or a small
glass is fixed, in which the ball lands
after being flung up.

Strategy

Seemingly easy, Bilboquet requires
remarkable skill in gauging the movement of the wrist in first casting the ball
upward, and then directing the point of
the handle toward the hole of the ball.
Repeated practice is the only means to
become an expert.

MATCHES

Games with matches have very old origins (in the past, of course, rather than matches, decorated sticks or pebbles were used to play). Brain teasers, solitaires, games to play in twos, puzzles and riddles to present to friends are all entertaining pastimes that require very few instruments!

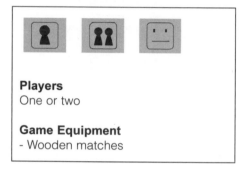

Players
One or two

Game Equipment
- Wooden matches

Start & Object of the Game

One of the oldest games with matches is Nim, adapted at the beginning of the century in Nimbi. It is a game to play in twos. The matches must be laid out in an established pattern: then, the two players alternate in removing the matches from the patterns.

The Play

The pattern in Figure 1 features a certain number of small groups of one's choice; each group is formed with a different number of matches. The players decide by luck of the draw who starts the game, and they alternate in picking up the matches.

The player can pick up as many matches as he wants, provided that they all belong to the same group. Whoever picks up the last match or matches wins.

GEOMETRIC SHAPES

The pattern of Figure 2 provides the shape of a square or rectangle of any dimensions. The players pick up, at their turn, one or more matches, either from a row or a column. The matches must be adjacent to each other, which is to say,

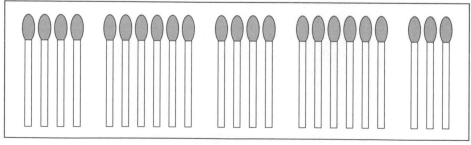

Fig. 1 - Initial pattern of the match game Nim.

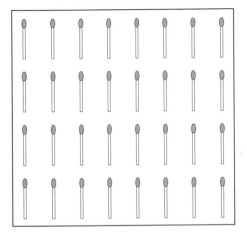

Fig. 2 - Nimbi, a variant of Nim.

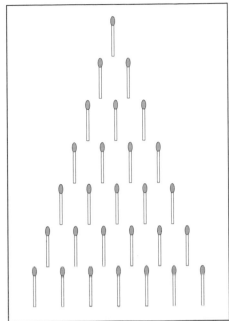

Fig. 3 - Variant of Nimbi

if one picks up three matches from the center of a row, the other player cannot pick up the remaining matches of the same row in one move. However, in two separate moves, he can pick up the matches preceding the "gap" and then the other matches following it.

On the contrary, an entire row or column can be picked up in only one move. Whoever picks up the last match or matches wins.

The pattern of Figure 3 is played and won according to the above-described rules, but, obviously, the matches can only be picked up horizontally.

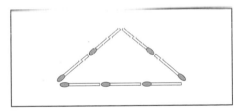

Fig. 4 - With these matches three adjacent triangles must be formed.

PUZZLES WITH MATCHES

Puzzles with matches may be played alone or, once they are solved, presented to a friend. With the same matches *(Fig. 4)*, three adjacent triangles must be formed.

From Figure 5, six matches must be removed to form three squares.

From Figure 6 on page 304, five matches must be removed in order to obtain five triangles.

The pattern of Figure 7 on page 304 provides the starting point of three

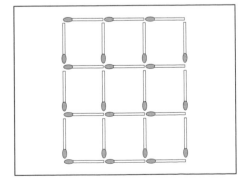

Fig. 5

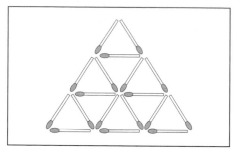

Fig. 6 - Five matches must be removed in order to obtain five triangles.

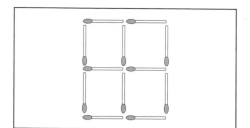

Fig. 7

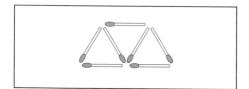

Fig. 8 - Solution of Figure 4.

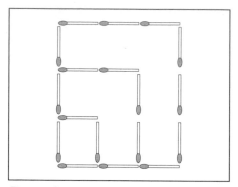

Fig. 9 - Solution of Figure 5.

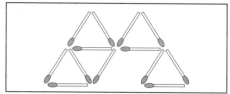

Fig. 10 - Solution of Figure 6.

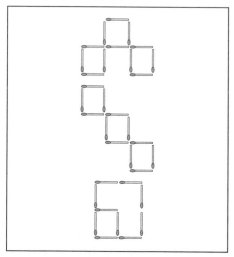

Fig. 11 - Solutions of the three problems contained in Figure 7.

different problems: moving three matches to get three squares; moving four matches to get three squares; moving two matches to get two squares.

Solutions are shown in Figures 8, 9, 10, and 11.

■ Strategy

For the game of Nim one must consider the possible moves of the opponent in order to anticipate him or, if one is skilled enough, to make the opponent lose the game.

Puzzles require a bit of reasoning but once you have found the solution, they will will seem much easier than you expected.

PENTAMINOES

*The name of this game of Greek origin implies that the patterns
are formed by the connection of five squares.
Pentaminoes is therefore, by definition, a geometrical puzzle
that offers numerous clues and almost infinite solutions!*

Players
One

Game Equipment
- Twelve pentaminoes,
shown in Figure 1

■ Start & Object of the Game

Gather the pentaminoes on a table, and
try to reassemble the Figure of the problem that one has decided to solve.

■ The Play

Watch out! For each problem there is
not just one way to solve it, but many
possible ways to find a solution!

For example, a rectangle that is ten
squares long by six suares high can be
assembled in 2399 different ways!

In Figures 2, 3, and 4 on page 306 we
propose three solutions . . . a drop in the
ocean!

Your task is to discover at least a hundred more!

Another problem is forming two rectangles each 5 squares long by 6 squares
high, each made of 6 pieces. One solution of this problem, of course, is shown
in Figure 5, on page 306.

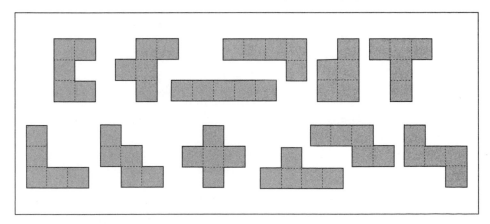

Fig.1 - The twelve Pentaminoes.

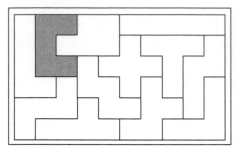

Fig. 2 - A possible solution of the problem to compose a rectangle of ten squares of base and six squares of height.

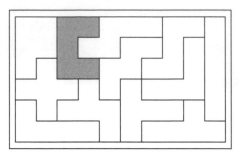

Fig. 4 - Another variant of the solution of the problem shown in Figure 1.

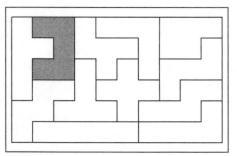

Fig. 3 - A variant of the solution of the problem shown in Figure 1.

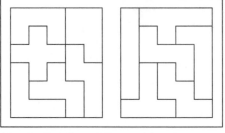

Fig. 5 - Solution of the problem to assemble two rectangles of six squares of height and with a base of five, each composed by six pieces.

■ Strategy

Patience, ability and reasoning: these qualities are all involved in the solutions of the problems.

Finally, do not underestimate the power of engaging your creativity, which allows you to guess at solutions that are difficult to find. Like Tangram, Pentaminoes can be played even by younger players, giving them the freedom to "create" any nuber of interesting figures, a pastime that will stimulate their imagination and logic.

POLYOMINOES

A game of logic and geometry invented by the American mathematician Solomon Golomb at the beginning of the 1950s, it is the progenitor of the Pentaminoes and is based on cards made of squares connected to each other only by one side.

Players
One

Game Equipment
- A gameboard that has six squares on each side *(Fig. 1)*
- Ten polyminoes, pieces made of one or more squares (with a maximum of five), connected to each other by only one side.

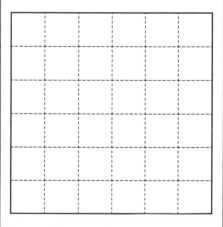

Fig. 1 - The gameboard is divided into squares, with six on each side.

■ Start & Object of the Game

Cover the whole gameboard connecting the ten pieces to each other.

■ The Play

The polyominoes *(Fig. 2)* are described, according to their squares, as monominoes, duominoes (both single pieces, made of one or two squares), triominoes (two pieces made of three squares each), tetraminoes (three pieces made of four squares each) and pentaminoes (three pieces made of five squares each).

Fig. 2 - The ten Polyominoes.

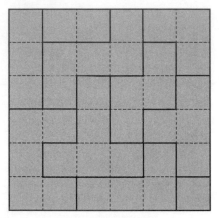

Fig. 3 - Solution of the game.

The solution of the game is shown in Figure 3.

Polyominoes can stimulate a child's creativity, by inviting her to form any number of figures, or patterns of figures like those in Tangram and Pentaminoes.

■ Strategy

Sharp logic and imagination are the characteristics needed for this extremely demanding game—one that will without a doubt tanatalize the those fascinated by geometrical puzzles.

SQUARES

*Squares is a mathematical puzzle that in the past was believed
to have magical and divinatory powers. The game of the Squares has been
in more recent times preferred by scientists, architects and inventors
such as the American Benjamin Franklin.*

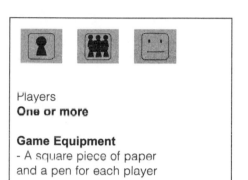

Players
One or more

Game Equipment
- A square piece of paper
and a pen for each player

▬ Start & Object of the Game

Each player draws a square made of
three small squares per side on the
paper. Object of the game is to fill the
squares with numbers from one to nine
in a way such that the sum of the three
numbers horizontally, vertically, and
diagonally always equals 15.

▬ The Play

Each player must fill the square with the
numbers in the aforementioned way.
The first who completes his square wins.

▬ Strategy

This is a puzzle that requires mathematical skill if played in a square made of 9

squares, but the bigger the area of the
square gets the more interesting the
game becomes. However, there is a trick.

On the large square, dvidied into 9 ,
we can ideally draw "pyramids," one per
side which, with each side composed of
three little squares, merge to make up a
single central little square *(Fig. 1)*.

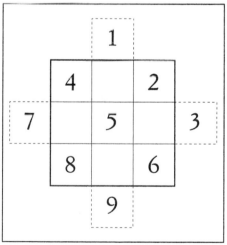

Fig. 1 - On the large square squared off
into 9 we can ideally draw "pyramids,"
one per side which, with each side
composed of three little squares, merge
to make up a single central little square.

In the first of the top squares we write
the number 1, then, going down diagonally we proceed with 2 and 3.

4	9	2
3	5	7
8	1	6

Fig. 2 - Solution of the game.

We skip a diagonal and we fill the next one with 4, 5, and 6, finally we complete the last diagonal with 7, 8 and 9; at this point, move the numbers of the external squares into the empty space directly opposite and the complete scheme of Figure 2 will appear: the solution of the game.

We do the same with a five-sided square *(Fig. 3)* with the pyramids formed by 3+1 squares and the diagonals alternately filled with numbers from 1 to 25; then the numbers of the external pyramids will be slid to their place, just as in the square of 9: the sum of every horizontal, vertical or diagonal row will be, in this case, 65.

Shown in bold are the numbers that have come from the external pyramids.

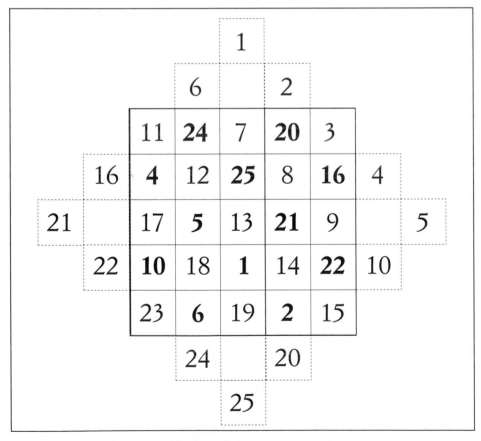

Fig. 3 - Continuing with the example: visualization of the development of the problem.

STAR
OF NAPOLEON

*This is a game of solitaire which is said to have been much loved
by the great historical character, who is renowned as a great connoisseur
of every kind of puzzle and game of skill.*

Players
One

Game Equipment
- A pattern in the shape
of a five-point star with 10 points
of intersection (Fig.1)
- 9 playing pieces

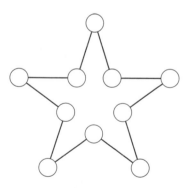

Fig. 1 - The basic scheme.

Start & Object of the Game

Put a piece on one of any of the points of
intersection. The object of the game is to
set the nine pieces on as many points of
intersection as you can.

The Play

The move of the first piece is free.

From the second piece on, this rule
has to be followed: the piece must be put
on a free point of intersection, then
moved to a second point adjacent to the
first (free or occupied) and finally placed
on a third point, which must be free and
adjacent to the previous point.

The solitaire is won when all pieces
have been put down.

A variation recalls classical solitaire:
once the nine pieces are set down on as
many points of intersection (leaving one
point out as preferred), only one piece
must remain on the pattern after having
removed all the others, by jumping them
as in the solitaire version.

Strategy

Logic and reasoning are fundamental to
solving all the puzzles. According to the
point from which one starts, the game
will have a different course.

Test yourself by starting from every
point of the star.

Of course, sometimes you will be able
to win, sometimes you won't, but the
game won't be boring or repetitive.

TANGRAM

*A game of patience and fantasy which probably derives from ancient China,
Tangram is right for children but also for grown ups
and even mathematicians because of the incredible series of clues
and problems that these seven pieces can offer.*

Players
One

Game Equipment
- Seven pieces (typically of wood or plastic) in the shape of polygons as those illustrated—forming a square—in Figure 1.

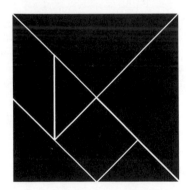

Fig. 1 – The square composed by the seven pieces of the Tangram.

■ Start & Object of the Game

Tangram can be played in three ways: using only your imagination and trying to create figures of humans, objects, and animals, without following any rules except that one must use all the seven pieces *(Fig.2)*; resolving puzzles, which is to say, fill the given outline of a shape with the pieces of the Tangram; finally, resolving geometrical problems, trying to form regular geometrical figures, always using all seven pieces.

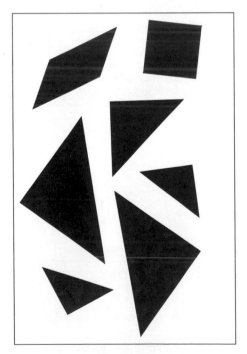

Fig. 2 - The seven Tangram pieces.

■ The Play

The shapes shown in Figures 3 (rabbits), 4 (cat), 5 (faces), 6 (dog), 7 (bat), and 8 (candles) are all assembling puzzles (the solutions are given in Figures 9, 10, 11, 12, 13, and 14 on page 314). A geometrical problem that is particularly demanding is to form the square without looking at Figure 1.

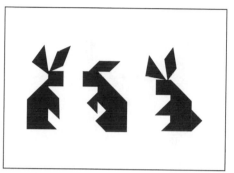

Fig. 3   Rabbits.

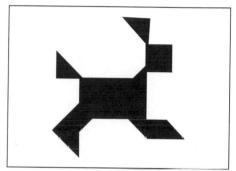

Fig. 6 - Dog.

Fig. 4 - Cat.

Fig. 7 - Bat.

Fig. 5 - Faces.

Fig. 8 - Candles.

■ Strategy

Using your imagination helps not only with inventing figures but also with resolving puzzles and problems. In order to deal with those two aspects (that is, puzzles and problems) one must have a great deal of patience and logic.

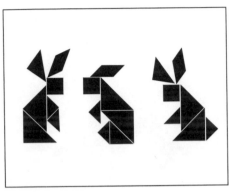

Fig. 9 - Solution of Figure 3.

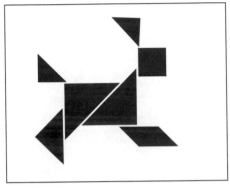

Fig. 12 - Solution of Figure 6.

Fig. 10 - Solution of Figure 4.

Fig. 13 - Solution of Figure 7.

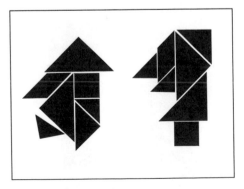

Fig. 11 - Solution of Figure 5.

Fig. 14 - Solution of Figure 8.

TOWER OF HANOI

*The Tower of Hanoi is solitaire and brain teaser that can be (actually must be!)
dealt with at different levels of difficulty, requiring logic and reasoning.
Its solution, like many games, is based on rigorous mathematical patterns.*

Players
One

Game Equipment
- A pattern with three circular holes, as shown in Figure 1.
- 9 pieces of decreasing diameter

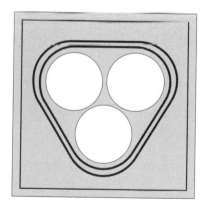

Fig. 1 - The basic pattern of the game.

■ Start & Object of the Game

Form a tower of 9 pieces, one above the other, from the biggest to the smallest in one of the three holes.

The object of the game is to rebuild the tower in another hole, using the third one to move the pieces.

■ The Play

The player can move only one piece at a time.

A piece can be moved only if it does not have another piece on top of it.

A bigger piece cannot be placed on a smaller one.

The solitaire is won not only when the tower is rebuilt in another hole but also when—and this makes the problem even more difficult—the operation is done in the least amount of moves.

■ Strategy

In order to learn the game, it is best to start with 3 pieces: it takes at least seven moves to rebuild the tower.

With 4 pieces, 15 moves will be needed; with 5 pieces, 31 moves, and so on, until 511 minimum moves are needed to solve the puzzle with all 9 pieces.

The mathematical formula of the solution is in fact two to the power of the numbers of the pieces used in the game minus one, which means:

$2^3 = 8 - 1 = 7$ moves for 3 pieces;
$2^4 = 16 - 1 = 15$ moves for 4 pieces;
$2^9 = 512 - 1 = 511$ moves for 9 pieces.

INDEX